Web Designing and Development

Training Guide

Plan Your Next Web Design Project

Prof. Satish Jain
Ambrish K. Rai
M. Geetha Iyer

www.bpbonline.com

FIRST EDITION 2015

REVISED & UPDATED EDITION 2021

REPRINT 2026

ISBN: 978-81-8333-579-9

LIMITS OF LIABILITY AND DISCLAIMER OF WARRANTY

The information contained in this book is true to correct and the best of author's & publisher's knowledge. The author has made every effort to ensure the accuracy of these publications, but cannot be held responsible for any loss or damage arising from any information in this book.

All trademarks referred to in the book are acknowledged as properties of their respective owners but BPB Publications cannot guarantee the accuracy of this information.

Distributors:

BPB PUBLICATIONS
20, Ansari Road, Darya Ganj
New Delhi-110002
Ph: 23254990 / 23254991

DECCAN AGENCIES
4-3-329, Bank Street,
Hyderabad-500195
Ph: 24756967 / 24756400

MICRO MEDIA
Shop No. 5, Mahendra Chambers,
150 DN Rd. Next to Capital Cinema,
V.T. (C.S.T.) Station, MUMBAI-400 001
Ph: 22078296 / 22078297

To View Complete BPB Publications Catalogue Scan the QR Code:

Published by Manish Jain for BPB Publications, 20 Ansari Road, Darya Ganj, New Delhi-110002 and Printed by him at Manipal Technologies Limited
www.bpbonline.com

Dedicated to

Mata Raj Rajeshwari and Sri Sai Baba

whose blessings overcome all hurdles in life

Preface

The objective of this book is to meet the growing need of the computer users and Web designers to build their Websites using Dreamweaver. This book tries to explore the four very versatile software packages namely, Dreamweaver, Photoshop and Flash. In addition, the Programming Language for Web Design called HyperText Markup Language (HTML) is also described in easy to understand manner.

It is observed that most of the books available in the market do not explain these packages and HTML in a step-by-step manner from the first time user's point of view. We have pressed into service all our Teaching and Professional experience in writing this book in an easy-to-understand Language along with use of examples and Figures. A very useful feature of this book is that different types of HTML tag are explained with practical examples, so as to enable a reader to understand them without any outside help.

We shall feel obliged to the readers if they send us their critical opinion of the presentation, readability and coverage in this book and send us suggestions at *sales@bpbonline.com* in improving the subject matter.

17th February, 2021 *Authors*

Table of Contents

Web Designing and Development Training Guide

This guide is a step-by-step training manual for learning a very versatile to create a Web page design. The book covers the basics process of planning and maintenance of Web pages and Websites in **Chapter 1**. It also discusses the basic structure and layout of a Website.

Chapter 2 covers Setting up a Websites and its files. It explains how to create a Dreamweaver Site file, set up a local testing server and a remote FTP server for your website.

Chapter 3 covers creating a Web page using Dreamweaver. It explains formatting Web page using Cascading Styles Sheets (CSS). It also covers different types of Style Sheets and various CSS properties.

Chapter 4 covers adding graphics to a Web page using Dreamweaver. It includes setting image properties, creating rollover images and image maps.

Chapter 5 covers Creating Forms and Frames in Dreamweaver. It is an easy way to collect and organize information from your Website's visitors.

Chapter 6 covers Using HTML to create Web pages using HTML tags to display information in a Web browser. It also explains how to set margins, add graphics and tables and to link in different pages in a Web browser.

Chapter 7 covers basics of Photoshop.

Chapter 8 covers Flash Animation.

Chapter 9 covers the basics of Adobe XD.

The notable features of this book are:

- Detail explanation of using FrontPage's wizards enables you to generate a design of Web page.
- A guide to learning this creative packages namely Dreamweaver.
- Step-by-Step description of HTML tags.
- A brief description of using Flash and Photoshop.

1 Web Publishing

Learning Objectives

After studying this chapter, you should be able to do:

• Explain web publishing • Discuss about hosting your site • Explain Website layout and structure • Discuss about search engine • Know about web server, Apache web browser, IIS, Internet and WWW

Introduction

Web publishing is the process of publishing content on the Internet. It includes creating and uploading Websites, updating the associated Web Pages, and posting content to these Web pages online. The content meant for Web publishing can include text, videos, digital images, artwork, and other forms of media.

Publishers must possess a Web server, a Web publishing software, and the Internet connection to carry out Web publishing.

Web publishing is also known as **online publishing**. To publish content on the Web, you need three things:

• Website development software • Internet connection • Server to host the Website

The Website development software can be a professional Web design application like Dreamweaver or a straightforward Web-based content management system like **WordPress**. Publishers require the Internet connection to upload the content to the Web server. Major sites may utilize a dedicated server to host them; however, many smaller Websites usually reside on shared servers that host an array of Websites.

Since Web publishing does not demand physical materials like ink and paper, it costs practically nothing to publish the content. Thus, anyone fulfilling the above three requirements can become a Web publisher. In addition, Web publishing brings countless visitors as the published contents are accessed by global visitors. These benefits of Web publishing opened a new era of personal publishing, which was unimaginable before.

E-book and blog publishers utilize almost the same Web publishing tools used by the Website developers. People who do not have the required Web publishing skills seek the services of professional Web publishing individuals or organizations to host, maintain, and modify their **Websites, e-books** and **blogs**.

Web Server

A Web server is a system that delivers content or services to end users over the Internet. A Web server consists of a physical server, server **Operating System (OS)** and software used to facilitate **HTTP (HyperText Transfer Protocol)** communication.

The collection of all your Web pages is called **Website.** To let others view the Web pages, you must **publish your Website.** To publish your work, you must **copy your site to a Web server.** Your own PC (Personal Computer) can act as a Web server if it is **connected to a network.** Most common is to use an **Internet Service Provider (ISP).**

The simple definition is that a Web server runs a Website by returning **HTML (HyperText Markup Language)** files over an HTTP connection. For example, a server that delivers an **XML (Extensible Markup Language)** document to another device can be a Web server. A better definition might be that **a Web server is any Internet server that responds to HTTP requests to deliver content and services.**

Depending on context, the term "Web Server" can refer to the hardware or Web server software on the server. For example, saying that you have "10 Web servers at the Web farm" is just as accurate as, "The **IIS (Internet Information Services)** Web server is on the machine that has 32 GB of **RAM (Random Access Memory)**."

In terms of software, there have been literally hundreds of Web servers over the years, but Apache and Microsoft's IIS have emerged as two of the most popular systems.

Apache Web Server

Apache Web Server is an open source Web server creation, deployment and management software. Initially developed by a group of software programmers, it is now maintained by the Apache Software Foundation.

As of 2013, with over **100 million Websites** and over 50 percent of the global market share. Apache Web Server is one of the most commonly used applications for Website hosting.

Apache Web Server is designed to create Web servers that have the ability to host one or more HTTP-based Websites. Notable features include the ability to support Multiple Programming Languages, server side scripting, an authentication mechanism and database support. Apache Web Server can be enhanced by manipulating the code base or adding multiple extensions/add- ons. It is also widely used by Web hosting companies for the purpose of providing shared/ virtual hosting.

Note: The Apache HTTP server, colloquially called Apache.

Internet Information Services (IIS)

Internet Information Services (IIS), formerly known as Internet **Information Server,** is a Web server produced by **Microsoft**. IIS is used with Microsoft Windows OS (Operating System) and is the most popular Web Server used with UNIX/Linux-based systems.

IIS was initially released for Windows NT and, along with ASP (Active Server Pages), finally made a Windows-box a usable alternative for Web-hosting. It was completely wide-open out of the box and required significant configuration to be secure. This IIS is now generally considered by many to be a stable and usable product. As of **2011**, the most current version is IIS 7, which includes pretty much all modern features you would expect to see in a Web server, including tight integration to ASP.NET. Though, as with any Microsoft vs Linux debate, some would argue that Apache is the only way to go.

Memorize

HTTP, NNTP, HTTP/2, HTTPs, SMTP, FTP and FTPS all are supported by IIS.

Internet

The Internet is a globally connected network system that uses **TCP/IP (Transmission Control Protocol/Internet Protocol)** to transmit data via various types of media. The Internet is a network of global exchanges - including private, public, business, academic and government networks - connected by guided, wireless and fiber-optic technologies.

The terms Internet and **World Wide Web (WWW)** are often used interchangeably, but they are not exactly the same thing. The Internet refers to the global communication system, including hardware and infrastructure, while the Web is one of the services communicated over the Internet.

World Wide Web (WWW)

The World Wide Web (WWW) is a network of online content that is formatted in HTML and accessed via HTTP. The term refers to all the interlinked HTML pages that can be accessed over the Internet.

The World Wide Web is most often referred to as the Web. The World Wide Web is what most people think of as the Internet. It is all the Web pages, pictures, videos and other online content that can be accessed via a Web browser. The Internet is the underlying network connection that allows us to send e-mail and access the World Wide Web. The Web was a collection of text-based sites hosted by organizations that were technically set up a Web server. It has continued to evolve since the original design, and it now includes interactive (social) media and user-generated content that requires little but no technical skills.

FACT

WWW was invented by Sir Tim Berners-Lee in 1989.

Hosting your Site

Once you have finalized which site you need to create, you will need to host it, which in turn make your site online.

Web Hosting

Hosting is also known as **Web hosting** or **Website hosting**. Web hosting is a service that allows individuals and organizations to have a Website made available via the **World Wide Web (WWW)**. Web hosts are usually based of a data center that contains servers used to store the data that makes up the client Websites.

At the most basic level, clients upload their Website files to the host server via **File Transfer Protocol (FTP)** or a Web interface that mimics FTP functions. Web hosts may own their own servers or may simply rent servers from other Web hosts and resell the space. Most Web-hosting services are shared, meaning that multiple Websites owned by different clients share space on the same server. Dedicated hosting is also available, in which the client rents an entire server for itself that it has full remote control over, but this is generally much more expensive than shared hosting. Managed hosting is a slightly less expensive service that gives a client a dedicated server but only limited control over its function.

A lot of people want to know how to host their Website so here is the step- by-step tutorial for hosting your Website. There are three basic requirements to host your Website these are listed below.

1. Your Website files
2. A domain name
3. Hosting space to store your files
4. A FTP client (FileZilla)

Now let us discuss step-by-step for the tutorial.

Step 1: You need to buy a suitable domain name for your Website which will be the primary URL of your Website. You can buy a domain name from **GoDaddy**. GoDaddy is the Internet domain name registrar and Web hosting company which manages the reservation of the Internet domain names. You also need a hosting space to store your Website files and for that you can buy a paid hosting space or you can use some free Web hosting providers to host your files. To buy a paid hosting space for your Website you should get better support and flexibility. A paid Web hosting space may cost you around few dollars per month.

Step 2: After completing step one you have your Website hosting space and your domain name. So you need to print your domain name to hosting space. For that you need know the hosting accounts name servers. You can ask it from your Website hosting provider. After getting the name servers you need to go to your domain control panel. There you will get an option to manage DNS. If you are unable to find the DNS manager you can ask your domain providers. So under DNS manager you need to submit the name servers provided by your Website hosting provider. It may take up to **48 hours** to point your domain name to your hosting space.

Step 3: You need to prepare your Website files at this step. If you know how to create a Website then fine otherwise you can hire a Website designer to create and design the Website. If you already have the files, then you need to set up a FTP user in your hosting panel. You also need a FTP client to upload your files however most Web hosting providers have their own program to upload files but it will be a lot easier to transfer your Website files using a FTP client. The most popular FTP client is **FileZilla**. You can get it free from their Website. Install FileZilla and login to your hosting space using your FTP login information. Using FileZilla, you can drag and drop your file to your hosting space.

Definition: HSP is a business which delivers a combination of traditional IT functions like monitoring, website hosting, web development, security over the WAN or Internet.

Hosting Service Provider (HSP)

A Hosting Service Provider (HSP) is a type of IT (Information Technology) service provider that serves a remote, Internet-based IT resource to individuals and organizations for hosting their Websites. A hosting service provider delivers hardware, software, storage, network and/or their combined solutions to enable Web hosting services. A hosting service provider is also known as **Web hosting service provider**.

Hosting service providers are the key IT entities behind the millions of Websites on the Internet. They build and deliver complete infrastructure for deploying Websites and maintaining their functionality. HSP creates hosts or hosting servers that have the ability to serve and operate as Web servers. Each host may house one or more Websites depending on its type and/or delivery mode. A hosting service provider delivers a simpler and more cost effective for Website hosting. A hosting service provider generally provides two different types of hosting services:

- Shared hosting
- Dedicated hosting

Let us discuss each of them in brief.

Shared Hosting

Shared hosting is a type of Web hosting service that allows multiple Websites to share a physical Web server and its resources among the hosted Websites. Shared hosting logically distributes a Web server to accommodate, serve and operate more than one Website.

Shared hosting may also be referred to as **virtual shared hosting**. Shared hosting is one of the most common and popular forms of Web hosting service. It is generally provided by Web hosting service providers, which usually have multiple Web servers on-site. Signup with the provider, each Website's logical partition/space is created on the Web server, which houses data for that Website only. Other Websites are also present on the same Web server, simultaneously sharing the storage, computing power, network and other resources. Because it is a shared service, shared hosting is a cheaper alternate to dedicated hosting.

Dedicated Hosting

Dedicated hosting is an Internet hosting option in which an organization leases an entire server, which is often housed in a data center. The host not only provides the server equipment, but may also provide administration and other services. This is considered a more flexible arrangement for the client because unlike in shared server arrangements, it gives the organization total control over the server, its software and security systems. In some cases, a dedicated server can be less expensive.

Dedicated hosting is also known as a **dedicated server** or **managed hosting service**. In the case of dedicated hosting, server administration is often provided by the hosting organization as an add-on service. The dedicated hosting providers will have a service level agreement with the client that outlines all the service guarantees. Server hardware is usually owned by the provider and in certain cases, it also provides support to operating systems, software applications and security systems.

Extra Byte

GoDaddy is a most popular hosting service provider in India.

Signing with ISP

To get your site, it is necessary to sign up with an Internet Service Provider (ISP). The Internet Service Provider is a company that offers Internet access to individuals and businesses for a **monthly** or **yearly fee**. In addition to Internet connection, ISPs may also provide related services like Website hosting and development, e-mail hosting and domain name registration, etc.

ISPs, offer have different types of Internet connections namely, **dialup**, **cable** and **DSL (Digital Subscriber Line)** broadband. Hardware, such as dialup modem or a wireless modem and router are usually provided by the company. When you register with an ISP for its services, an account is created and you are provided with the login details – **username** and **password**. You connect to the Internet via your account and this way the company keeps a watch on your online activities.

ISPs can be both regional, and national, servicing the entire country and they are connected with each other through **Network Access Points (NAPs)**. ISPs are also referred to as **Internet Access Providers.**

Using the Internet Service Provider

Renting a server from an Internet Service Provider is a common option. Most small companies store their Website on a server provided by an ISP. Here are some advantages.

1. **Connection Speed:** Most ISPs have very fast connections to the Internet.
2. **Powerful Hardware:** ISPs often have powerful Web servers that can be shared by several companies. You can also expect them to have an effective load balancing, and necessary backup servers.
3. **Security and Stability:** ISPs are specialists on Web hosting. Expect their servers to have more than 99% up time, the latest software patches, and the best virus protection.

Things to consider with an ISP

1. **24-hour Support:** Make sure your ISP offers 24-hours support.
2. **Daily Backup:** Make sure your ISP runs a daily backup routine, otherwise you may lose some valuable data.
3. **Traffic Volume:** The ISP's traffic volume restrictions that you do not have to pay a fortune for unexpected high traffic if your Website becomes popular.
4. **Bandwidth or Content Restrictions:** The ISP's bandwidth and content restrictions plan to publish pictures or broadcast video or sound.
5. **E-mail Capabilities:** Make sure your ISP supports the e-mail capabilities you need.

6. **Front Page Extensions:** If you use FrontPage to develop your Website, make sure your ISP supports FrontPage server extensions.
7. **Database Access:** If you plan to use data from databases on your Website, make sure your ISP supports the database access.

Types of the Internet access

Most ISPs offer several types of Internet access which essentially differ in connection speeds – the time taken for download and upload. Many also offer different plans or "packages" that vary in the download limit, number of e-mail accounts, etc.

Dialup Internet access is probably the slowest connection and requires you to connect to the Internet via your phone line by dialing a number specified by the ISP. Cable Internet access can be obtained from the local cable TV operator. However, ask them for a demo first or check with your neighbours on the quality of service. Internet access via DSL broadband is indeed very fast and ISPs can offer different download speeds – quicker the speed, higher will be the price. If you are planning for a DSL Internet connection, ask the ISP if they would also install a wireless modem and router at your location. A wireless Internet connection gives you freedom and flexibility – you need not be confined to one place and can access the Internet from any spot as long as the computer can catch the wireless signal. However, ensure that the provider secures the wireless connection with a password.

In many countries, the ISPs may put a limit on the amount of data exchanged over a connection. **For example**, one may be allowed only a few **GB (Gigabytes)** of download and upload each month.

How to choose an ISP?

Here is some advice in helping you choose an ISP.

- Monthly or yearly charge
- Type of Internet access
- Regional or national ISP
- Extra services from the ISP

Choosing your Domain Names

To use a domain name, it must be registered with a registry. **ICANN (Internet Corporation for Assigned Names and Numbers)** maintains a current directory of accredited registrars. The domain name is registered for a specified period of time, i.e., one year, up to a maximum of ten years, and is renewable on an ongoing basis. When you purchase a domain name, it only belongs to you for the specified time. As long as you continue to renew it in a timely period because if the domain name is not renewed, it can be registered by anyone for own use.

During the registration process you may be asked for information for different "contacts," i.e., technical, administrative. Your domain name record will be available to the public in what is called a **WHOIS** (a query and response protocol) database (a public database mandated by ICANN). The information is categorized under different areas in order for the proper contact information to be available in any given situation (technical difficulties, copyright infringement, etc.). The contact information can be the same for each position; some registrars will have a check box to enable the duplication of the information in each section.

Document Interchange Standards

Every network and every computer in the networks exchange information according to certain rules called **protocols**. These different computers and different networks are united with the common thread of protocols to exchange their information over the network.

Connectionless and Connection-Oriented Protocols

With a connectionless protocol, clients connect to the server, make a request, get a response, and then disconnect. For the Internet, HTTP is a connectionless protocol. With a connection-oriented protocol, clients connect to the server, make a request, get a response, and then maintain the connection to handle future requests. An **example** of a connection-oriented protocol is **File Transfer Protocol (FTP)**. When you connect to an FTP server, the connection remains open even after you download a file. The maintenance of this connection consumes system resources. A server with too many open connections quickly gets overloaded. Consequently, many FTP servers are configured to allow only **250 open connections at one time**, so only **250 users** can access the **FTP server at a time**.

Extra Byte

UDP is a connectionless Protocol whereas TCP/IP is a connection-Oriented Protocol.

Stateless and Stateful Protocols

There are two kinds of protocols for the processed transactions on the Internet. These are **stateless** and **stateful protocols**. In a stateless protocol, no information about a transaction is maintained after a transaction has been processed. In a stateful protocol, state information is kept even after a transaction has been processed.

Servers using stateful protocols maintain the following information:

- Status of the connection
- Processes running
- Status of the processes running

Generally, this state information resides in the memory and consumes system resources. When a client breaks a connection with a server running a stateful protocol, the state information has to be cleaned up and is often logged as well.

Document Management

The action of identifying, acquiring, processing, storing, updating and distributing the document is called **document management**. It may include file organization, uploading, etc. These are described in the following sections:

File Organization

When organizing the files on your site, keep files in separate folders. That way, the site is easier to update. The site maintains separate folders for images, HTML files, video, sound and **CGI (Common Gateway Interface)** scripts. The site has different folders name too; so, files related to the jobs section are arranged and put in a folder called **jobs**.

Uploading

Uploading means transferring files from your computer to the Internet server. When you are uploading files from your site, do not forget that you need to upload them in the correct file format. HTML and text files should be uploaded in **ASCII** (**American Standard Code for Information Interchange**) format, while images, CGI scripts, Flash files, sounds and video should all be uploaded in the Binary format.

File Names

When you are naming the files for your site, stick to what is known as **8.3** file names, i.e., **8 characters** for file name and **3 characters** for extensions. Some people may still be looking at your site on older machines. Use the *.htm ending rather than *.html. You would like as many people as possible to see your Website, so do not exclude those who cannot see long file names.

Backups

Whatever you do, be sure to back up your files on your Website. Put them on to a Zip disk or **CD** (**Compact Disk**) and then store it away in a safe place. If you lose everything, at least you have a backup ready to upload the site again.

Planning your Website Design

When you decide to have a Website for your business or personal interest there are a number of things you have to consider before you start actually building your Website. Website planning has various steps:

- Creating goals for your site
- Organizing the site structure
- Creating your design look
- Designing the navigation scheme
- Planning and gathering your assets

Creating goals for your site

Decide your site goals at the first step and then create a Website. Ask yourself, that what you hope to accomplish by having a Website. Write down your goals so that you remember them as you go through the design process. Goals help you focus and target your Website to your particular needs.

Organizing the site structure

Organizing your site carefully from the start can save the time later on. To set up a site is to create a folder on your local hard disk that contains all the files for your site (referred to as the local site), and to create and edit documents within that folder. You then copy those files to a Web server when you are ready to publish your site and allow the public to view it. This approach is better than creating and editing files on the live public Website itself, because it allows you to test changes in the local site before making them publicly viewable. When you finish, you can upload the local site files and update the entire public site.

This type of organization will make your site easier to maintain and navigate. Decide where to put items, such as images and sound files. For example, it is convenient to place all your images in one location, so that when you want to insert an image into a page, you know where to find it. Designers sometimes place all of the non-HTML items to be used on a site in a folder called **Assets**. This folder may contain other folders, for example Images folder, a Macromedia Shockwave folder, and a Sound folder. Or you might have a separate Assets folder for each group of related pages on your site, if there are not many assets shared among such groups.

Creating your design look

You can save a lot of time later if you plan your design and layout before you begin working in **Dreamweaver**. You can simply create a mock-up drawing on paper of how you want the site layout to look and then follow it as you build your site; or you can create a composite drawing of your site using software, such as **Macromedia FreeHand** or **Macromedia Fireworks**.

Maintaining consistency in your page layout and design helps to ensure a good user experience. The user should be able to click through the pages in your site without getting confused. If all the pages have a different look, or the navigation is in a different place on each page, it might frustrate the user. Make sure your site provides a consistent look for your user.

Designing the navigation scheme

As you design your site, think about the experience you want your visitors to have. Think about how a visitor to your site will be able to move from one area to another. Navigation should be consistent throughout your site. If you place a navigation bar across the top of your home page, try to keep it there for all the linked pages. Consider the following points:

- Visitors should know where they are in your site and how to return to your top-level page.
- Search features and indexes make it easier for visitors to find information they are looking for.
- Feedback features provide a way for visitors to contact the Webmaster if something is wrong with the site, and to contact other relevant people associated with the company or the site.

Planning and gathering your assets

Once you know what your design and layout will look like, you can create and gather the assets, such as images, text, or media. Make sure you have all of these items gathered and ready to go before you begin developing your site.

If you are using images and graphics from a ClipArt site or someone else is creating them, make sure you collect them and put them in a folder on your site. If you are creating the assets yourself, make sure you create them all before you start development, including any images you need if you are using roll-overs.

Then organize your assets so you can access them easily while creating your site in Dreamweaver.

You can reuse page layouts and page elements in various documents by using templates and libraries in Dreamweaver. However, it is easier to create new pages with templates and libraries than it is to apply them to existing documents.

Use templates if many of your pages will use the same layout. Plan and design a template for that layout, and then you can create new pages based on that template. If you decide to change the layout for all the pages, you can simply change the template.

Basic Website layout and structure

Your basic Website structure should follow a logical pattern of organization. It easy for visitors to search for the information they are seeking and for search engines to index your Website. Also, the basic layout of a Website that is logically organized will be much easier to maintain and edit.

The basic structure and layout of a Website

The layout of your Website should look as shown in Figure 1.1. The Website basic divisions shown below reflect the linking network must used by Web masters.

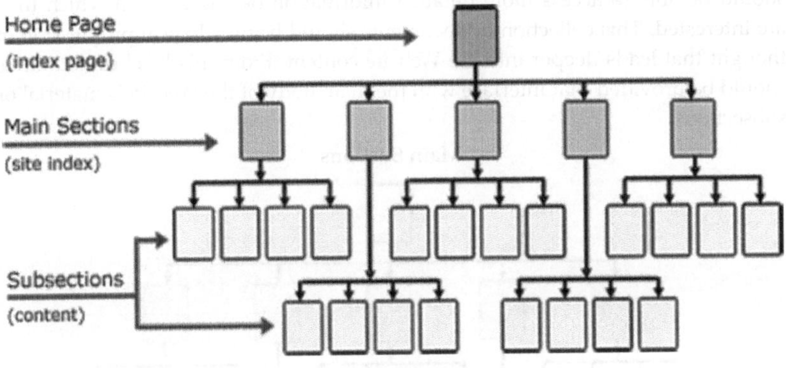

Figure 1.1: Basic of a Website layout

The basic divisions of a Website layout are as follows:

Home page

The home page is the first tier of Website content and leads into the interior of the Website. It links directly to the main sections of a site. In other words, from the home page links are introduced that access the internal Website sections or main subject areas of a Website.

The home page is first introduced to your Website (See Figure 1.2). As you go about designing your Website it put a large part of your efforts into perfecting this home page. It is important that the home page clearly conveys the essence of what your Website is all about.

Homepages

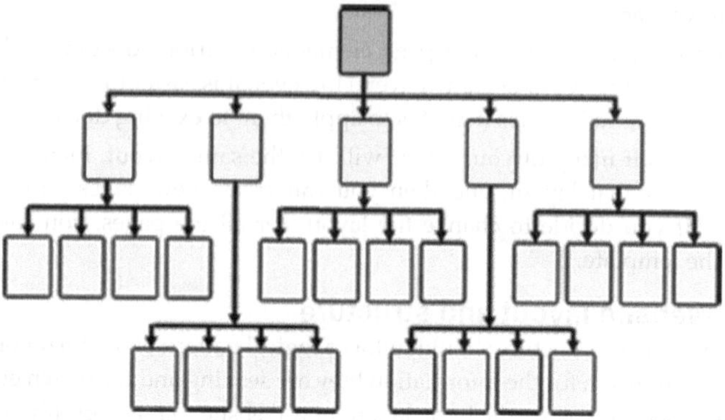

Figure 1.2: The Home page

Main Sections

The main sections or subject areas of a Website should be identified in this second layer of content (See Figure 1.3). Here is where the people visiting your Website should be able to access more detailed information on the topic in which they are interested. This collection of documents should begin a logical progression of thought that leads deeper into the Website content. From this level of data links should be provided that interface with the main body of the Website's material or subsections.

Main Sections

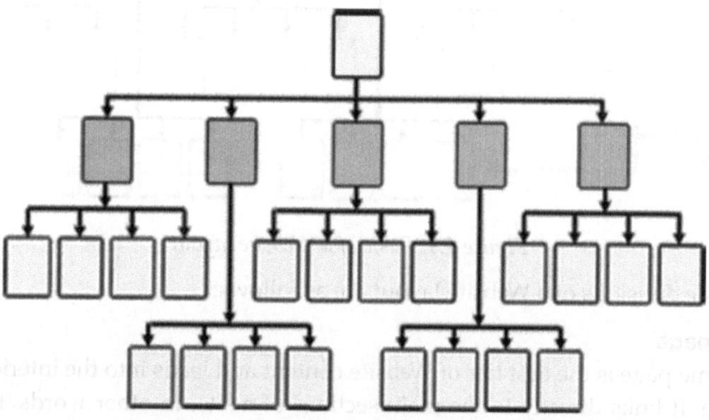

Figure 1.3: The Main Sections

Links coming from the home page should lead to the main sections of your Website. In other words, your index page should provide links that interface with specific subject areas of Website content.

Subsections

Subsections should be placed in their proper categories and the content tied to the main sections of the Website (See Figure 1.4). This is where the main body or database of your Website content resides.

Subsections

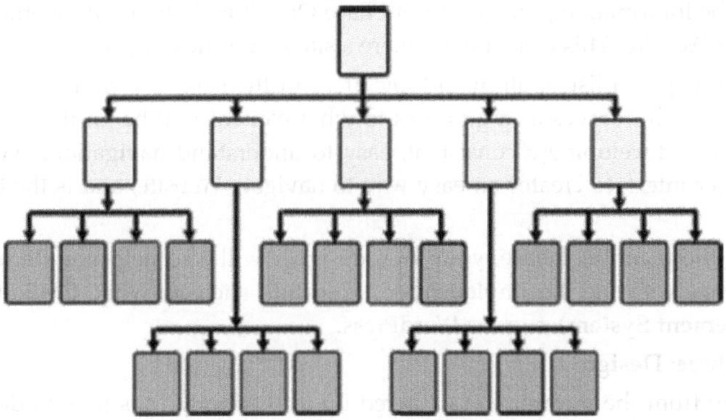

Figure 1.4: The Subsections

The subsections of a Website are the areas in which a collection of supporting material for the Website's main sections is accumulated. This is the heart and soul of your Website. These basic divisions of a Website should also be in a constant state of expansion.

The Website Design and Development Process

There are numerous steps in the Website design and development process. From gathering initial information, to the creation of your Website, and maintenance, you need to keep your Website up-to-date and current.

The exact process will vary slightly from designer to designer, but the basics are the same, which are discussed below.

- Information Gathering
- Planning
- Design
- Development
- Testing and Delivery
- Maintenance

Information Gathering

The first step in designing a successful Website is to gather information. It is actually the most important one, as it involves a solid understanding of the company it is created for. It involves a good understanding of you – what your business goals and dreams are, and how the Web can be utilized to help you achieve those goals. Certain things to consider are:

Phase One

Purpose: What is the purpose of the site?

Goals: What do you hope to accomplish by building this Website? Two of the more common goals are either to make money or share information.

Target Audience: Is there a specific group of people that will help you reach your goals? It is helpful to picture the "ideal" person you want to visit your Website.

Content: What kind of information will the target audience be looking for on your site? Are they looking for specific information, a particular product or service, online ordering, etc.,

Phase Two: Planning

Using the information gathered from Phase One, it is time to put together a plan for your Website. This is the point where a site map is developed.

The site map is a list of all main topic areas of the site, as well as sub-topics, if applicable. This serves as a guide as to what content will be on the site, and is essential to developing a consistent, easy to understand navigational system. A good user interface creates an easy way to navigate Website, and is the basis for this.

During the planning phase, your Web designer will also help you decide what technologies should be implemented. Elements such as what **CMS (Content Management System)**, such as WordPress.

Phase three: Design

Drawing from the information gathered up to this point, it is time to determine the look and feel of your site. As part of the design phase, it is also important to incorporate elements, such as the company logo or colors to help strengthen the identity of your company on the Website.

Your Web designer will create one or more prototype designs for your Website. This is typically a **.jpg** image of what the final design will look like. Either way, your designer should allow you to view your project throughout the design and development stages. The most important reason for this is that it gives you the opportunity to express your likes and dislikes on the site design.

In this phase, communication between both you and your designer is crucial to ensure that the final Website will match your needs and requirement. It is important that you work closely with your designer, exchanging ideas, until you arrive at the final design for your Website.

Phase Four: Development

The developmental stage is the point where the Website itself is created. At this time, your Web designer will take all of the individual graphic elements from the prototype and use them to create the actual, functional site.

This is typically done by first developing the home page, followed by a "**shell**" for the interior pages. The shell serves as a template for the content pages of your site, as it contains the main navigational structure for the Website. Once the shell has been created, your designer will take your content and distribute it throughout the site, in the appropriate areas.

Elements, such as CMS like, interactive contact forms, or e-commerce shopping carts are implemented and made functional during this phase, as well.

This entire time, your designer should continue to make your in-progress Website available to you for viewing, so that you can suggest any additional changes or corrections you would like to have done.

Phase Five: Testing and Delivery

Your Web designer will attend to the final details and test your Website. They will test things, such as the complete functionality of forms or other scripts, as well last testing for last minute compatibility issues (viewing differences between different

Web browsers), ensuring that your Website is optimized to be viewed properly in the most recent browser versions.

A good Web designer is one who is well-versed in current standards for Website design and development. The basic technologies currently used are **HTML** and **CSS (Cascading Style Sheets)**. As part of testing, your designer should check to be sure that all of the code written for your Website validates. Valid code means that your site meets the current Web development standards – this is helpful when checking for issues, such as cross-browser compatibility.

Once you give your Web designer final approval, it is time to deliver the site. An **FTP (File Transfer Protocol)** program is used to upload the Website files to your server. Other final details include plug-in installation (for WordPress or other CMS-driven Websites and **SEO (Search Engine Optimization)**. SEO is the optimization of your Website with elements, such as title, description and keyword tags which help your Website achieve higher rankings in the search engines. The previously mentioned code validation is something that plays a vital role in SEO, as well. There are many WordPress plug-ins available that further enhance the default WordPress functionality – many of them are directly related to improving your SEO, as well.

Phase Six: Maintenance

Many designers offer maintenance packages at reduced rates, based on how often you anticipate making changes or additions to your Website. If you prefer to be more update your own content, there is something called a **CMS**, such as can be implemented to your Website. This is something that would be decided upon during the Planning stage.

A Website determined by a CMS gives you the ability to edit the content areas of the Website. You are given access to a back-end administrative area, where you can use an online text editor. You will be able to edit existing content and you can even add new pages and content yourself. Other maintenance type items include regular site backups, WordPress upgrades, additional plug-in installation, etc.

How to Develop a Website?

The design and development of a Website should be a thorough going and premeditated process. One of the most effective ways of doing this is to generate a Website outline. The construction and maintenance of a Website outline is imperative for the proper design and development of an efficient Website. In this way, you can keep track of the physical data that comprises your site. In other words, a Website outline helps you keep control of the growing database of files that accumulate as you develop your site.

1. **Organize your files:** Keep your Website files organized on your hard drive just as you are presenting it on the Internet. This simple step will save you hours of wasted effort as your Website takes shape.
2. **Create a root directory:** Keep files that link directly to your index page and files that are used repeatedly in your root directory. But do not overload this directory. Make use of sub folders, of content, that link to these main pages. Place only prime pages in your root directory.

3. **Develop subdirectories:** Create a subdirectory of related pages or Website sections. Keep all relevant information together in individual sub folders. This will help you and the search engines follow threads of thought and provide quick access to information for your visitors.
4. **Plan for the expansion of your Website:** If you think a page on a particular theme will expand into a number of pages, create a subdirectory for it during the development phase.
5. **Organize your directory links:** Keep files that link to individual pages, of your root directory, in unique subdirectories. Do not put files from your root directory into subdirectories, keep them separate and link them to folders that contain related content.
6. **Use simple file names:** Name your subdirectories and files in an easy to identify manner. Make good use of your keywords when naming sub folders and files. This will unite the content of your Website. All of your Website's file names should tie together in a logical way.
7. **Develop and maintain permanent file addresses:** Do not change your subdirectory or file names, or HTML page addresses. Name and address are indexed and arranged in a manner that these can easily be maintained in the future. This will help to prevent broken links as your Website grows.

   If you do have to change an address after your Website, then place a redirect page or link in the old location. This will help your visitors find the information they are seeking with a minimum of effort and direct new visitors and search engines to the modified address.

Search Engines

Since the Internet is a vast collection of information, it is tedious to find specific information you actually need. Therefore, the search feature in a Web browser, such as Internet Explorer provides an easy access to a special facility called **search engine**. Search engines scan the Internet for the words or topics you are looking for.

Extra Byte

Google is the topest search engine.

Find Information using a Search Engine

There are many search engines available on the Web. The searching process is the same for all these search engines. Now we will describe the information searching process in Yahoo!.

1. Go to the **Yahoo! Home page** by logging on to www.yahoo.com as shown in Figure 1.5.
2. Type, the information to be searched for in the box provided for it and then click the **Search Web** button as shown in Figure 1.5.
3. Within a few seconds, the search engine will display the available links to the Web page as shown in Figure 1.6.

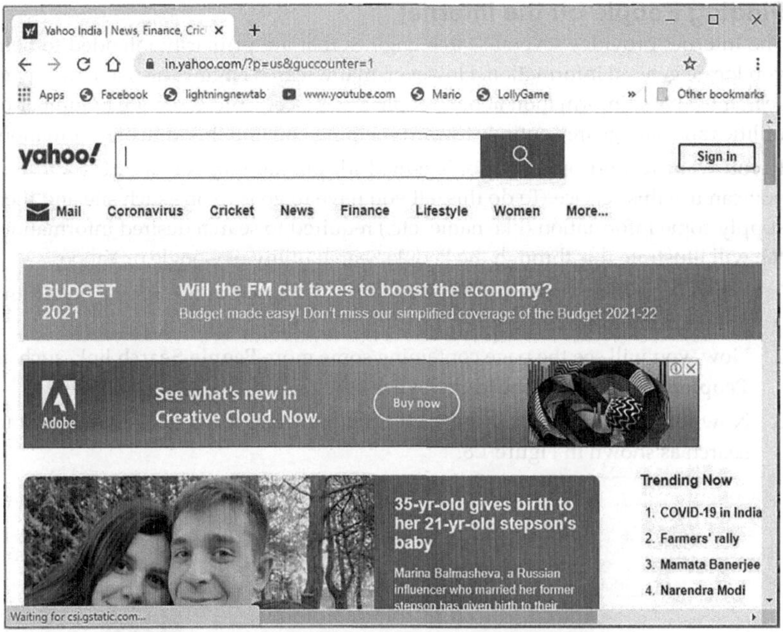

Figure 1.5: Yahoo! Home page and Query typed in the box

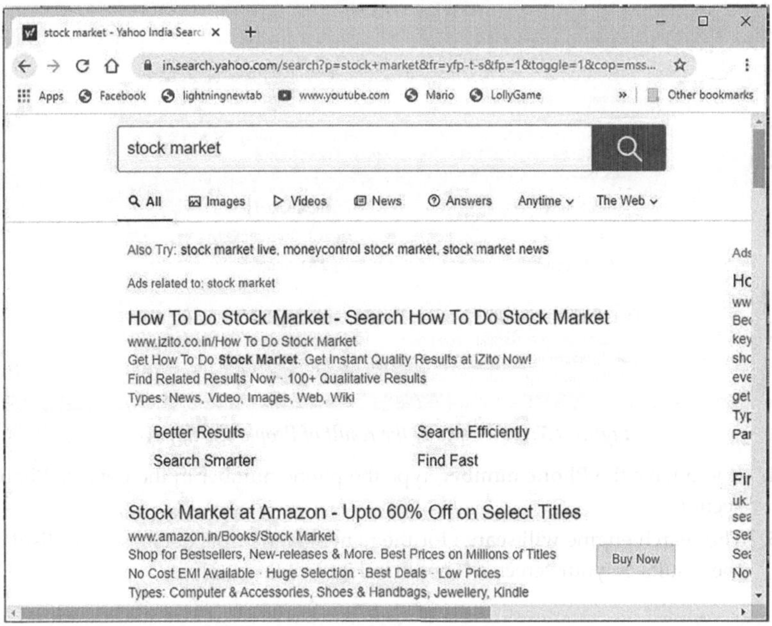

Figure 1.6: Result of Query

Finding People on the Internet

The Internet provides several search engines that are primarily intended to help you locate general information. However, many search engines also offer a way to search for basic information about people and places. And there are a number of utilities and sites geared entirely towards helping you find this kind of information.

If you want to find out a person's e-mail id, phone, number or street address, you can use this service. To do this, all you have to go is to one such site and then supply some information (like name, etc.) required to search desired information. We will illustrate this through the People Search utility of Google or Yahoo!

1. Log onto **www.yahoo.com**. Type the **People Search** in the Search box in the Yahoo Home page as shown in Figure 1.7.
2. Now, you will see the page containing some more **People Search** link, such as **Peoplefinders.com** as shown in Figure 1.8.
3. Now type the first and last name and city and state of the person you want to search as shown in Figure 1.8.

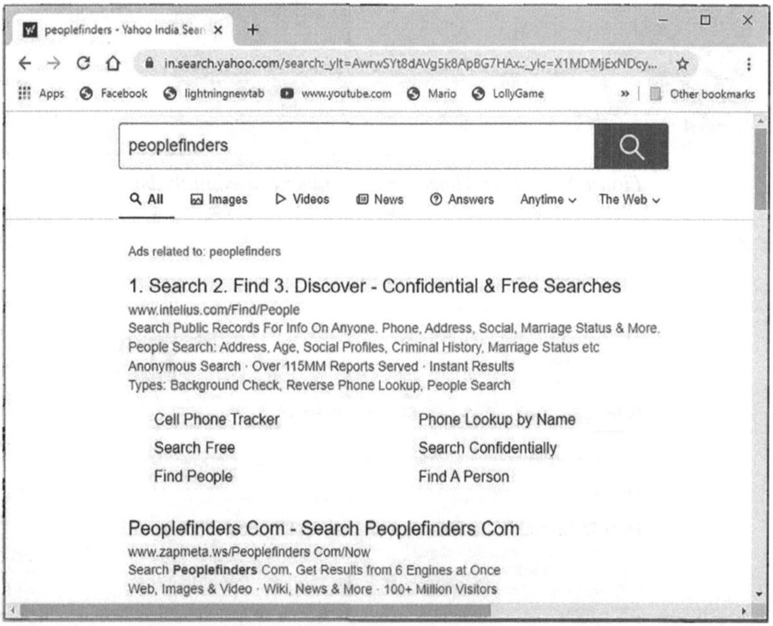

Figure 1.7: *Yahoo search the result of People search page*

4. If you have the **Phone number,** type the phone number in the Reverse Phone section.
5. The search engine will search for the name given on its database and display the results on your screen as shown in Figure 1.9.

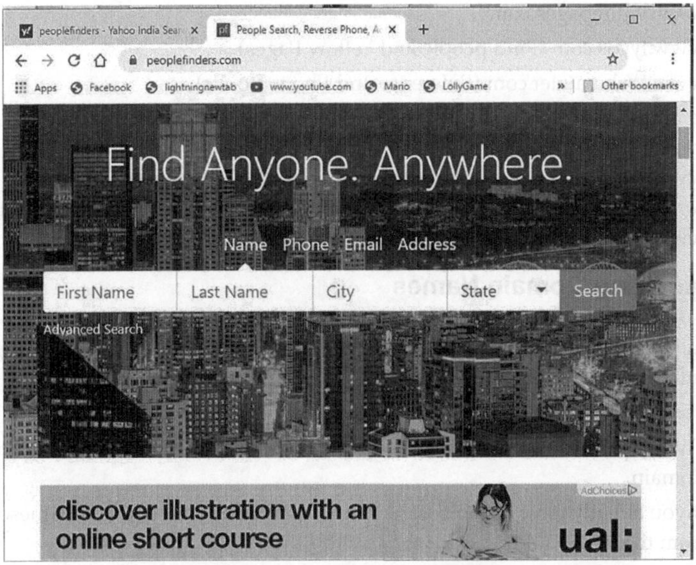

Figure 1.8: People Search Web page

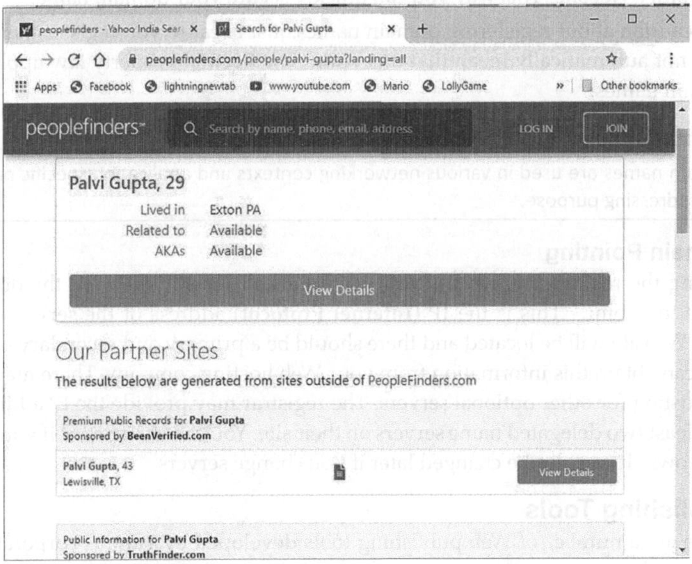

***Figure 1.9:** The search engine displays the results*

Apart from Yahoo! you may also try the following Websites:

- www.excite.com (people Finder, E-mail Lookup, and Yellow Pages)
- www.infoseek.com (Find Business, Find People and Find E-mail)

- www.whitepages.com
- www.lycos.com (Find people and Yellow Pages)
- www.Webcrawler.com (Reference and Phone Books)

Some popular online e-mail and phone directories listed here can also be used for searches.

- www.bigfoot.com
- www.bigyellow.com
- www.forall.com
- www.infospace.com
- www.whowhere.com
- www.peoplesmart.com
- www.worldpages.com

Registering Domain Names

To use a domain name, it must be registered with a registry. The maximum period of registration for a domain name is 10 years. Some of the required steps to register a domain name are as follows:

- Think of a good domain names that you would like to use.
- Then you will need either a **credit card** or a **PayPal account** to pay for the domain.
- If you already have a Web host obtain the primary and secondary nameservers from there.
- If you do not have a Web host, you can get space for your domain name at a temporary Website. This way you can quickly secure your domain name.

One caution about registering domain names: just because you register the name does not automatically mean that it is yours. Intellectual property law applies to domain names.

Extra Byte

Domain names are used in various networking contexts and application specific naming and addressing purpose.

Domain Pointing

During the registration process you will be asked where you want the domain name to "point." This is the **IP (Internet Protocol)** address of the server where your Website will be located and there should be a primary and secondary server. You can obtain this information from your Web hosting company. There may also be a listing for other optional servers. The registrar may provide the IP addresses of at least two delegated name servers on their site. You can change this if you have your own. It can also be changed later if you change servers.

Publishing Tools

There are a number of Web publishing tools developed by various corporations. Some of the more popular ones are:

- Netscape Navigator Gold
- Macromedia's Backstage Desktop Studio
- Adobe's PageMill and SiteMill
- Other Web Publishing Tools, such as **HotDog**, **HoTMetal** and **WebEdit**.

Netscape Navigator Gold

As Visual Editor: Netscape Gold offers a visual editing environment that closely approximates that of a Web page and at the same time adopts many of the concepts used by word processors and document publishing tools.

Netscape Gold provides a Web publishing environment that looks and feels like a Web page.

Netscape Gold generates true HTML code, but during the editing phase, this code is hidden from the user by the graphical interface. When creating complex Web pages, you will need to understand the principles behind the HTML language and its various constructs. Using Templates and the Page Wizard, Netscape has reduced the amount of work you need to do when designing a Web page.

Macromedia's Backstage Desktop Studio

Backstage Desktop Studio consists of a suite of tools to assemble and manage an end-to-end Website. The advantage of Macromedia is its excellence in multimedia Web authoring. By combining that experience in imaginary with the simplicity of a point-and-click, drag-and-drop, **WYSIWYG (What You See Is What You Get)** strategy for the implementation tools, Macromedia has one of the best tools for designing Web pages. Macromedia's Backstage Desktop Studio is one of the new generation of tools that combine dynamic Web page authoring facilities with Website management features.

Adobe PageMill and SiteMill

PageMill and SiteMill from Adobe feature a **WYSIWYG interface**, which makes operating them easy. At the same time, it incorporates typical Macintosh ease of use.

SiteMill

SiteMill is the perfect choice for both managing and editing Web pages on the server. It catalogues a Website, checks each link, and displays all errors. Currently, both programs support **HTML** as well as **Netscape plug-ins** (a software component that adds a specific feature to an existing software application).

Using PageMill

PageMill is an excellent choice for creating Web pages. It allows even a novice to create a Web page complete with forms, graphics and formatting. PageMill can be operated in two separate modes: **Browse** and **Edit**. The **Browse mode** is the default mode when you are opening a saved page. It shows a view of the page as though it were being served over the Internet to your browser. The **Edit mode** is for creating and editing your page. You can toggle between the two modes by simply clicking the Browse/Edit icon at the screen's upper right corner. PageMill lets you easily create Web pages that have **forms, backgrounds, internal links, external links, images, image maps**, and **detailed text formatting**.

You can accomplish all of this without any knowledge of HTML. PageMill supports normal cut-and-paste operation. If the dragged or copied text is (**Rich Text Format**) RTF-formatted, the attributes and styles are preserved; otherwise, you have to reformat the text.

Other Web Publishing Tools

There is a wide variety of Web publishing tools. Many of these tools offer value for low price. These are described in the following subsections:

GoLive

Adobe GoLive boasts drag-and-drop authoring features that will have you building your own site in no time. Although Adobe was one of the first big software developers to release a drag-and-drop Web authoring package in the shape of PageMill, it did not offer a real contender until the release of GoLive. GoLive incorporates cutting-edge features.

HotDog and HotDog Pro

HotDog supports **HTML**, **Netscape extensions** to **HTML**, and **Internet Explorer** extensions to **HTML**. When you have multiple documents open in the editor, you can switch between them quickly using tabs at the bottom of the editor window. HotDog has a **friendly interface**.

HotDog lets you preview your pages without having to save the page. Other features include an advanced correction system that automatically replaces text and file paths when you publish your pages. HotDog is designed for beginners and experts alike. You will know this immediately when you start HotDog. In addition to being able to insert many common tags into a page directly from the toolbar, HotDog has a dialog box for adding tags.

Creating forms with HotDog is easy just click the Forms icon on the toolbar and HotDog displays a form builder. The form builder provides a friendly interface for selecting the type of element you want to add to a form.

HotDog has other friendly tools for managing links, building tables and creating frames. With HotDog Pro, not only you can customize the toolbar, but also you can select the icons and labels for toolbar buttons. Another nice feature of HotDog Pro is the ability to define your own tags or tag sets that can be accessed via the menus.

HoTMetaL and HoTMetaL Pro

HoTMetaL is an editor of **SoftQuad Software**, the specialized (**Standard Generalized Markup Language**) SGML editor. There are two editions of HoTMetaL. HoTMetaL is available free! What is even better is that SoftQuad has made a serious commitment to continue to develop and improve this freeware editor.

HotMetaL Pro supports features that put it in the same league as Microsoft FrontPage and Macromedia Backstage. Still, SoftQuad has the market experience to back its offerings with solid support and continual upgrades. Versions of this editor are available for **Windows, Macintosh, Power Macintosh**, and **UNIX**.

HoTMetaL Pro is an advanced authoring system that supports the most current HTML specification and extensions. It supports **HTML**, **Java**, **ActiveX**, **objects**, **scripts** and even **Shockwave**. HoTMetaL Pro follows an integrated WYSIWYG and tag marker approach.

Dreamweaver

In the space of two short years, **Macromedia Dreamweaver** has become the standard Web authoring tool for **creative designers**. Now in its latest version, the package is still in a position to take advantage of future developments on the Web. In the industry, e-business and e-commerce have become buzzwords and Dreamweaver acknowledges this with Roundtrip Coded data import. The program can be customized for specific projects so that team members and clients alike can use the same package in the development cycle. Dreamweaver also prepares us for Web development with a core built around **XML (eXtensible Markup Language)**, **CSS (Cascading Style Sheet)**, the **eXtensible Scripting Language (XSL)** expected to go mainstream as browser support comes online. Dreamweaver lets you keep one eye on the future without forgetting what is important now.

Choosing the right software to build your own Website

You have taken the decision to build your own Website, but the next step is which software should you use to build and design Website?

XsitePro is one of the most popular pieces of Web building software available on the market. Launched in **2004** it quickly became a firm favourite, with critical acclaim from hundreds of delighted customers. XsitePro recently released an upgrade to the original software, **XsitePro Version 2.5**.

XsitePro Features

XsitePro has a wealth of features, with too many to list here. However, some of the best features are as follows:

1. **Simple and straight forward design interface:** The user has complete control over the design of the page so you can create a site which looks and functions just has you want it to.
2. **Hundreds of Website templates available:** If you want to create a professional Website in a hurry, then you can choose from a catalog of Website templates, all of which have been professionally created by XsitePro designers.
3. **A well thought through, interactive layout:** You can create your Website easily thanks to the simple and easy to follow layout.
4. **Create unlimited Websites:** There is no limit to the number of Websites you can create with XsitePro.
5. **Scripts:** Scripts can be run on a number of pages. This allows you to track events on your pages and report factors, such as on the return, on investment, on your Web pages.
6. **No HTML coding required:** Perfect for the novice, XsitePro delivers a built-in WYSIWYG designer, meaning no coding is ever required.
7. **Audio and Video in a few simple clicks:** Set your site apart from your competitors by adding an audio or video feature (or both), which can be added with a few clicks of your mouse.

8. **Easy linking:** Websites become more powerful when they have relevant links to other sites. With XsitePro you can create multipage directories of your links, with categories, sub categories, automatically generated screen shots and more.
9. **Use host and domain name of your choice:** XsitePro will work with any hosting account and domain name.
10. **Ideal for sites of any size:** XsitePro can handle sites with small amounts of content, right up to sites with thousands of Web pages.
11. **Windows compatibility:** XsitePro works well with all versions of Windows 2000, plus Windows XP and Windows Vista (note, it is not Mac compatible).

Adobe Dreamweaver

The newest version of Dreamweaver is **Adobe Dreamweaver CC2021**, and there are four different solutions to chose from so you can buy the package that best meets your needs.

Features of Dreamweaver

Live View: You can design your Web pages under real world browser conditions with this new function. Simple code editing is required, and the effects of changes can be seen in real time.

3D Transformation Tools: Bring your Websites to life using the Flash Professional software.

Faster design tools: The Photoshop Extended software allows you to exercise greater precision with images whilst making changes quickly.

Compatible with Windows and **Mac Operating Systems**, unlike **XsitePro**, which is only Windows compatible.

FACT

Adobe Dreamweaver was created by Macromedia in 1997.

Microsoft Expression Web (formerly FrontPage)

Microsoft Expression Web, formerly Microsoft FrontPage, is another leading and well-respected software package which allows the user to create professional Websites quickly and effectively. The most current version is Expression Web 3, and as with XsitePro and Dreamweaver, Microsoft claims that Expression Web 3 is suitable for all types of user. However, in reality Expression Web 3 is aimed at professional Web designers and developers and the user must have an understanding of coding in order to have any degree of success.

Microsoft Expression Web 3 is packed full of useful features, such as:

Professional Code Editor

This allows the user to debug effectively, as coding is colour coded for **HTML, JavaScript, CSS** and **PHP (Hypertext Preprocessor)**.

Professional Design Surface

Users can create an impressive design layout with a design surface which allows for easy manipulation of images, copy positioning, sizing and margins.

See effects of changes in real time

Any changes can be viewed in a real time Web browser, which can be viewed alongside the screen you are making the changes in.

Ideal for building standards-based Websites

With Expression Web 3, professional developers and designers can easily take advantage of the best of dynamic Web technologies to quickly and efficiently design, develop, and maintain standards-based Websites with seamless integration with **ASP.NET 3.5** (server-side Web application framework), **ASP.NET AJAX** (a set of extensions to **ASP.NET** developed by **Microsoft** for implementing Ajax) and **Visual Studio 2008** (used to develop Websites, Web applications and Web services).

Drag-and-Drop Controls

These controls simplify the process of adding rich media. Combined with advanced Photoshop the user has complete control over imported file layers.

Memorize

Dreamweaver is an HTML editor and general web design software product. It is used for publishing, designing and developing the website.

EXERCISES

A. Multiple Choice Questions.

1. The full form of HTTP is:
   (a) HyperText Transfer Protocol (b) HyperText Trans Protocol
   (c) HyperText Transfer Press (d) HyperText Trans Press
2. Adobe Dreamweaver was created by Macromedia in ____________.
   (a) 1996 (b) 1997 (c) 1998 (d) 1999
3. ____________ is the topest search engine.
   (a) Yahoo! (b) Bing (c) Google (d) Baidu
4. Another name of shared hosting is:
   (a) Machine shared hosting (b) Website shared hosting
   (c) Dedicated shared hosting (d) Virtual shared hosting
5. There are ____________ types of hosting services.
   (a) 2 (b) 3 (c) 4 (d) 5

B. Fill in the blanks.

1. The full form of FTP is ____________.
2. Another name of dedicated hosting is ____________.
3. ____________ means transferring files from your computer to the internet server.

4. ____________ is a connection-oriented protocol.
5. Home page is also known as ____________.

C. State whether the following statements are True or False.

1. SEO is Search Engine Optimization.
2. Dreamweaver is an HTML editor and general web design software product.
3. GoDaddy is a most popular hosting service provider in India.
4. WWW was invented by Sir Tim Berners-Lee in 1988.
5. An example of Connection-oriented protocol is FTP.

D. Answers the following questions.

1. What is the difference between connection-oriented and connectionless-oriented protocol?
2. How to plan your website design?
3. How to develop a website?
4. Write down the steps to find people on the internet.
5. Explain Adobe Dreamweaver and its features.

2 Setting up a Website and its Files

Learning Objectives

After studying this chapter, you should be able to do:

• Understanding a website structure • How to organise the root folder • Explain Dreamweaver file types • Discuss to prepare to set page properties • How to create a website

Introduction

A Website is a collection of Web pages that contains several elements, such as text, special characters, graphics, hyperlinks, and e-mail links, etc. Using the Setup dialog box you can set the information of your Website, such as the name of the Website, the path of the directory where the files of the Website are stored. A Website can be created in three different types of folders, namely, **Local**, **Remote** and **Testing server**. Generally, first create and edit your Web pages in the Local folder on your computer. After you complete your Website, copy the Web page files to the folder where the user can access your Website.

Understanding a Website Structure

To define the structure set up a Local folder. Create Web page files with complete information given to the Local folder. Later, copy these files to the Remote and Testing server folders to transfer the files on a Web server for developing the Website. The structure of a Website retains three folders which are discussed below.

Local root Folder: It stores the files you are working on. Dreamweaver refers to this folder as your "Local site." This folder is typically on your Local computer, but it can also be on a Network Server.

Remote Folder: The Remote folder has the same name as the Local folder. The files and subfolders that you post to your Remote folder are copies of the files and subfolders that you create in the Local folder.

Testing Server: This folder can present in the Local computer. The Testing Server folder is an alternative location where you can test your Web page. If you want to test dynamic pages during development, you also need a testing server folder, which provides aplace to generate and display dynamic content while youwork.

> **Definition:** Website refers to the way a website is setup i.e. how homepages and other important a pages are interconnected.

Extra Byte

There are four types of website structure namely Hierarchical Model, Sequential Model, Matrix Model and Database Model.

Organizing the Root Folder

To set up a Local folder, decide the structure of a Website, such as establishing hyperlinks between Web pages. Each Web page of a Website has its own unique address known as the **URL (Uniform Resource Locator)**, such as www.yahoo.com. When you make a Local hyperlink that is a hyperlink from one Web page to another on the same Website, you do not need to specify the complete URL of a Web page. You need to set the relative path, the path from a Web page to the linked Web page.

There are three different ways to specify a link path: absolute, document-relative, and site root-relative.

Absolute Path: Provides the complete URL for linking the Web pages, including the protocol to use (**http://**) here http represents **HyperText Transfer Protocol**. You must use an absolute path to link a Web page on another server. A generic absolute path is as follows:

Protocol name://Website name/path/file name

For example, http://www.priintek.in/Unnamed Site 3/public.html. An absolute path is used to link to a Web page on another server.

Document-relative path: Links different Web pages by defining the path through the folder hierarchy from the current document to the linked document. The document-relative path is mainly used for Local hyperlinks on a Website. These hyperlinks are particularly useful when the current and linked Web pages are in the same folder. A generic document-relative path is given as follows:

"common folder name/file name"

For example; <img src="images/flower.gif">

Site Root-relative Path: A site root-relative path provides a path from the site's root folder to a document. A site root-relative folder starts with a **forward slash** (/), which indicates the root folder. For example, if you want to link to od_pictures.htm, you can use the site root-relative path/pictures/ od_pictures.htm.

Dreamweaver File Types

To create Web pages based on different file types by using Dreamweaver CC2021. Table 2.1 shows some of the file types that you can use in Dreamweaver CC2021.

Table 2.1 *File Types supported by Dreamweaver and their Description*

Dreamweaver File Types	Description
HTML	HyperText Markup Language (.html or .htm) files. It displays Web pages in a browser.

Dreamweaver File Types	Description
CSS	Cascading Style Sheet (.css) files. It is used to format and position HTML content in a consistent manner.
GIF	Graphics Interchange Format (.gif) files. It is used for graphics, such as logos, containing maximum of 256 colors.
JPEG	Joint Photographic Expert Group (.jpeg) files. It is used for graphics, such as photographs, requiring more than 256 colors.
XML	Extensible Markup Language (.xml) files contain data in raw form that can be formatted using XSL (eXtensible Stylesheet Language).
XSL	Extensible Stylesheet Language (.xsl or .xslt) files. It is used to create style for XML data.
CFML	ColdFusion Markup Language (.cfm) files. It is used to process dynamic Web pages.
ASPX	ASP.NET files (.aspx) files. It is used to process dynamic Web pages.
PHP	Hypertext Preprocessor (.php) files. It is used to process dynamic Web pages.

Creating a Website

Before you create a Website, you need to create a Local root folder where you will store all the elements that make up the site. Websites are more than just a bunch of Web pages. All the images, videos, navigational buttons, documents, scripts, etc., are separate files that must be uploaded in those pages. Defining a Website instructs Dreamweaver that the Local root folder is the folder location that contains all the elements of your site. Dreamweaver will keep track of the files within the folder, automatically update them as needed, and give you access to them, while you are working.

You can create a Website by using the Site Setup dialog box that contains three main categories. These are:

Site: You can specify the name for your Website and the name of the Local folder in which you want to keep all the Web page files.

Note: Dreamweaver supports the most important languages for web design (HTML, CSS, JavaScript and PHP) and a lot more.

Server: The server hosts the Web pages over the Web. If you want to create the Website, you do not want to publish it on the Internet.

Version Control: Subversion is a version control system that works along with Dreamweaver to help you maintain version histories of your site files. Subversion maintains a repository of the file and folder structure of your site.

Advanced Settings: It lets you perform functions related to a Website, such as defining production collaboration and deployment capabilities.

To create a Website by using the Site Setup dialog box, do this:

1. Click the **Site** menu and choose **New Site...** .
2. The **Site Setup for Unnamed Site 2** dialog box appears, as shown in Figure 2.5.

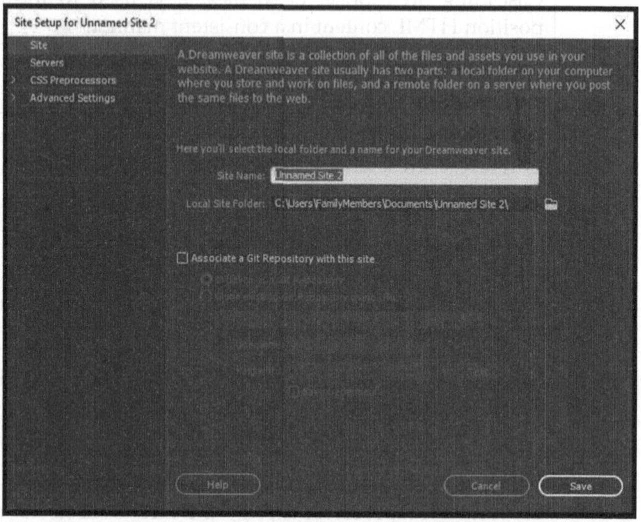

Figure 2.1: Site Setup for Unnamed Site 2 dialog box

3. In the left pane of **Site** category, enter a name for your Website in the **Site Name:** text field.
4. Specify the folder to server as the **Local Site Folder:** by either typing the pathname directly or click the Browser for folder icon to open the Choose **Root Folder** dialog box (See Figure 2.2).
5. Select the Folder in the **Select:** drop-down list and then click the **Select** button.

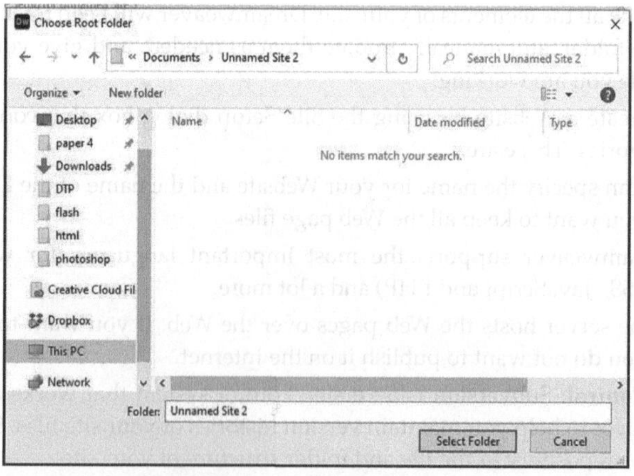

Figure 2.2: Choose Root Folder dialog box

6. Slide on **Save** button.

Working with a Website

After creating the Website, you may sometimes discover that you have included incorrect information in it. You can create a duplicate copy of your Website for further reference and make necessary changes in the original Website. You can delete the Website in case you do not want it. In addition, you can manage your Website by importing and exporting it also.

Duplicating a Website

You can create duplicate copies of an existing Website using the **Duplicate** button present on the Manage Sites dialog box. Dreamweaver copies all the settings and creates a new Website with the same document name appended with the text copy. The Duplicate button does not copy the actual documents, rather it just creates a new Website within Dreamweaver that can be manually modified easily. The copied Website appears in the Website list of the Mange Sites dialog box.

To duplicate a Website, do this:

1. Select the **Site** menu and choose **Manage Sites...** . The **Manage Sites** dialog box appears (See Figure 2.3).

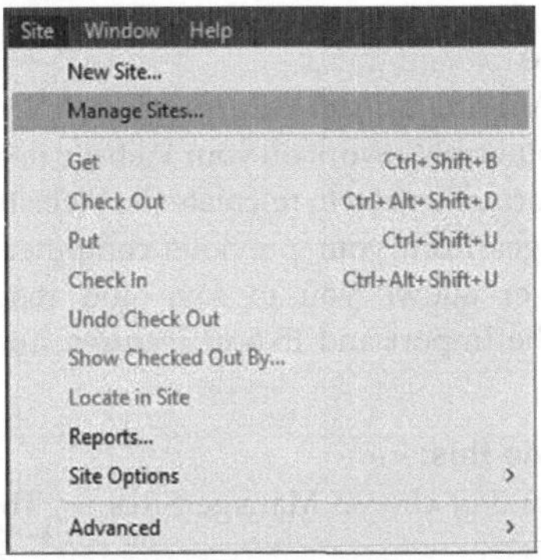

Figure 2.3: Selecting Manage Sites dialog box

2. Select the Website that you want to duplicate from the **Manage Sites** list box. For example, we have selected **New MyWebsite** (See Figure 2.4).
3. Click the **Duplicate** button in the **Manage Sites** dialog box, as shown in Figure 2.4.

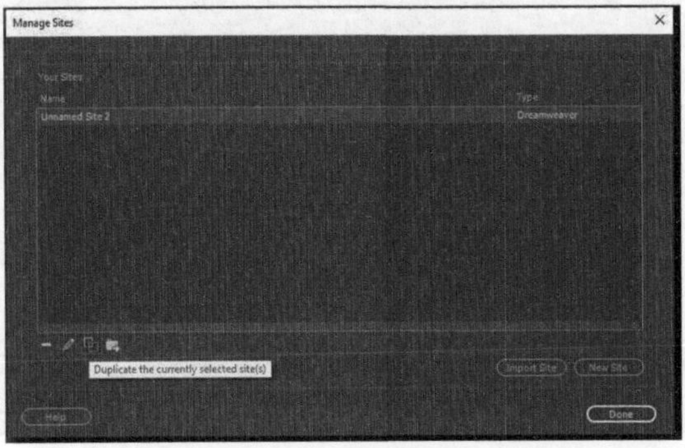

Figure 2.4: Selecting Site name from the Manage Sites

4. The duplicate copy of the **NewWebsite** Website is added in the list in the **Manage Sites** dialog box.
5. Click the **Done** button in the **Manage Sites** dialog box as shown in Figure 2.5.

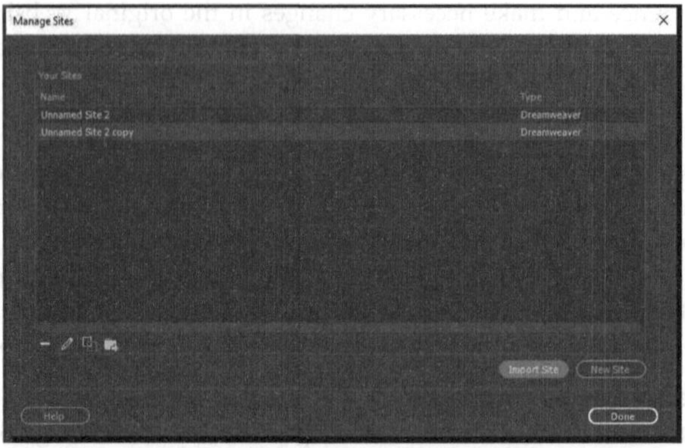

Figure 2.5: Manage Sites dialog box

Exporting a Website

When you create a Website, Dreamweaver stores it in a Local PC (Personal Computer) folder. If you want to work on your Website using a different computer in future, you would normally need to re-create the Website with the same settings and copy the Web pages from your previous computer to the new computer. However, Dreamweaver allows you to save and reopen Websites as XML documents by using the Import and Export features. You can export a Website with all of its settings.

To export a Website, do this:

1. Click the **Site** menu and choose **Manage Sites...** . The **Manage Sites** dialog box appears.
2. Select the Website that you want to export from the Manage Sites list box. For example, here to select the **MyWebSite.**
3. Click the **Export...** button (See Figure 2.6).

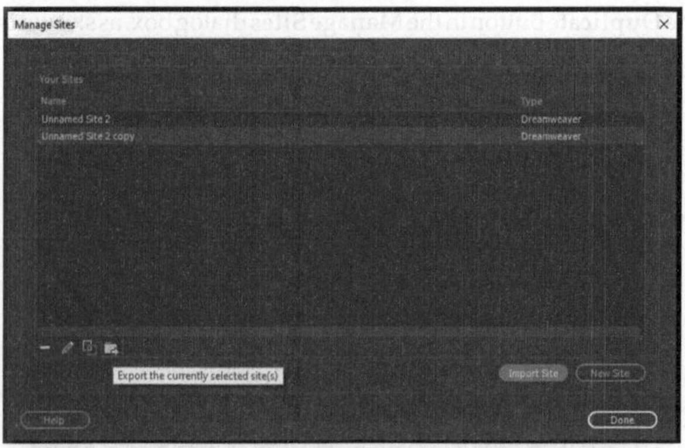

***Figure 2.6:** The Selected Site name get duplicated containing Export… button*

4. A Export Site dialog box appears as shown in Figure 2.7.

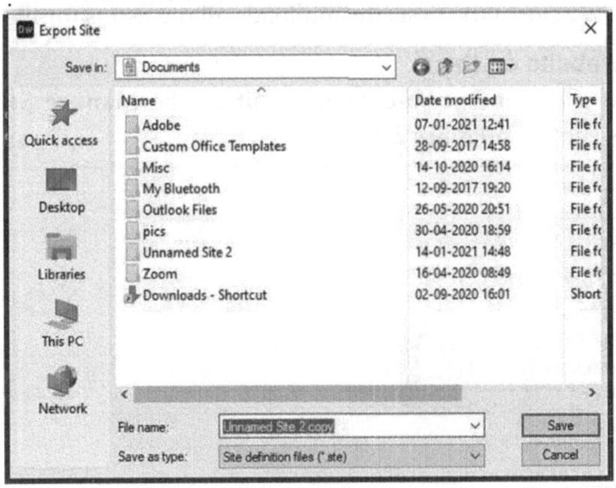

Figure 2.7: Export site dialog box

5. Select the folder which you want to export the Website.
6. Click the **Save** button.

Extra Byte

Edit tool allows you to change the site name, the local site folder, or the remote site definition.

Opening or Importing a Website

Dreamweaver allows you to manage multiple sites. When you open Dreamweaver it will load the Website last used. If, however, you need to work on another Website it is a simple matter to redirect Dreamweaver to the needed site using the Manage Sites dialog box, which you can also use to **create**, **edit**, **duplicate**, **remove**, **export**, and **import sites**.

To open Predefined Sites, do this:

1. Click the **Site** menu, and then click **Manage Sites**.
2. Select the site from the listed options as shown in Figure 2.8.

Figure 2.8: Manage site dialog box

3. Click **Done**.
4. Dreamweaver closes the first site and loads all the assets for the selected site.

To import a Website do this:

1. Select **Site** menu and choose **Manage sites**. The **Manage Sites** dialog box appears as shown in Figure 2.9.

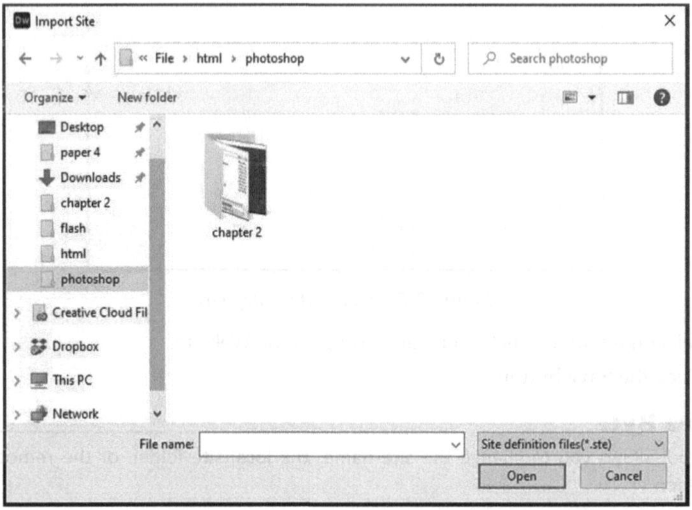

Figure 2.9: Import site dialog box

2. Click **Import** button.
3. Select one or more sites—defined in files with an **.ste** file extension—whose settings you want to import in the **Look in:** drop-down list.
4. Click **Open** and then click **Done**.
5. After Dreamweaver imports the site settings, the site names appear in the **Manage Sites** dialog box.

Deleting a Website

You can remove a Website from the list of Websites by using Dreamweaver. You can also retrieve and use this information whenever you require.

To delete a Website, do this:

1. Click **Site** menu and choose **Manage Sites**. The Manage Sites dialog box appears.
2. Select the **Website** that you want to delete from the Site pane.
3. Click the **Remove** button as shown in Figure 2.10. The Dreamweaver message box appears that prompts you to confirm the deletion.

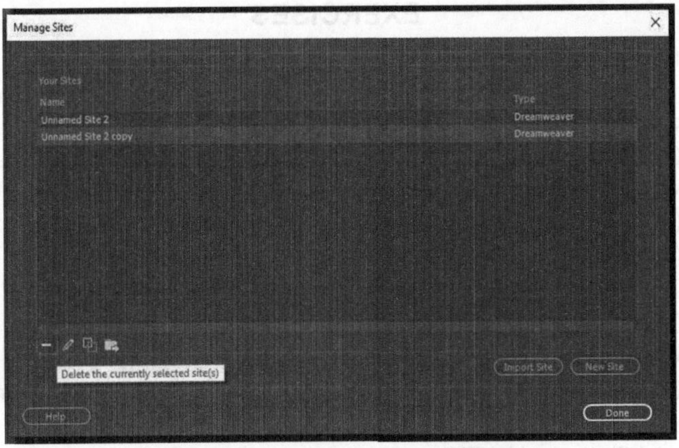

Figure 2.10: *Manage site dialog box*

4. Click the **Yes** button. The message box is closed and the selected Website is removed from the list as shown in Figure 2.11.

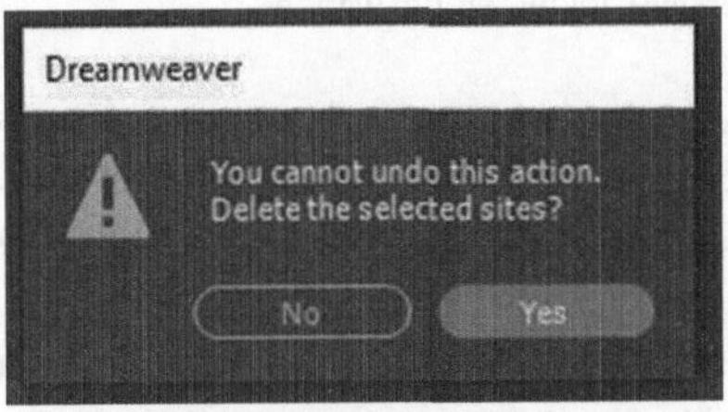

Figure 2.11: *Message box*

5. Click the **Done** button in the **Message Sites** dialog box. as shown in Figure 2.12.

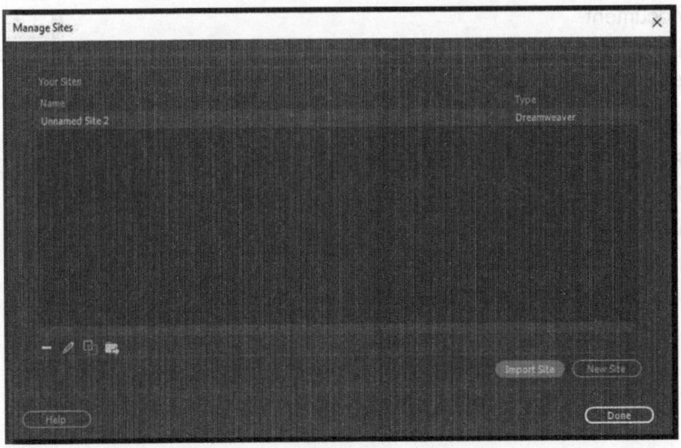

Figure 2.12: *Manage site dialog box*

EXERCISES

A. Multiple Choice Questions.

1. ____________ refers to the way a website is setup i.e. how homepages and other important a pages are interconnected.
   (a) Website (b) Local root folder (c) Remote folder (c) Testing server
2. What is the full form of URL?
   (a) Uniform Recourse Location (b) Uniform Resource locator
   (c) Unicorm Resource Location (d) Unicorn Resource Locator
3. There are ____________ different ways to specify a link path.
   (a) Two (b) Three (c) Four (d) Five
4. Which folder can present in the local computer?
   (a) Website (b) Local root folder (c) Remote folder (c) Testing server
5. ____________ is used to create style for XML data.
   (a) XSL (b) HTML (c) CSS (d) XML

B. Fill in the blanks.

1. ____________ displays web pages in a browser.
2. A site root relative folder starts with a ____________, which indicates the root folder.
3. ____________ is used to process dynamic web pages.
4. The ____________ hosts the web pages over the web.
5. ____________ is used for graphics, such s logos, containing maximum of 256 colors.

C. State whether the following statements are True or False.

1. The remote folder has the same name as the local folder.
2. A web page is a collection of website that contain several elements.
3. HTTP stands for HyperText Transfer Protocol.
4. A site root relative path provides a path from the sites root folder to a document.
5. Local root folder is the folder location that contains all the elements of your sites.

D. Answers the following questions.

1. Explain Dreamweaver file types.
2. How to duplicate a website in Dreamweaver?
3. Discuss a website structure.
4. How to organise the root folder?
5. How to delete a website in Dreamweaver?

3

Creating Web Page using Dreamweaver

Learning Objectives

After studying this chapter, you should be able to do:

• Understanding for creating a New page • How to saving and closing the file • Explain to preview the file • Discuss to add a Page title setting page font • How to create ordered/unordered list • Identify how to add horizontal rule using Tables in a web page • Explain CSS and its rule

Introduction

Dreamweaver is a frequently used Web editor that you can use to create and maintain Website. This chapter introduces you to design Web pages visually with multiple columns, pictures and text, create and manipulate tables and style sheets and also update the Web pages design.

Dreamweaver is also used to create a Web page and to store them on your own computer.

Creating a New Page

To create a new blank HTML Web page, do this:

1. Select the File menu and choose **New...** . *Alternatively*, press **Ctrl + N** keys together.
2. The **New Document** dialog box appears as shown in Figure 3.1.
3. In the **Blank Page** category of the **New Document** dialog box, select the kind of page you want to create from the **Page Type** column. For example, select HTML (HypterText Markup Language) to create a plain HTML page.

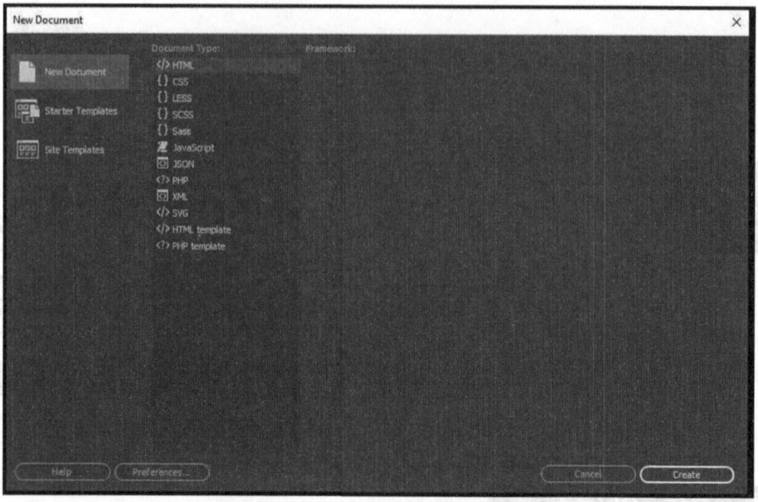

Figure 3.1: New Document dialog box

4. Select the desired layout from the **Layout:** column. For example, here to Select 2 column fixed, left sidebar, centered (See Figure 3.1).
5. Click **Create** to create a new blank document to the selected type as shown in Figure 3.2.

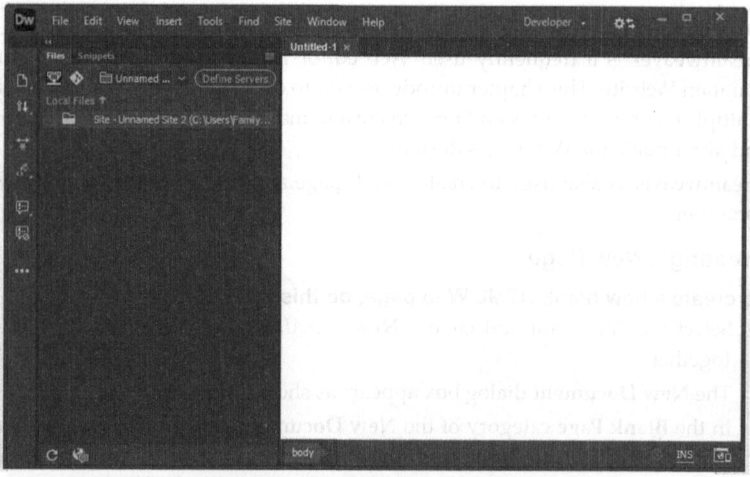

Figure 3.2: The new document with untitled

Extra Byte

To launch Dreamweaver CC2021:

1. Click on the start button.
2. Type Dreamweaver on the search bar.
3. Click on the Dreamweaver to open the application.

Saving the File

When you save a Web page, an image or other files on your site, there are certain rules that you must follow. For example, you should give the file name with the appropriate file extension. You should also include an extension at the end of the file to identify the file type, such as **.html** for HTML files or **.xml** for XML documents.

Filenames are important in Websites because they are included in the HTML code when you set links in the Web pages.

To Save a Web page, do this:

1. Select the File menu and choose **Save**. The **Save** as dialog box appears as shown in Figure 3.3.

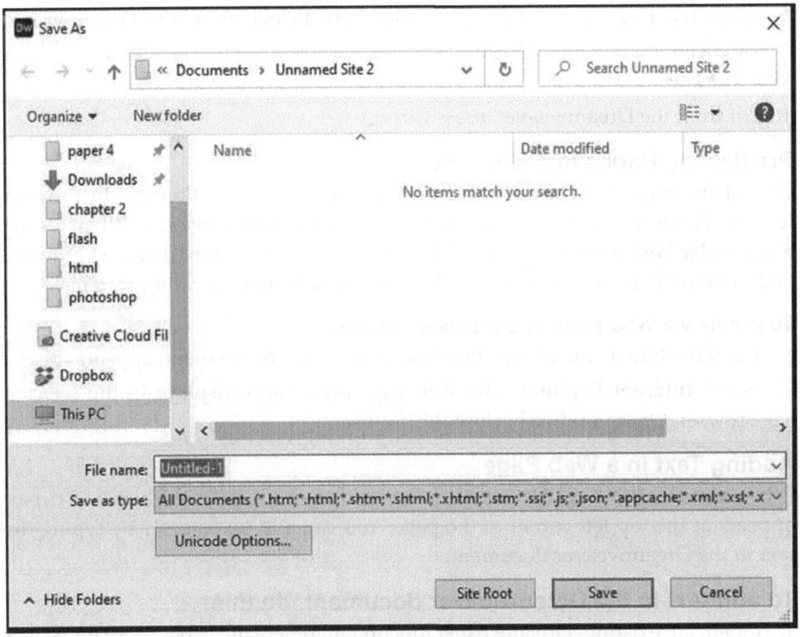

Figure 3.3: Save As dialog box

2. Select a location where you want to save the file.
3. Type a name in the **File name:** text box, for example, **Untitled-1**.

Memorize

The local root folder is the name for the folder where you are storing all of your websites contents.

Shortcut key

To save the program in Dreamweaver, press Ctrl+S.

Closing the File

When you have finished your project, you can close the Web page.

To close the file, do this:

1. The **File** menu and choose **Close**. *Alternatively*, press **Ctrl+W** keys together.
2. The **Test.html** page closes and the Welcome screen of the Dreamweaver application.

Extra Byte

To close the Dreamweaver program, click on the  in the upper corner of the Dreamweaver window.

Quitting the Program

After you have completed the work done, you can **Quit** the program.

To quit the program, do this:

1. Click the **File** menu and then choose **Exit**, to exit from the Dreamweaver application.

Shortcut key

To exit from the Dreamweaver, press Ctrl+Q.

Previewing Pages in a Browser

One of the most used features for testing your site is the Preview In Browser feature. This is one of the most used when working in Dreamweaver. When testing a particular Web page, it is a good idea to check it out in more than one browser, and in more than one version of the browser on different operating systems.

To preview a Web page in a browser, do this:

1. Click the **File** menu, choose **Preview in Browser**. A sub menu appears.
2. Select **Internet Explorer**. The Web page opens and displays in the selected browser. Once you finish, close the browser.

Adding Text in a Web Page

When you create a new document in Dreamweaver CC2021, the blinking cursor appears at the top left corner of the page. You can add text simply by typing the text in the Dreamweaver document.

To add text in the Dreamweaver document, do this:

1. Open an existing Dreamweaver document or create a new Dreamweaver document. In our case, we open an existing document as Untitled.html as shown in Figure 3.4.
2. Type some text in the document window, as shown in Figure 3.4. For example, here we have typed **This is a Sample page** to make text Bold, Italics, etc.
3. From the **Window** menu and choose **Properties**. The **PROPERTIES Inspector** at the bottom of the page.
4. Select the text and make the changes to the text using the **PROPERTIES** Inspector.

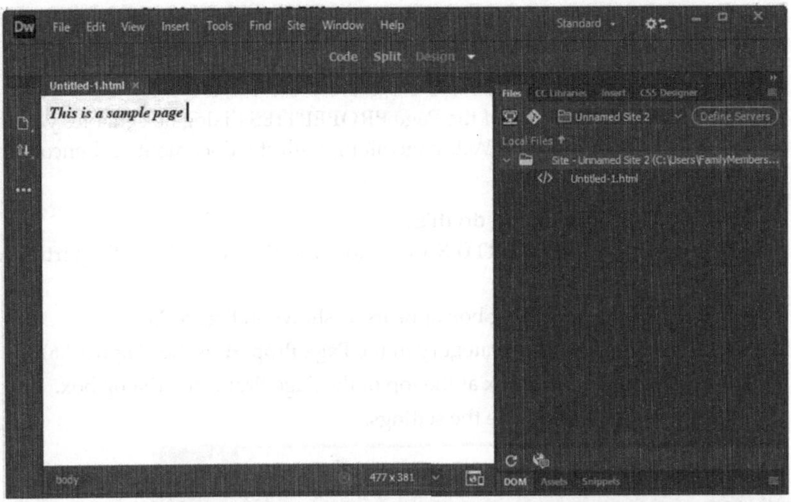

Figure 3.4: Opening a saved document Untitled.html

HTML Properties

You can make changes in the text that appears in the Web page with the help of HTML properties. You can also set various properties of the text, such as listing, paragraph, heading level, title from the Properties inspector using the HTML PROPERTIES inspector. The following options are available (See Figure 3.5):

Figure 3.5: HTML Properties

Format: Set the paragraph style and heading level of the selected text.

ID: It assigns an ID to the selected text.

Bold: It sets the font style of the selected text as **bold.**

Italic: It sets the font style of the selected text as *italic.*

Unordered List: It creates a bulleted list of the selected text.

Ordered list: It creates a numbered list of the selected text.

Text Indent: It applies <blockquote> HTML tag or block quotation to the paragraph, list or block of text.

Text Outdent: It removes the <blockquote> HTML tag or block quotation to the paragraph, list or block of text.

Link: It creates a hyperlink to the selected text.

Title: It specifies the textual tooltip for the hyperlink text.

Target: It specifies the frame or window in which the linked document loads.

Page Properties: It opens the Page Properties dialog box from which you can modify the properties, such as default font face, background, etc.

Adding a Page Title

The Title/Encoding category of the Page **PROPERTIES** dialog box enables you to set the document title for the Web page along with the document and encoding types.

To add a title to a document, do this:

1. Select the HTML **PROPERTIES** Inspector, and then click **Page Properties...** button.
2. The **Page Properties** dialog box appears as shown in Figure 3.6.
3. Select the **Title/Encoding** category in the **Page Properties** (See Figure 3.6).
4. Type a title in the **Title:** box at the top of the Page Properties dialog box.
5. Click the OK button to save the settings.

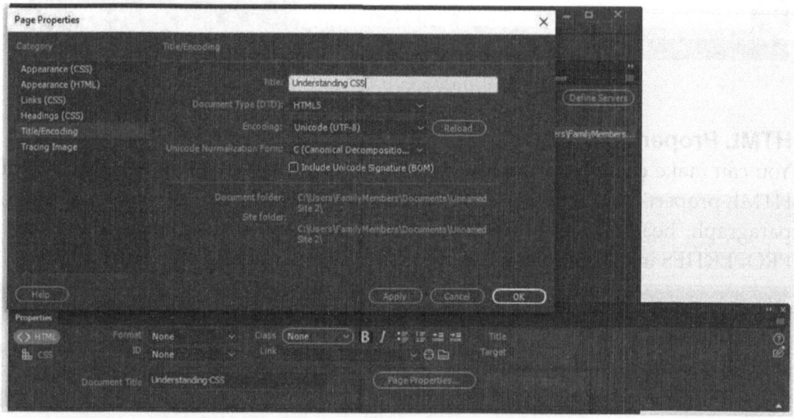

Figure 3.6: Document title appears in the title bar

Note: Page title should not more than 60 characters.

Setting Page Font/Font Size and Color of Text

Select the Appearance (CSS) category in the **Page Properties** dialog box by clicking the category name on the left side of the dialog box. You can select the default page font for the entire page along with the default text size and color.

To set the page font and font size properties, do this:

1. Click the **Page Properties...** button. The **Page Properties** dialog box appears as shown in Figure 3.7.
2. Select the **Appearance (CSS)** category from the left side of the Page Properties.
3. Select the font family you want from the **Page font:** drop-down menu.
4. You can also set the text to be bold, italic, or both.

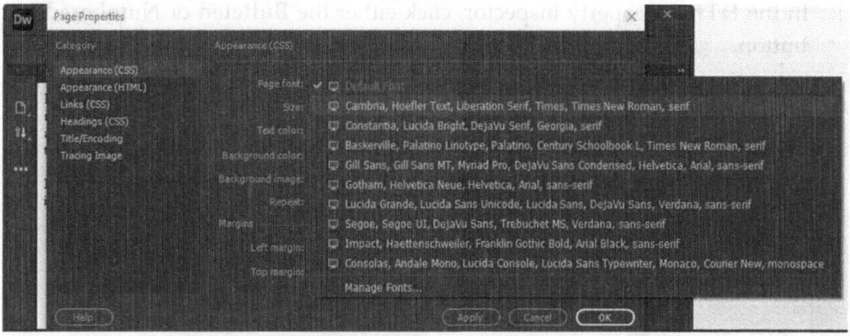

Figure 3.7: Selecting page font and size in the Page Properties dialog box

5. Select the font size in the **Size:** drop-down menu.
6. Click the **Apply** button at the bottom of the **Page Properties** dialog box to view the font changes you have changed so far. The **Apply** button enables you to view your changes without closing the **Page Properties** dialog box.
7. The changes applied in the Page Properties are shown in Figure 3.8.

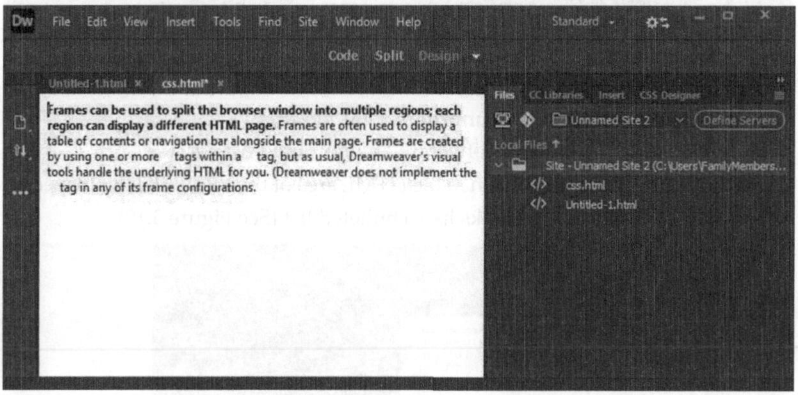

Figure 3.8: Applied font type and size in the paragraph

To set the text color, do this:

1. Click the **Page Properties...** button.
2. The **Page Properties** dialog box appears.
3. Click the **Text color:** (a small arrow) as shown in Figure 3.7.
4. Color swatches palette appears. Use the eyedropper to pick up any color on-screen by simply clicking the eyedropper on it.
5. The selected color appears in the Dreamweaver text.

Creating Ordered/Unordered List

You can create bulleted (unordered) lists, numbered (ordered) lists, and definition lists from existing text or from new text as you type in the Document window. In the Dreamweaver document, place the insertion point where you want to add a list, and then do the following:

1. In the **HTML** Property inspector, click either the **Bulleted** or **Numbered** List button.
2. Select the type of list desired—**Unordered** (bulleted) List, **Ordered** (numbered) List, or **Definition List**.
3. The specified list item appears in the Document window (See Figure 3.9)

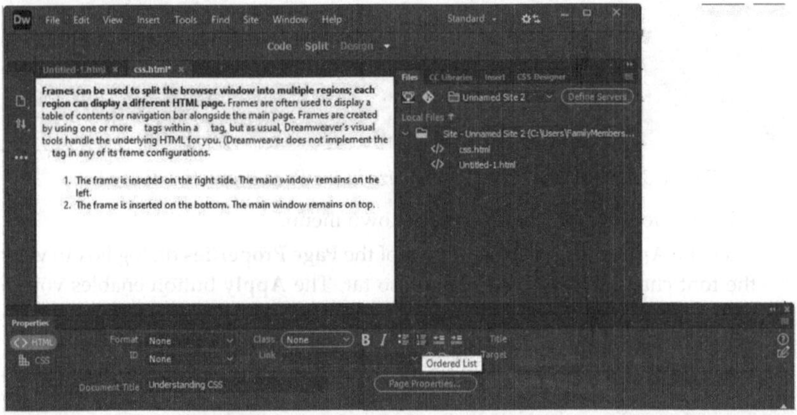

Figure 3.9: The Ordered list appears in the document window

To convert selected text into unordered list, do this:

1. Select the text you want to convert to an unordered list. Or
2. Click the **Unordered List** icon in the HTML area of the PROPERTIES Inspector.
3. The Unordered List icon looks like a bulleted list (See Figure 3.10).

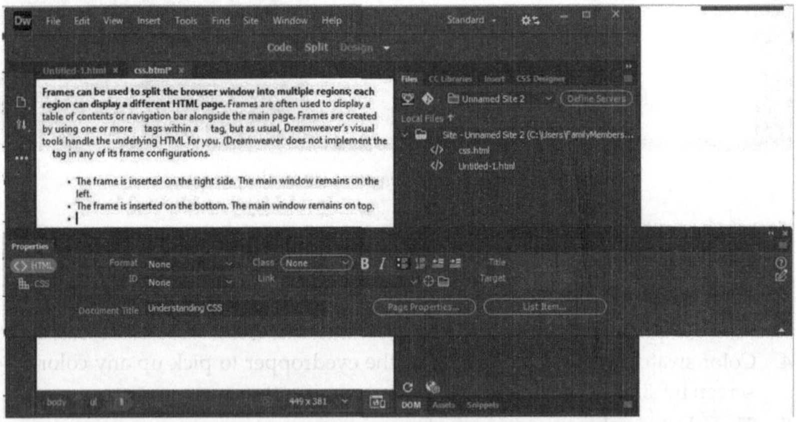

Figure 3.10: Selecting Unordered list in the HTML PROPERTIES Inspector

4. If you want to apply the bullet style, deselect the text by clicking the cursor inside any list item.
5. When the list is deselected, the **List Item** button becomes active in the PROPERTIES Inspector.

6. Click the **List Item** button in the **PROPERTIES Inspector**. The **List Properties** dialog box appears as shown in Figure 3.11.

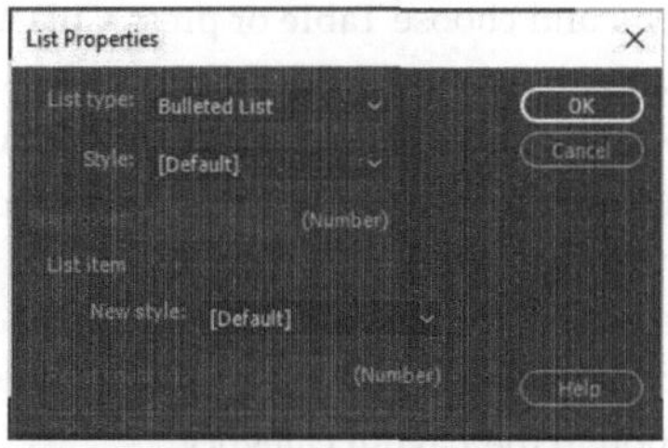

Figure 3.11: List Properties dialog box

7. Choose the desired list from the **List type:** drop-down list.
8. Click **OK** to close the List Properties dialog box.

Adding Horizontal Rule

Horizontal rule (lines) is useful for organizing information. On a page, you can visually separate text and objects with one or more rules.

To create a horizontal rule, do this:

1. In the Document window, place the insertion point where you want to insert a horizontal rule as shown in Figure 3.12.
2. Click **Insert** menu highlight HTML. A sub menu appears select **Horizontal Rule.**

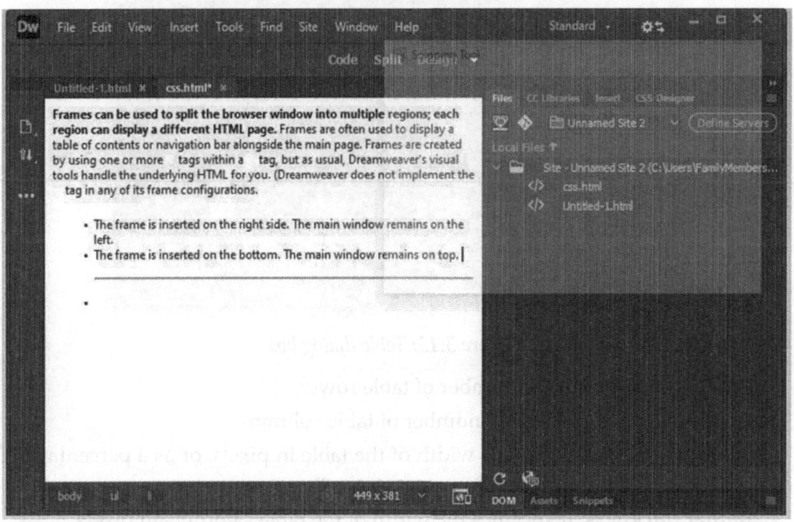

Figure 3.12: Modify the horizontal rule in the PROPERTIES Inspector

Using Tables in a Web Page

In the past, tables were designed manually by using the HyperText Markup Language (HTML) code. Now, with the help of Dreamweaver, you can easily create tables in the Design view.

To create a table in Dreamweaver, do this:

1. Open an existing document in Dreamweaver.
2. Click the **Insert** menu and choose **Table** or press **Ctrl+Alt+T** keys together.
3. Or in the **Layout** category of the **INSERT** panel, as shown in Figure 3.13, you can choose from two layout modes when working with tables:

   Standard: By default, Dreamweaver uses Standard mode, which shows tables as a grid of rows and columns.

   Expanded: For even easier editing, try using the Expanded mode, which adds temporary cell padding and cell spacing for more precise selections.
4. Click the **Table** option in the **Layout** category.
5. The **Table** dialog box appears as shown in Figure 3.13.
6. The following attributes to set the table using **Table size** Section are:

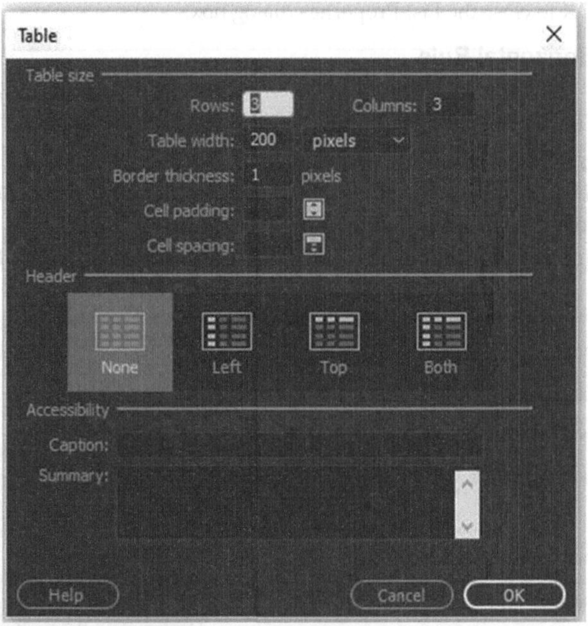

Figure 3.13: Table dialog box

Rows: It determines the number of table rows.

Columns: It determines the number of table columns.

Table width: It specifies the width of the table in pixels, or as a percentage of the browser window's width.

Border thickness: It specifies the width of the table's borders in pixels.

Cell padding: It determines the number of pixels between a cell's border and its contents.

Cell spacing: It determines the number of pixels between adjacent table cells.

7. The **Header** Section contains the following attributes:

   None: It does not enable column or row headings for the table.

   Left: It makes the first column of the table a column for headings, so that you can enter a heading for each row of the table.

   Top: It makes the first row of the table a row for headings, so that you can enter a heading for each column of the table.

   Both: It enables you to enter column and row headings in the table.
8. The **Accessibility** Section contains the following attributes:

   Caption: It provides a table title which displays outside area of the table. Align Caption specifies where the table caption appears in relation to the table.

   Summary: It provides a table description. Screen readers read the summary text, but the text does not appear in the user's browser.
9. Specify the required number of rows and columns in the table in the **Rows:** and **Columns:** text boxes.
10. Specify the width of the table in the **Table width:** text box.
11. Select the desired table header from the **Header** Section options.
12. Click the **OK** button in the **Table** dialog box.
13. The table is inserted in the Dreamweaver document as shown in Figure 3.14.

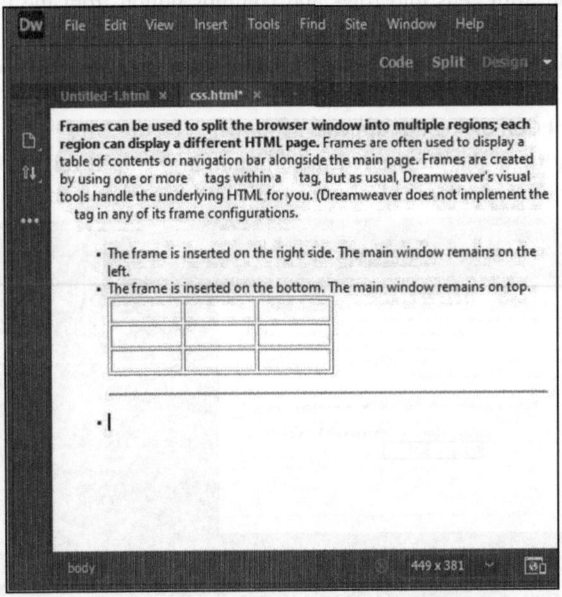

Figure 3.14: Table is inserted in the Dreamweaver document

Editing Tables

After creating a table, you can modify it by merging and splitting cells, and sorting data in the table.

Merging and Splitting Table Cells

You can merge any number of adjacent cells—as long as the entire selection is a line or a rectangle of cells—to produce a single cell that spans several columns or rows. You can split a cell into any number of rows or columns, regardless of whether it was previously merged. Dreamweaver automatically restructures the table (adding any necessary `colspan` or `rowspan` attributes) to create the specified arrangement.

> **Definition:** Merging of cells means to combine two or more cells to make it single.

To merge a cell of a table, do this:

1. Select the cells that you want to merge as shown in Figure 3.15.
2. Click on **Merge Cells** button from the **PROPERTIES Inspector** as shown in Figure 3.15.
3. The selected cells are merged and appear as a single cell as shown in Figure 3.16.

To Split a cell, do this:

1. Select the cell that you want to split as shown in Figure 3.17.
2. Click the **Split** cells into rows and columns button from the PROPERTIES Inspector, as shown in Figure 3.17. Or
3. Click **Modify** menu highlight **Table.** A sub menu appears choose **Split Cell.** *Alternatively* **Ctrl+Alt+S** keys together.
4. The **Split Cell** dialog box appears as shown in Figure 3.18.
5. Select either of the the desired radio button in the **Split cell into** option. For example, here we use the **Columns** radio button as shown in Figure 3.18.

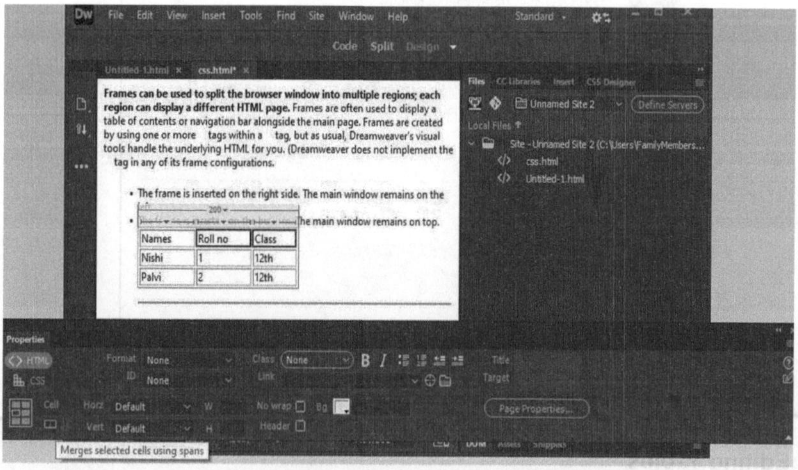

Figure 3.15: Selecting the cells

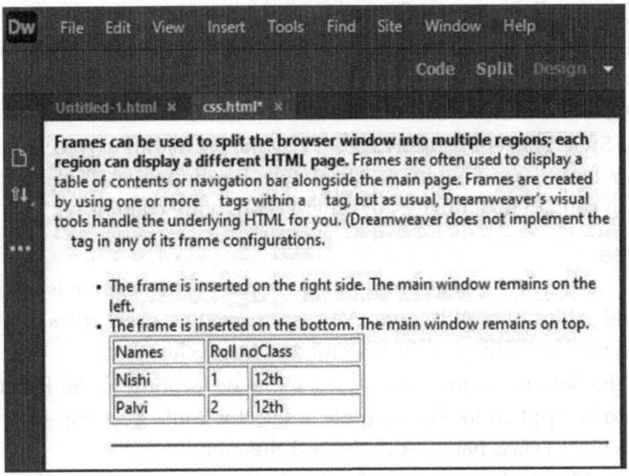

Figure 3.16: The selected cells gets merged

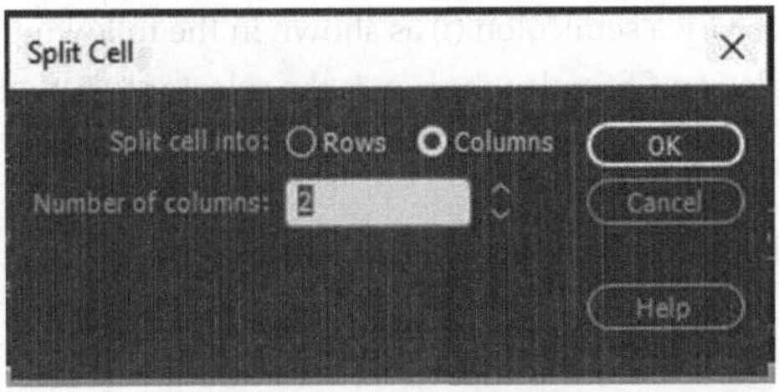

Figure 3.17: Selecting the cell

6. Specify the number of columns you want to insert in the **Number of columns:** spinner box.
7. Click **OK** button in the **Split Cell** dialog box.
8. The selected cell is split into two columns, as shown in Figure 3.18.

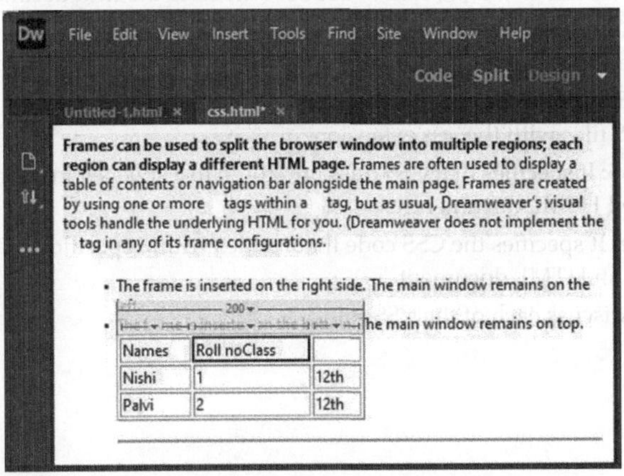

Figure 3.18: The selected cell gets split into two columns

Using Cascading Style Sheets

Cascading Style Sheets refers to CSS rules collection, to control how the content appears on the Web page. Coding of these styles are placed either within the `<body>` tag of an element or in an external CSS file.

Cascading Style Sheets-Positions (CSS-P) elements within a Web page by using rectangular boxes, are known as Absolutely Positioned (AP) elements. An AP element can contain text, images, or other HTML body content.

CSS Rules

CSS rules are the styles that are applied on the HTML elements, such as font, images, and tables of a Web page. All cascading style sheet rules are written in two-part syntax consisting of the selector and the declaration.

Selector: The Selector defines the style's name or location in the HTML that the style should be applied to. For example, a selector could be a tag, such as `<p>` or `<h1>`, or a custom class name, such as `tableheader`.

Declaration: The declaration specifies all the style's elements, such as font face, size, color, margin, and padding. Rules can contain multiple declarations as long as each is separated by a semicolon (;) as shown in the following example.

Here is an example of a CSS rule where `p` is the selector and everything inside the curly brackets (`{ }`) is the declaration.

```
p {
font-family: Verdana, Arial, Helvetica, sans-serif;
font-size: 12px;
color: #993300;
}
```

Note that the declarations themselves have two parts separated by a colon (`:`), the property (such as `color`) and the value (such as `#993300`). In the rule for p in the preceding example, a style has been defined for all `<p>` tags, meaning that all content in the document between any pair of opening and closing `<p>` tags, is displayed as `Verdana`, `12px`, and `#993300` (which is the hexadecimal code for a deep brick red color).

CSS rules can be placed in the following locations:

External CSS: It specifies that all CSS rules are collectively stored in separate, external CSS files with the .css extension.

Internal CSS: It specifies that CSS rules are stored in a style tag in the head portion of the related HTML document.

Inline Style: It specifies the CSS code that resides within specific instances of tags throughout an HTML document.

Now let us discuss each of the CSS rules.

Internal Style Sheet

An internal style sheet should be used when a single document has a unique style. You define internal styles in the head section of an HTML page, by using the `<style>` tag.

To create an internal style sheet, do this:

1. Switch to the code view of the document.
2. Type the code, given in Example 1, under the `<head>` tag in the document as shown in Figure 3.19.

Example 1: Creating an internal style sheet

Solution:

```
<style type-"text/css">
body {background-color:#ff4500; /* Webpage background color */
color:#ffffff; /* text color #ffffff - color value for
white */ }
</style>
```

We have defined a style that changes background and text color of the paragraph element as shown in Figure 3.22.

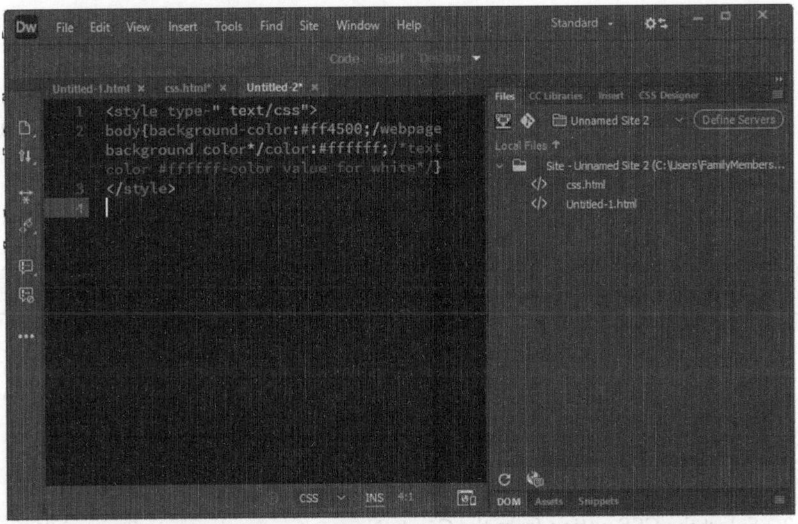

Figure 3.19: The above code entered in the code view in the document

You can view the change in the background color and text color of the paragraph element in the Design view of the document as shown in Figure 3.20.

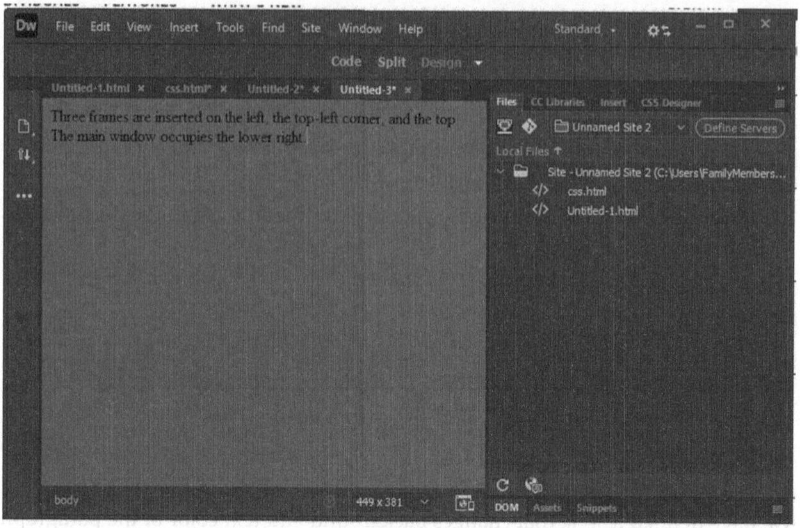

Figure 3.20: The output of the above code view in the Design code

Inline Style Sheet

An inline style sheet is used to apply a style to a specific element of a document. To use inline styles, you have to use the style attribute in the relevant tag. The style attribute can contain any CSS property. The Example 2 shows how to change the color and the left margin of a paragraph:

Example 2: Changing the color and left margin of a paragraph.

Solution:

```
<p style="color:blue;margin-left:40px">This is a paragraph.</p>
```

The above code sets the paragraph color to blue and the left margin to 40 pixels.

External Style Sheet

An external style sheet is ideal when the style is applied to many pages. With an external style sheet, you can change the look of an entire Website by changing one file. Each page must link to the style sheet using the <link> tag. The <link> tag goes inside the head section.

1. Open the Dreamweaver application. The **Welcome screen** appears.
2. Select the **CSS** option from the **Create New** group, as shown in Figure 3.21.

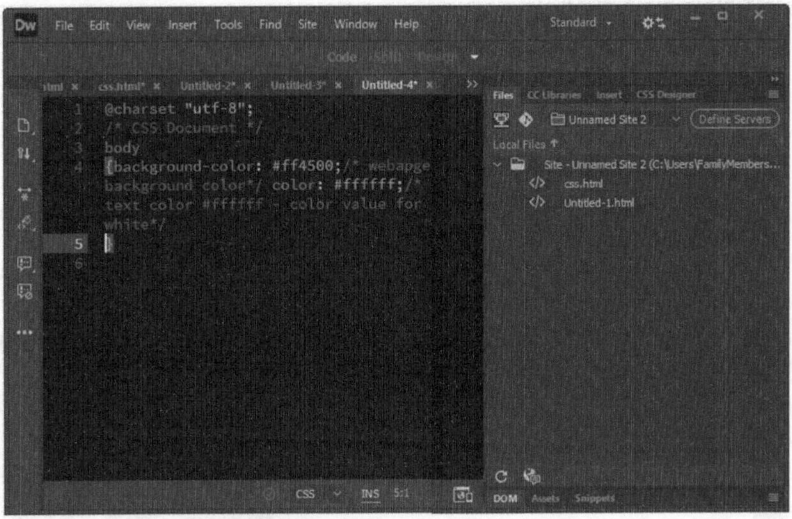

***Figure 3.21:** Type the code in the CSS file*

3. A new document is created.
4. Type the code, given in Example 3, in the CSS file (See Figure 3.21).

Example 3: Creating an External Style sheet.

Solution:

```
Body
{
background-color:#ff4500;  /* Web page background color */
color:#ffffff;     /* text color #ffffff - color value for white */
}
```

In above Example 3, the parameter for background and text color are written in external.css file.

5. Select the **File** menu and choose **Save**. For example, we have saved the file as **external.css.**

Each HTML document that requires the style sheet must link to the style sheet by using the `<link>` tag. The `<link>` tag is defined inside the `head` section, as shown in the following code.

To link the external style sheet to the HTML document, do this:

1. Open the HTML document on which you want to apply the style sheet. In our case, we are opening the exter.html document.
2. Type the code, as given in Example 4.

Example 4: Opening external style sheet to the HTML document.

Solution:

```
<head>
<link rel=”stylesheet” type=”text/css”
```

```
href="external.css" />
<body>
<p>Text Color will be changed in blue color when we use external CSS</p>
</body>
</head>
```

3. Click the **File** menu and choose **Save**. For example, we have saved the file as **exter.html**.
4. Now, you can view the background and text color in the Design view of the document as shown in Figure 3.22.

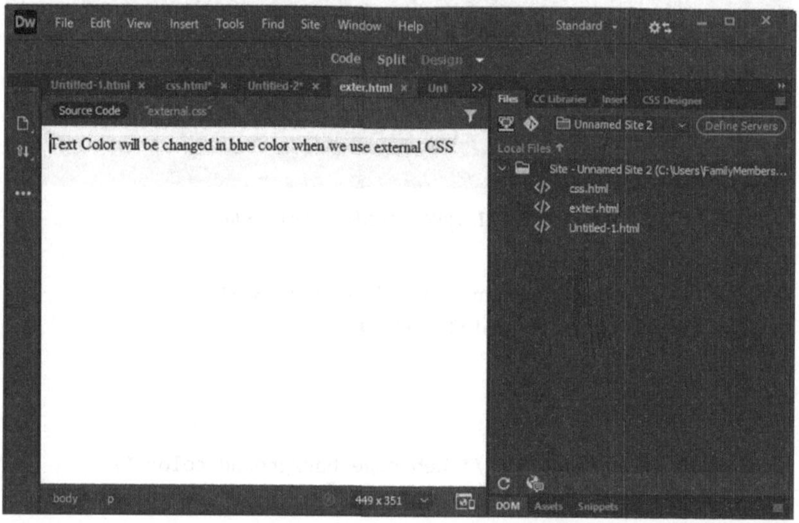

Figure 3.22: The background and text color in the Design view

EXERCISES

A. Multiple Choice Questions.

1. __________ is used to create a web page and to store them on your own computer.
   (a) Web browser (b) HTML (c) CSS (d) Dreamweaver
2. __________ is the name for the folder where you are storing all of your website's contents.
   (a) Website (b) Testing server
   (c) Local root folder (d) Remote folder
3. __________ shortcut key to open the save program in Dreamweaver.
   (a) Ctrl+S (b) Ctrl+V (c) Ctrl+C (d) Ctrl+D
4. __________ sets the font style of the selected text as italic.
   (a) Bold (b) Italic (c) ID (d) Format

5. ____________ creates the numbered list of the selected list.
   (a) Ordered list (b) Unordered list (c) Definition list (d) All of these

B. Fill in the blanks.

1. To exit from the Dreamweaver application, press ____________ key.
2. Page title should not more than ____________ characters.
3. ____________ provides a table description.
4. ____________ provides a table title which display outside area of the table.
5. ____________ determines the number of pixels between a cell's border and its contents.

C. State whether the following statements are True or False.

1. Row determines the number of table columns.
2. Merging of cells means to combine two or more cells to make it single.
3. The full form of CSS is Cascading Style Sheet.
4. CSS file is stored with an extension of .csv.
5. Dreamweaver provides the CSS design to create styles by using an abbreviated syntax, known as shorthand CSS.

D. Answers the following questions.

1. Write down the rules of CSS. How to create an internal style sheet?
2. Discuss HTML properties in detail.
3. How to save a web page on Dreamweaver? Write down its steps.
4. What is the difference between internal and external style sheet?

4 Adding Graphics to Web Page in Dreamweaver

Learning Objectives

After studying this chapter, you should be able to do:

• Understanding for inserting an image • Discuss in detail about the setting image attributes • Explain how to add image border • Discuss to add background image • How to create image map and rollover image • Identify multimedia files and flash file format • Explain how to insert SWF file, Flash video file and embedding a sound file on a web page • Discuss to work with hyperlink

Adding Graphics

A graphic can be defined as a visual representation of information in the form of pictures, graphs and images. Selecting appropriate graphics in Web pages help in communicating the intended message effectively.

Inserting an Image

Dreamweaver provides several ways to insert an image into an **HTML (HyperText Markup Language)** document. You can insert an image in the document simply by selecting the Image option from the Insert menu. In addition, you can use the Insert and Assets panels to insert an image in a Web page.

When you insert an image into an HTML document, a reference to the image file is automatically created in the HTML source code. You can save your image files in the root folder on your Website to keep a track of documents for easy Website management. This also helps in maintaining the reference of the image file in the HTML source code. However, if the image file is not located in the root folder of your Website, Dreamweaver asks you to copy the image file into the root folder.

To insert an image into a Web page, do this:

1. Place the cursor where you want to insert the image. You will see the insertion point blinking as shown in Figure 4.1.
2. Select **Insert** menu and choose **Image**. *Alternatively*, you can also select the image in the **Insert** panel.

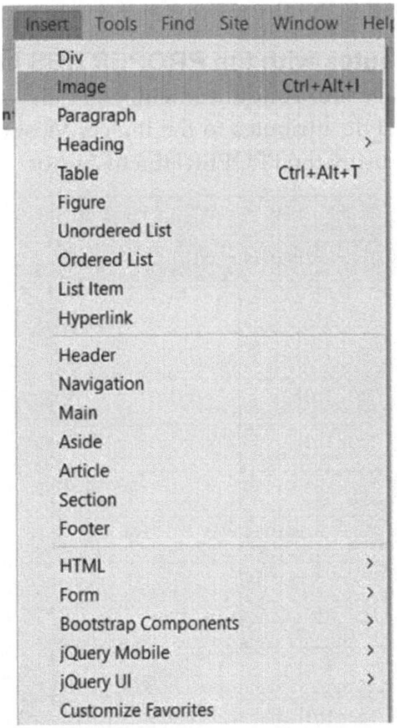

Figure 4.1: *Selecting Image options in the Insert menu*

3. The **Select Image Source** dialog box appears as shown in Figure 4.2.
4. Navigate the location of the image file.
5. Select the image and then click the **OK** button.

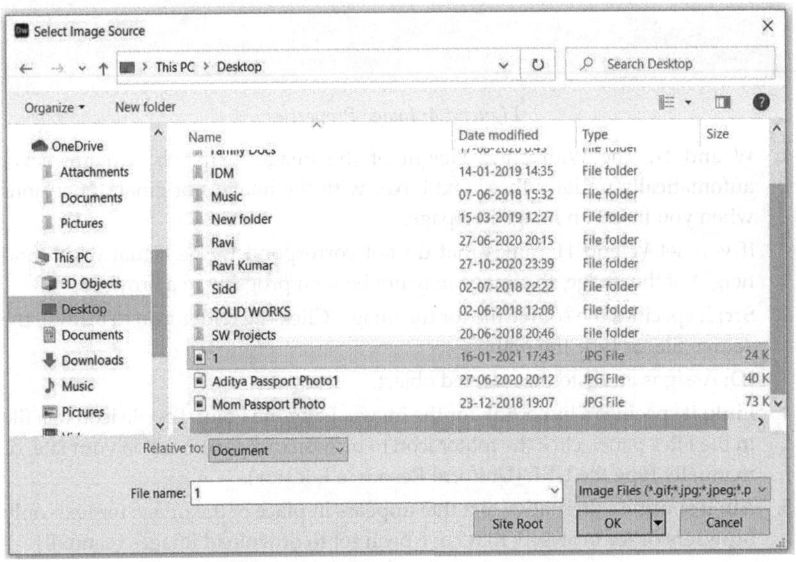

Figure 4.2: *Select Image Source dialog box*

6. The image is inserted in the Dreamweaver document.

Setting Image Attributes with the PROPERTIES Inspector

After you insert an image into your document, you will want to add other HTML markup and possibly style attributes to the image. Most of the attributes can be added to the image by using the PROPERTIES Inspector.

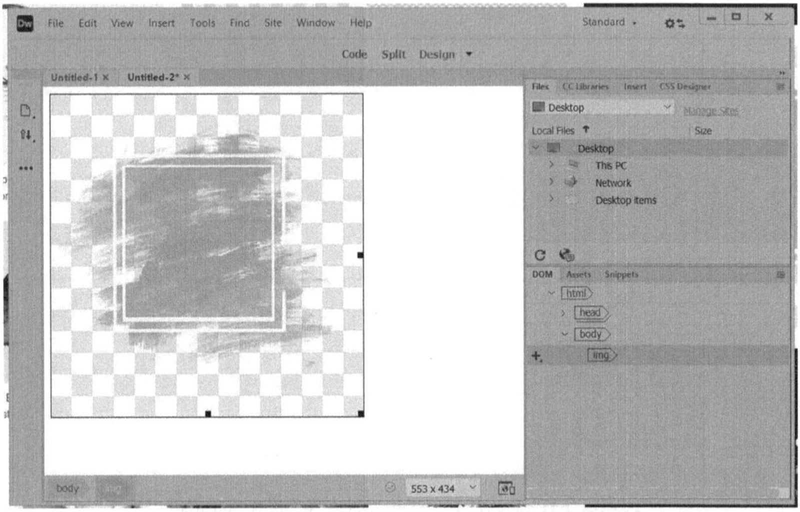

Figure 4.3: *The image has inserted in the Dreamweaver document*

Following options are available in the PROPERTIES Inspector as shown in Figure 4.4.

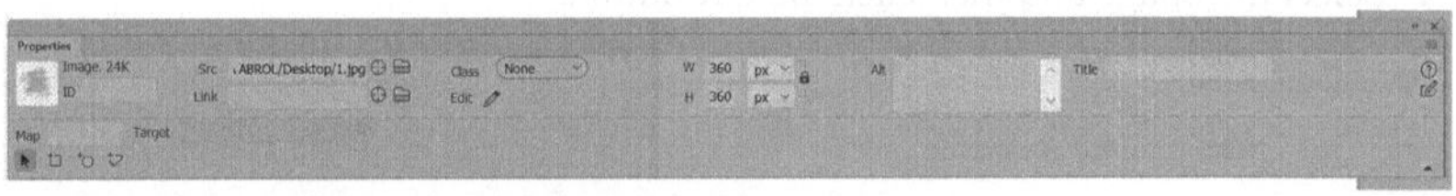

Figure 4.4: *Image Properties*

1. **W and H:** The Width and Height of the image, in pixels. Dreamweaver automatically updates these text boxes with the image's original dimensions when you insert an image in a page.

   If you set W and H values that do not correspond to the actual width and height of the image, the image may not be seen properly in a browser.
2. **Src:** It specifies the source file for the image. Click the folder icon to browse the source file, or type the path.
3. **ID:** Assigns an ID to the selected object.
4. **Link:** It specifies a hyperlink for the image. Drag the Point-To-File icon to a file in the Files panel, click the folder icon to browse to a document on your site, or manually type the URL (Uniform Resource Locator).
5. **Alt:** It specifies alternative text that appears in place of the image for text- only browsers or for browsers that have been set to download images manually.

6. **Target:** Specifies the frame or window in which the linked page should load. This option is only used when you set the hyperlink in the image.
   - _blank opens a linked Web page in a new browser window.
   - _parent opens a linked Web page in the parent frameset. If the parent frameset is not nested, the linked page will fill the entire browser window.
   - _self opens a linked Web page in the same window or frame that contains the link. This is the default setting.
   - _top opens a linked Web page in the entire browser window.

Resizing and Resetting the images

Resize images by either dragging the resize handles located on the right, bottom, and bottom-right corners of the selected image or by entering new image dimensions in the **W** and **H** fields in the Properties Inspector as shown in Figure 4.5. After you stretch or scrunch an image beyond its normal size, the **Reset Size** icon appears between the **W** and **H** fields in the **Properties Inspector** and the **W** and **H** values appear in bold. To revert an image to its normal size, click the Reset Size icon as shown in Figure 4.5.

Note: Dreamweaver is not a WYSIWYG (What you see is what you get) editor. That is, you can add or insert images using Dreamweaver, but you cannot move or position the images from the interface.

Adding Image Borders

By default, images with no links have no borders, but you can add black borders of any pixel width using HTML. Images with links have a border that takes on the properties of text links. For example, if the default text link color is blue, a linked image has a blue border. Although adding an HTML border by entering a number for the width of the border in the **Border** field in the **Properties Inspector**.

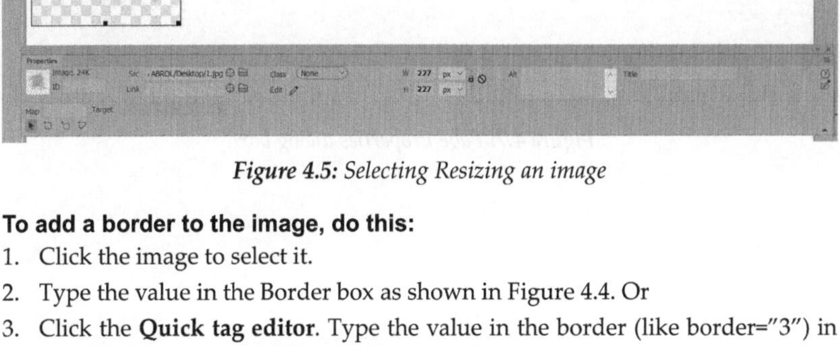

Figure 4.5: *Selecting Resizing an image*

To add a border to the image, do this:

1. Click the image to select it.
2. Type the value in the Border box as shown in Figure 4.4. Or
3. Click the **Quick tag editor**. Type the value in the border (like border="3") in the Quick tag editor as shown in Figure 4.6.

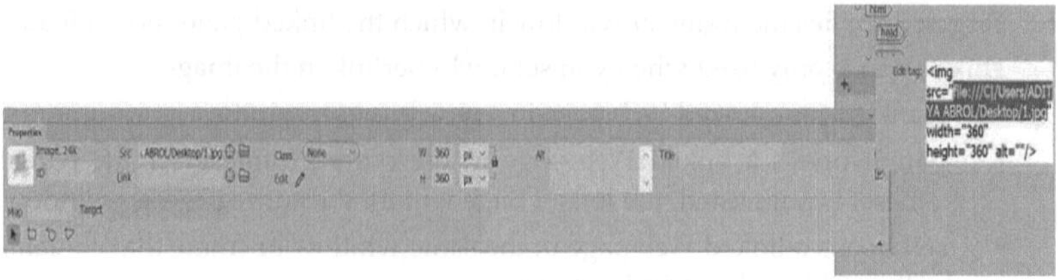

Figure 4.6: Select the Quick tag editor and then type the value in the border tag

Extra Byte

If you want to revert an image to its original size, Click the Reset size button in the image Property Inspector.

Adding Background Image

To insert an image as a background, do this:

1. Open a Web page where you want to insert a background image. In our case, we are inserting the image in the public.html.
2. Click the Page Properties button from the **CSS Properties Inspector**.
3. The **Page Properties** dialog box appears as shown in Figure 4.7.
4. Click the **Browse...** button to navigate the location where the image is saved.
5. The **Select Image Source** dialog box appears as shown in Figure 4.8.

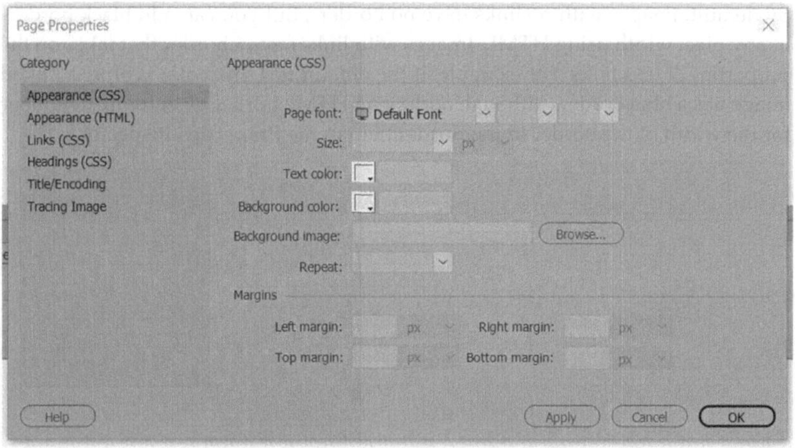

Figure 4.7: Page Properties dialog box

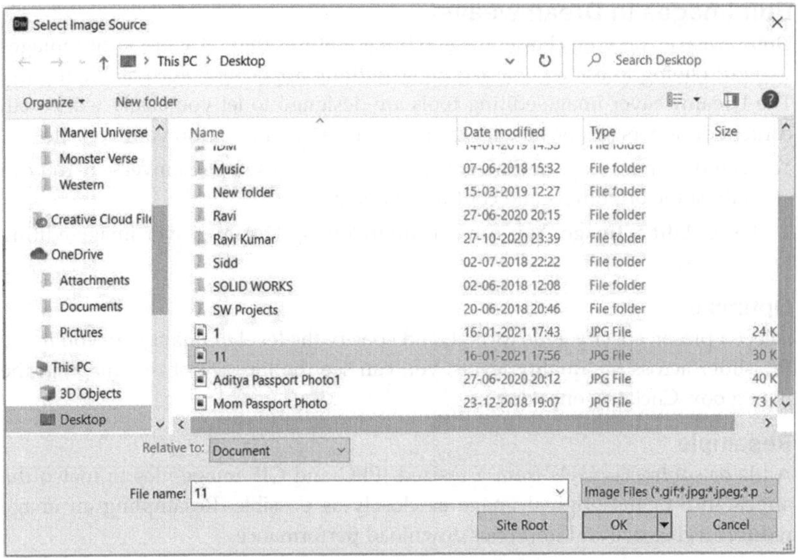

Figure 4.8: *Select Image Source dialog box*

6. Browse the location of the image. In our case, we have opened the default **Unnamed Site 3** folder.
7. Select the desired image from the **Contents** pane.
8. Click **OK** button.
9. The Background image is inserted in the Web page as shown in Figure 4.9.

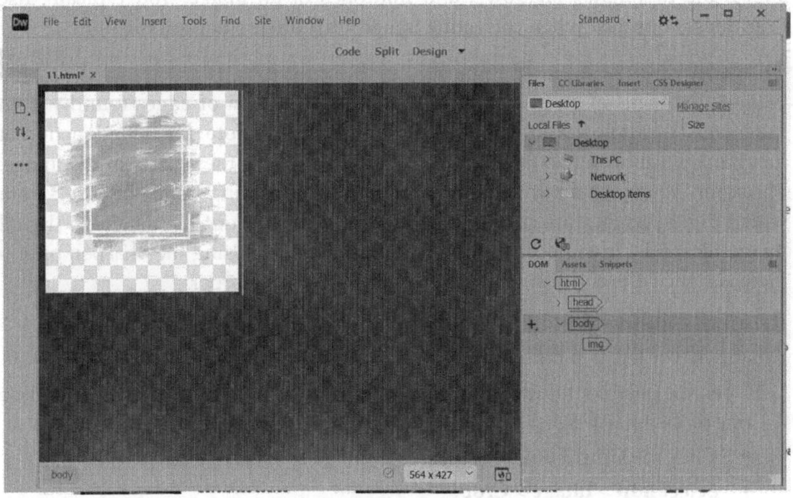

Figure 4.9: *The background image is inserted in the Web page*

Edit images in Dreamweaver

Dreamweaver provides basic image-editing features that let you modify images without having to use an external image-editing application such as Photoshop. The Dreamweaver image-editing tools are designed to let you easily work with content designers responsible for creating image files for use on your website.

You can resample, crop, optimize, and sharpen images in Dreamweaver. You can also adjust the brightness and contrast of images.

1. Select **Edit > Image**. You can set the following Dreamweaver image-editing features:

Optimize

Select a preset, specify a file format, and specify the level of quality. As you move the slider across the quality levels, you can see the file size of the image in the dialog box. Click OK once done.

Resample

Adds or subtracts pixels from a resized JPEG and GIF image files to match the appearance of the original image as closely as possible. Resampling an image reduces its file size and improves download performance.

Crop

Edit images by reducing the area of the image. You can use crop to place more emphasis on the subject of the image, and remove unwanted aspects surrounding the center of interest.

Brightness and Contrast

Modifies the contrast or brightness of pixels in an image. Brightness and Contrast affects the highlights, shadows, and midtones of an image. You typically use Brightness/Contrast when correcting images that are too dark or too light.

Sharpen

Adjusts the focus of an image by increasing the contrast of edges found within the image. When you scan an image, or take a digital photo, the default action of most image capturing software is to soften the edges of the objects in the image. The scanning prevents extremely fine details from becoming lost in the pixels from which digital images are composed. However, to bring out the details in digital image files, it is often necessary to sharpen the image. Using the Sharpen option increases the edge contrast, making the image appear sharper.

Crop an image

Dreamweaver lets you crop or trim bitmap file images.

1. Open the page containing the image you want to crop, select the image, and do one of the following:
    - Click the **Crop Tool** icon in the image Property inspector.
    - Select **Edit > Image > Crop.**
    - Crop handles appear around the selected image.

2. Adjust the crop handles until the bounding box surrounds the area of the image that you want to keep.
3. Double-click inside the bounding box or press Enter to crop the selection.
4. A dialog box informs you that the image file you are cropping will be changed on disk. Click **OK.**

   Every pixel in the selected bitmap outside the bounding box is removed, but other objects in the image remain.
5. Preview the image and ensure that it meets your expectations. If not, select **Edit > Undo Crop** to revert to the original image.

Create a rollover image

A *rollover* is an image that, when viewed in a browser, changes when the pointer moves across it. You must have two images to create the rollover. A primary image or the image displayed when the page first loads, and a secondary image or the image that appears when the pointer moves over the primary image. Both the images in a rollover must be of the same size. If the images are not the same size, Dreamweaver resizes the second image to match the properties of the first image.

Rollover images are automatically set to respond to the **onMouseOver** event. You can set an image to respond to a different event. For example, a mouse click or change a rollover image.

1. In the Document window, place the insertion point where you want the rollover to appear.
2. Insert the rollover using one of these methods:
   - In the **Insert** panel, select **HTML** from the drop-down list. Select **Rollover Image**, from the list of options.
   - Select **Insert > HTML > Rollover Image.**
3. In the **Insert Rollover Image** dialog box, select the images and set the properties for the rollover. You can set the following properties:

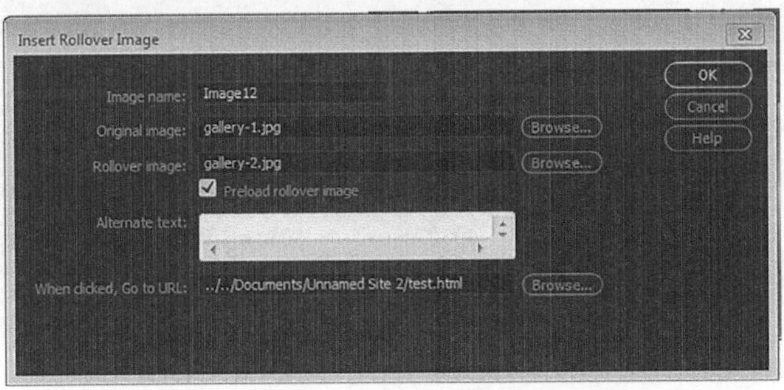

Figure 4.10: Setting properties of a rollover image

Image Name

The name of the rollover image.

Original image

The image you want to display when the page loads. Enter the path in the text box, or click Browse and select the image.

Rollover Image

The image you want to display when the pointer rolls over the original image. Enter the path or click Browse to select the image.

Preload Rollover Image

Preloads the images in the browser's cache so no delay occurs when the user rolls the pointer over the image.

Alternate Text

(Optional) Text to describe the image for viewers using a text-only browser.

When clicked, Go to URL

The file that you want to open when a user clicks the rollover image. Enter the path or click Browse and select the file.

1. To preview the rollover image, select **File > Real-time Preview**, or press F12.
2. In the browser, move the pointer over the original image to see the rollover image.

Creating an Image Map

An image map is an image divided into regions known as hotspots. For example, when a user clicks a hotspot, it opens a new Web page. In Dreamweaver, you can create hotspots in various shapes.

To add a Hotspot to an image map, do this:

1. Select the image on which you want to set the image map.
2. Specify the name of the image map in the **Map** text box located in the **PROPERTIES Inspector** (See Figure 4.11).

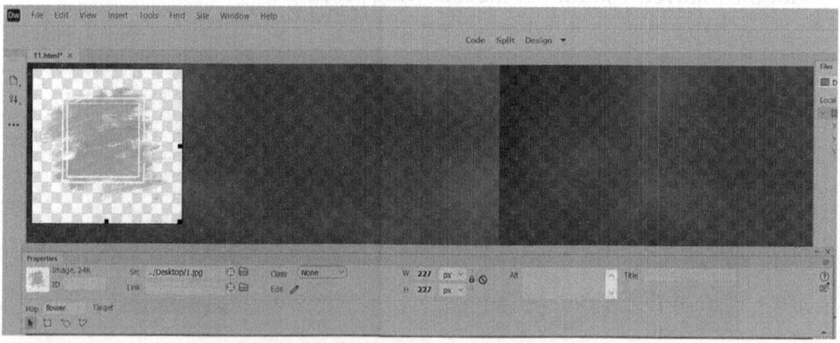

Figure 4.11: Specify the name in the Map text box

3. Click the **Circle** hotspot in the PROPERTIES Inspector as shown in Figure 4.11.
4. Drag the mouse-pointer in the image where you want to set the hotspot. The Dreamweaver message box appears as shown in Figure 4.12. This message box prompts the user to describe the image map in the Alt field on the PROPERTIES Inspector.

5. Click the OK button in the Dreamweaver message box, as shown in Figure 4.12.

Extra Byte

A video file that contains encoded audio and video data for delivery through Flash® Player.

6. The PROPERTIES Inspector displays the settings related to the hotspot.
7. Click the **Browse for File** button beside the **Link** text box located in the Properties inspector, as shown in Figure 4.12.
8. The **Select File** dialog box appears as shown in Figure 4.13.
9. Select the file in the **Look in:** drop-down list, and then click the **OK** button in the **Select File** dialog box.

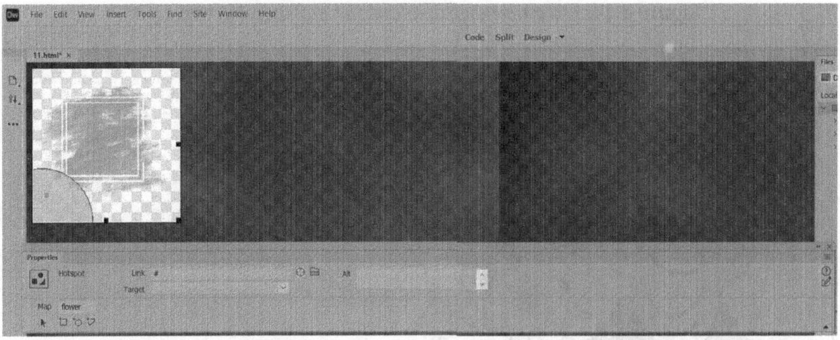

***Figure 4.12:** Selecting Browse for File in the Hotspot PROPERTIES Inspector*

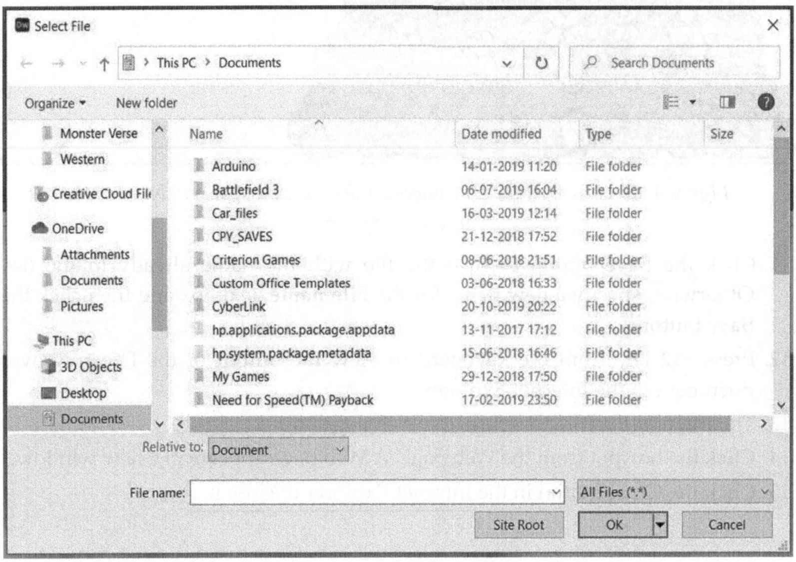

***Figure 4.13:** Selecting file using Select File dialog box*

Dreamweaver message box appears as shown in Figure 4.14.

10. Click the **Yes** button in the Dreamweaver message box to save the file in the root folder of the Website.

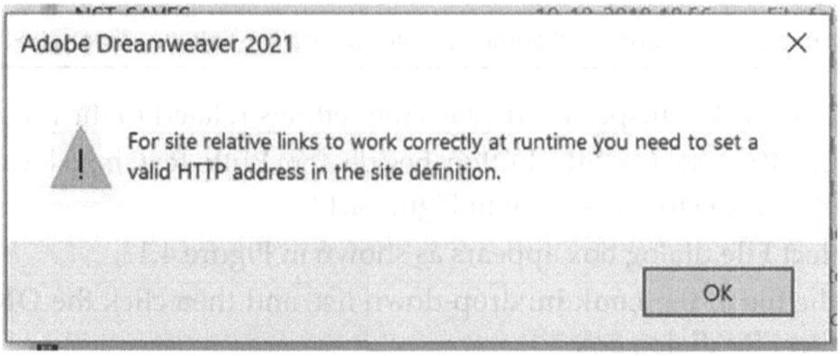

Figure 4.14: *Dreamweaver displays the message to copy a file*

Figure 4.15: *Output of the Dreamweaver document displays in browser like Internet Explorer*

11. Click the **Save** button to save the file with the name already in the list. Otherwise, specify a new name for the **File name:** text box and then click the **Save** button.
12. Press **F12** key from the keyboard to view the output of the Dreamweaver document in the Internet Explorer.
13. The Internet Explorer displays the Web page.
14. Click the hotspot from the Web page. A Web page appears in a new window.
15. Click the **Close** button in the Internet Explorer to close it.

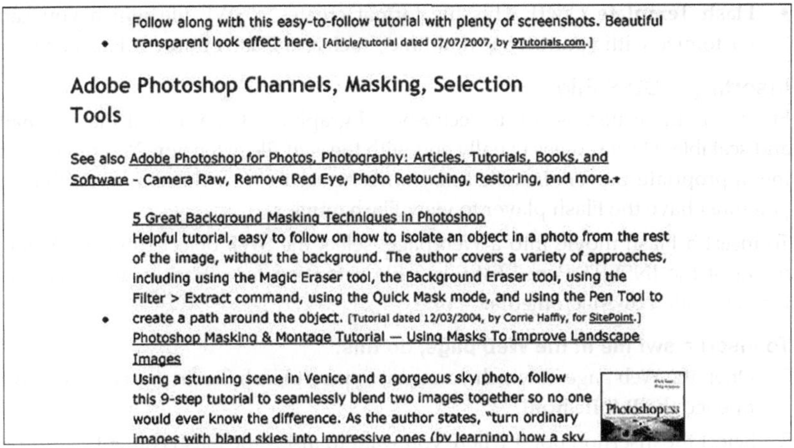

- Follow along with this easy-to-follow tutorial with plenty of screenshots. Beautiful transparent look effect here. [Article/tutorial dated 07/07/2007, by 9Tutorials.com.]

Adobe Photoshop Channels, Masking, Selection Tools

See also Adobe Photoshop for Photos, Photography: Articles, Tutorials, Books, and Software - Camera Raw, Remove Red Eye, Photo Retouching, Restoring, and more.

- 5 Great Background Masking Techniques in Photoshop
  Helpful tutorial, easy to follow on how to isolate an object in a photo from the rest of the image, without the background. The author covers a variety of approaches, including using the Magic Eraser tool, the Background Eraser tool, using the Filter > Extract command, using the Quick Mask mode, and using the Pen Tool to create a path around the object. [Tutorial dated 12/03/2004, by Corrie Haffly, for SitePoint.]
  Photoshop Masking & Montage Tutorial — Using Masks To Improve Landscape Images
  Using a stunning scene in Venice and a gorgeous sky photo, follow this 9-step tutorial to seamlessly blend two images together so no one would ever know the difference. As the author states, "turn ordinary images with bland skies into impressive ones (by learning) how a sky

Figure 4.16: Hotspot link opens in new window

Adding Multimedia Files

Not only text and graphics are displayed in your Web pages but also you can add multimedia files, like sounds and movies. It almost seems that every page you visit on the Web uses Flash or other multimedia in some way or another.

In addition to Flash elements, such as text and buttons, Dreamweaver lets you add user-defined Flash movies, Java Applets and ActiveX Controls (can be used to add specialized functionality, such as animation, pop-up menus, or Web pages). Most multimedia is controlled by specific plug-ins. For example, the Flash plug-in allows you to play flash movies, just as the QuickTime plug-in allows you to play QuickTime movies. Plug-ins are a part of the open application architecture of Web browsers.

Understanding Flash File Formats

Adobe Flash allows you to create a variety of file types—FLA(Macromedia Flash file extension), SWF (Small Web Format), SWT (Flash Template), SWC (Flash Element), and FLV(Flash Video)—for different purposes. The file formats provided by Dreamweaver are as follows:

- **The Flash file (.fla):** It is the source file format for the Adobe Flash program. This file format cannot be opened in Dreamweaver; you can only open this file format in Flash. You use the source Flash file (.fla) to create the other Flash file formats.
- **Flash SWF (.swf):** This file format creates a compressed movie of the Flash (.fla) file.
- **Flash Video file (.flv):** This file format creates a video file with audio and video encoding you can play in the Flash Player.

- **Flash Template (.swt):** This file format creates a SWF file which you can customize with your own text or links, such as a Flash button or Flash text.

Inserting a SWF File

Flash is popular because of its vector-based graphics. It is a format that is small and scalable. Flash movies usually end with the .swf file extension. You must have the appropriate players installed in your browser to view these movies; that is, you must have the Flash player to view Flash movies.

To insert a Flash movie into a Web page, select the SWF object from the Media menu of the INSERT Panel. SWF is a file extension for a Shockwave Flash file format created by Macromedia.

To insert a swf file in the Web page, do this:

1. Open the Web page in which you want to insert Flash file. In our case, we have opened the **Public.html**.
2. Select the insertion point where you want to insert the Flash content.
3. Select **Insert** menu highlight **HTML**. A sub menu appears; select **Flash SWF** as shown in Figure 4.17. *Alternatively*, you can press **Ctrl+Alt+F** keys together.

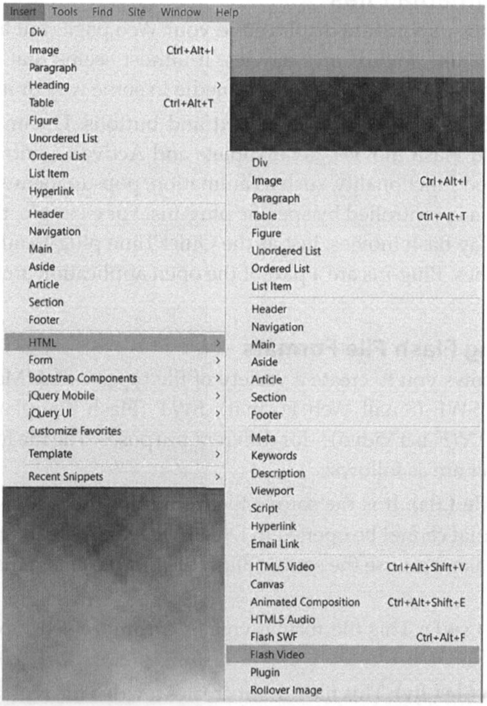

Figure 4.17: Selecting Media SWF option

4. The **Select SWF** dialog box appears as shown in Figure 4.18.
5. Select the File that you want to insert. In our case, we have selected the **Examples1**.

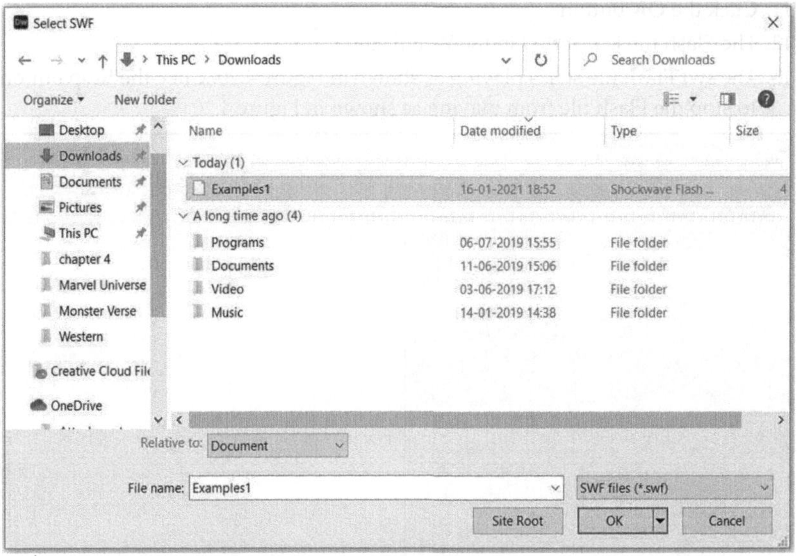

Figure 4.18: *Select SWF dialog box*

6. Click **OK** button as shown in Figure 4.18.
7. The **Object Tag Accessibility Attributes** dialog box appears as shown in Figure 4.19.

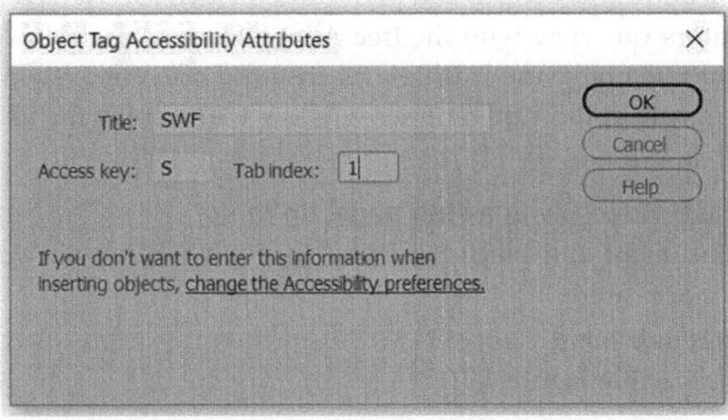

Figure 4.19: *Object Tag Accessibility Attributes dialog box*

8. Type the title in the **Title:** text box. In our case, we have typed the title as **SWF**.
9. Type the value for the access key in the **Access key:** text box. In our case, we have typed the value as **S**.
10. Type the value for the tab index in the **Tab index:** text box. In our case, we have typed the value as 1.

11. Click the **OK** button.
12. The Flash file is inserted in the Web page.
15. The swf Flash file starts playing as shown in Figure 4.20. Click the **Stop** button to stop the Flash file from playing as shown in Figure 4.20.

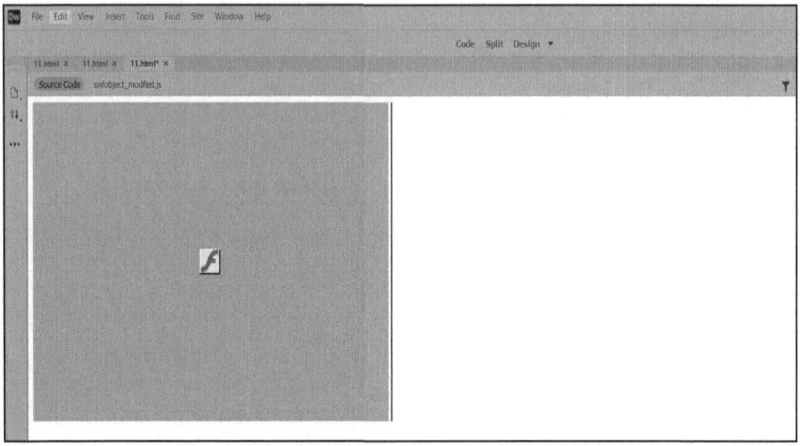

Figure 4.20: Inserting SWF file in the Web page

Inserting a Flash Video File

Flash video is different from a regular Flash movie in that a Flash video uses the FLV file format and allows you to add prerecorded video to a Web page in a format that most visitors can view with the free Adobe Flash player. However, to play these files, you must have the Flash player installed on your system. If the Flash player is not installed, the Web browser window will display the instructions for downloading it.

To inset a Flash video file in a Web page, do this:

1. Open a document and place the insertion point where you want the Flash video to be appeared.
2. Select **Insert** menu and choose **HTML**. A sub menu appears, select **Flash Video** option as shown in Figure 4.21.

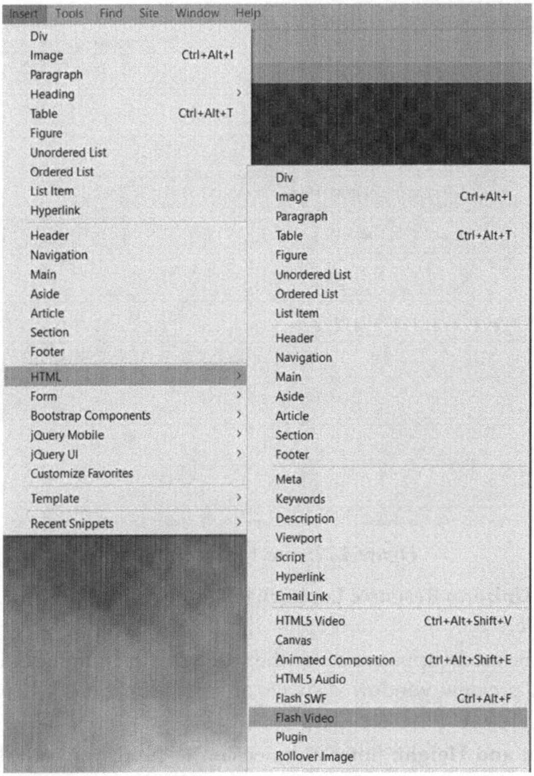

***Figure 4.21:** Selecting FVL option from the Insert menu*

3. The **Insert FLV** dialog box appears as shown in Figure 4.22. When inserting a Flash video, you have two options for the video type: **Progressive Download** and **Streaming**. The decisions you make for inserting Flash video vary slightly depending on which type you choose:
   - **Progressive Download Video:** Download the FLV file to the user's computer and play it there. The benefit of FLV is that the video starts to play during the download.
   - **Streaming Video:** Stream the Flash video and play it in the browser window. Streaming video typically buffers for a few seconds before playback. Streaming requires that the file to be served by your own Flash Media Server or by a hosted server running Flash Video Streaming Services.

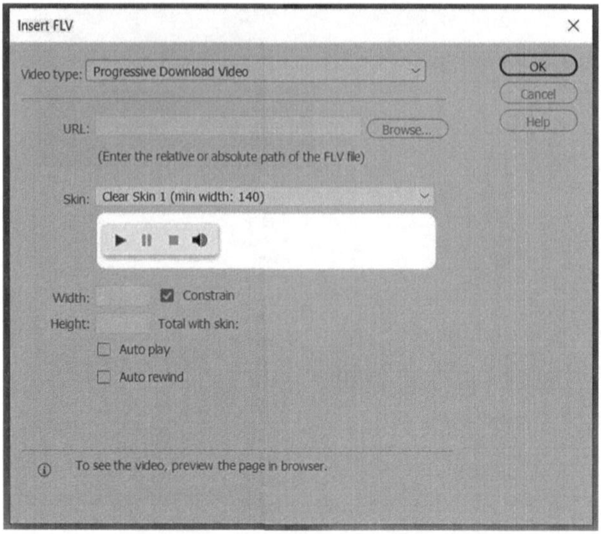

Figure 4.22: *Insert FLV dialog box*

- **URL (Uniform Resource Locator):** Enter the relative or absolute path of the FLV file.
- **Skin:** Select an appearance for the video player from the Skin drop-down list. A preview window displays an approximation of how each option looks.
- **Width: and Height:** Enter a dimension in pixels for both the width and height of the FLV file. Click the **Detect Size** button to automatically read the FLV file dimensions. If the dimensions are unreadable, manually enter Width: and Height: sizes. The Total with Skin dimensions displayed after the dimensions are detected represents the total Width and Height of the FLV file plus the Width and Height of the chosen skin.
    - o **Constrain:** Maintain the aspect ratio between the width and height of the FLV movie. This option is selected by default.
    - o **Auto Play:** Play the video as soon as the Web page loads in the browser window.
    - o **Auto Rewind:** Return the video playback to the start position when the video reaches the end.

4. Click the **Browse...** button to locate the path of the Flash video file as shown in Figure 4.23.
5. The **Select FLV** dialog box appears as shown in Figure 4.23.

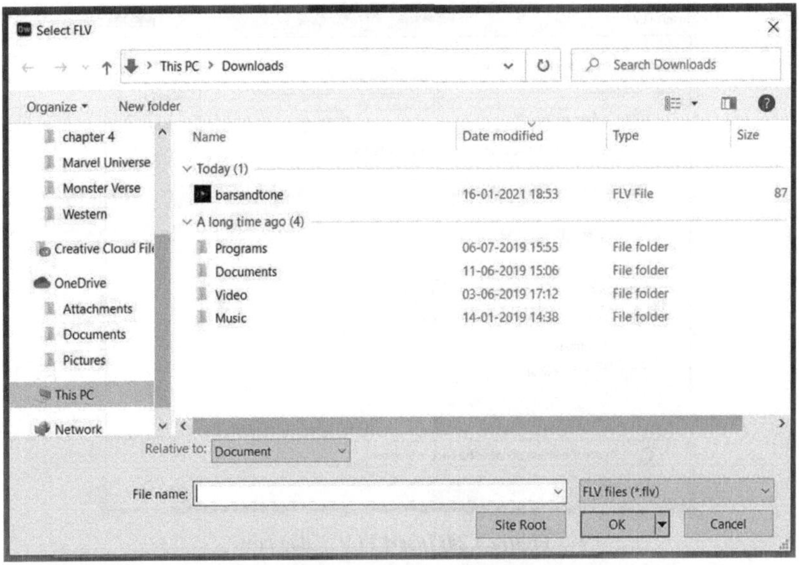

***Figure 4.23:** Select FLV dialog box*

6. Browse to the folder where the Flash video file is saved.
7. Select the desired Flash video file that you want to insert as shown in Figure 4.23.
8. Click the **OK** button to close the dialog box. The URL of the selected Flash video file appears in the URL text box in the **Insert FLV** dialog box as shown in Figure 4.24.
9. Click the **Detect Size** button to automatically set the height and width of the inserted Flash video file as shown in Figure 4.24.

   The height and width values appear in their respective text boxes.
10. Click the **OK** button as shown in Figure 4.24.
11. The selected file appears in the Web page as shown in Figure 4.25. Save the file as **.html** Web page.
12. Preview the Web page in the Web browser window. The Web page opens in the Internet Explorer window.

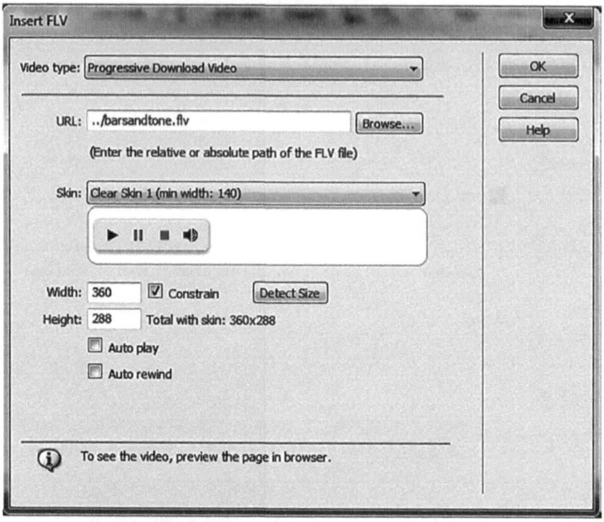

Figure 4.24: *Insert FLV dialog box*

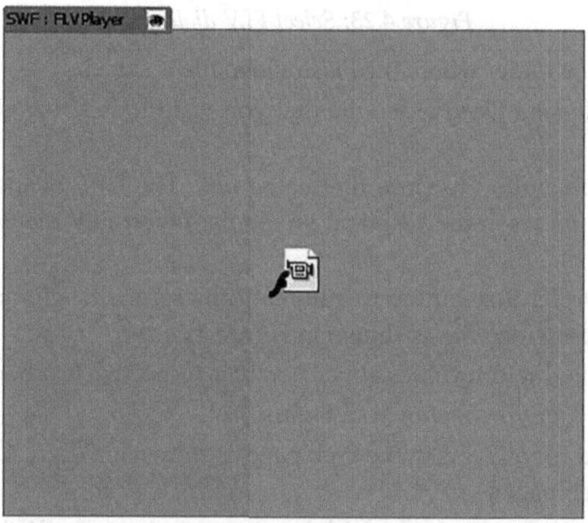

Figure 4.25: *The selected file appears in the Web page*

13. Click the **Play** button. The selected file .flv is played.

Adding Shockwave Movies, Java Applets, and ActiveX Controls

In Dreamweaver, you can add Shockwave movies, Java applets, ActiveX controls, and other sound and video files to any open, saved file. If the object you want to add is not one of these types, use a Netscape Navigator plug-in. You need to prepare these objects before inserting them on your page. Table 4.1 describes the type of objects you can add to your Web page.

Figure 4.26: *The selected video file appears in the Web page*

Table 4.1: *Objects to be added to Web Pages and their Description*

Media Type	Description
Shockwave movie	Adobe's standard for interactive multimedia files on the Web. Shockwave movies download fast and can be displayed in browsers.
Java applet	Lightweight Web page applications (applets) generated with the Java programming language.
ActiveX control	Reusable components like Netscape Navigator browser plug-ins. (ActiveX controls were formerly called OLE or Object Linking and Embedding controls). They run only in Windows versions of Internet Explorer. You can assign these controls, additional attributes and parameters in Dreamweaver.
QuickTime movie	A movie format created with Apple's QuickTime program that can include video, audio, and other bitstreams, such as images and animations.
Non-FLV video	Any non-FLV video, such as MPEG(Moving Picture Expert Group) or AVI(Audio Video Interleave). These movies can be linked to or embedded in your Web page.
Netscape Navigator plug-in	A plug-in, that allows a Netscape Navigator browser to display multimedia content (audio, video, animation, virtual reality, and 3D or Three Dimensional objects) in a range of file formats.

Embedding a Sound File on a Web Page

Dreamweaver supports adding sound to a Web page. You can choose from many types of sound files and formats, such as .midi, .wav, RealPlayer, and .mp3.

To insert a sound in a Web page, do this:

1. Open the Web page where you want to insert the sound.
2. Click the desired place to insert the sound.
3. Click Insert menu and choose **HTML**. A sub menu appears. Select **Plugin** as shown in Figure 4.27.

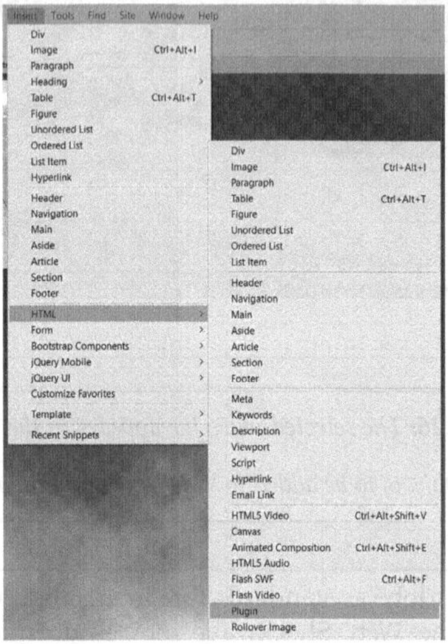

Figure 4.27: Selecting Plugin in the Insert menu

4. The **Select File** dialog box as shown in Figure 4.28.
5. Select the desired sound file.
6. Click the **OK** button as shown in Figure 4.28.

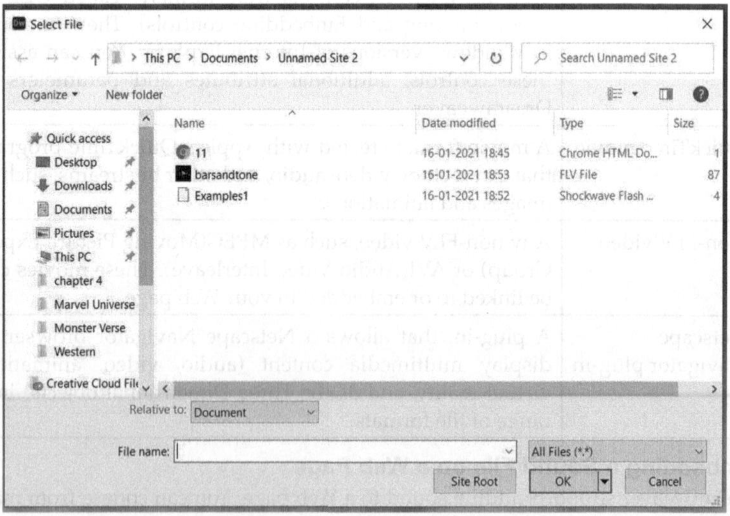

Figure 4.28: Select File dialog box

7. The sound file is inserted. Set it to required size as shown in Figure 5.40.
8. Click the **File** menu and choose **Preview in Browser**. A sub menu appears select **IExplore** to preview the Web page in Internet Explorer.
9. The selected sound file appears in the browser. You can click the **Play** button to play the sound file.

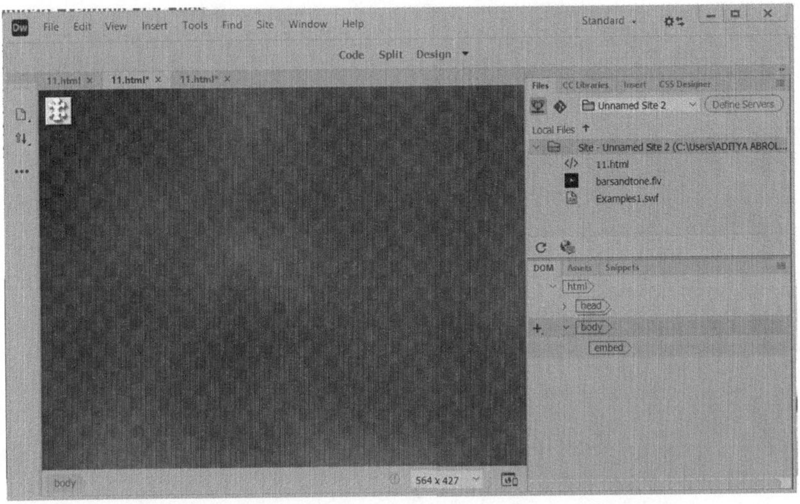

Figure 4.29: *The selected sound file is inserted in the Web page*

Working with Hyperlinks

A hyperlink is a segment of text or graphical item that serves as a cross-reference between different Web pages or different locations of the same Web page. The region from which a hyperlink can be activated is called an anchor, and the destination page of the hyperlink is known as a target. Hyperlinks can also point to any resource on graphic, sound, documents, and other files.

Creating a Hyperlink

In Dreamweaver, you can create a hyperlink from a word, paragraph or even the entire text of the Web page document. You can select the required text and create a hyperlink using the PROPERTIES Inspector. After creating the hyperlink, the selected text is highlighted. When you place the mouse pointer on the highlighted text, it displays the Hand tool that directs to the referenced document.

To create hyperlink, do this:

1. Select the text in the HTML that you want to set as hyperlink. For example, we have selected the **HTML Links** as shown in Figure 4.30.

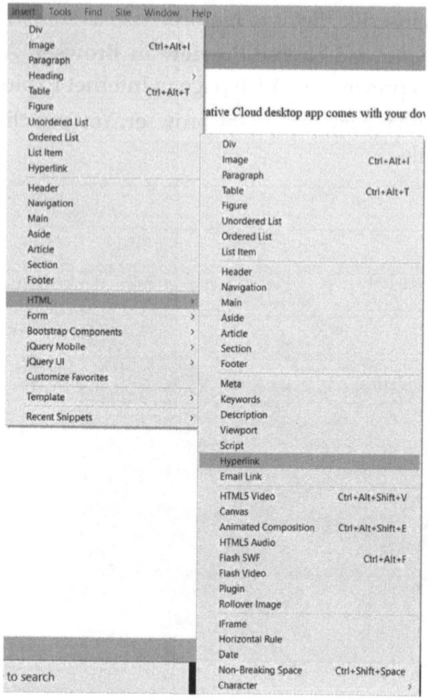

Figure 4.30: Select the text to set as hyperlink

2. Click the **Insert** menu and choose **Hyperlink**. The **Hyperlink** dialog box appears as shown in Figure 4.31.

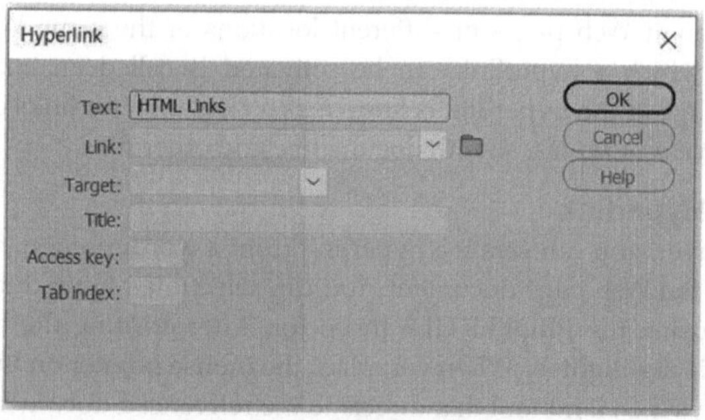

Figure 4.31: Hyperlink dialog box

3. Click the **Browse** button in the **Hyperlink** dialog box, as shown in Figure 4.32.
4. The **Select File** dialog box appears as shown in Figure 4.32.

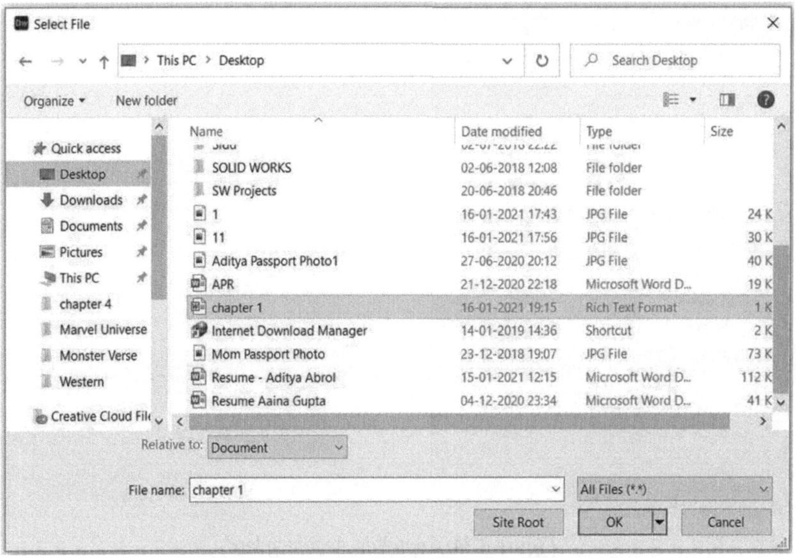

Figure 4.32: Selecting file in the Select File dialog box

5. Browse to the folder where the HTML document that you want to set as a hyperlink is stored. For example, we have selected the file **chapter 1**.
6. Click **OK** button to close the **Select File** dialog box.

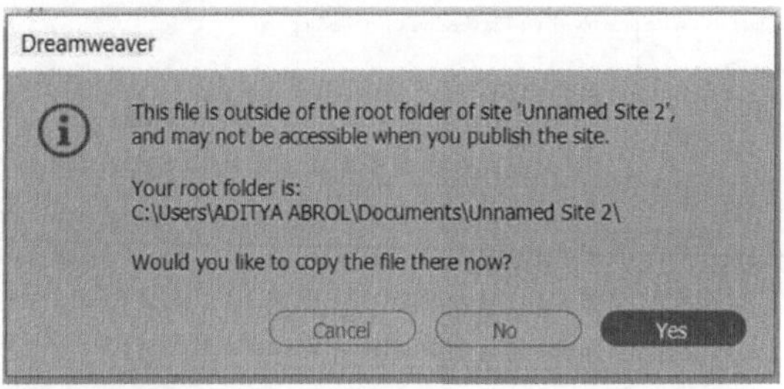

Figure 4.33: Dreamweaver message dialog box

8. Click the **Yes** button to copy the image file into the root folder of your Website.
9. The **Copy File As** dialog box appears as shown in Figure 4.34.
10. Click the Save button to save the file with the same name. Otherwise specify a new name for the file in the **File name:** text box.

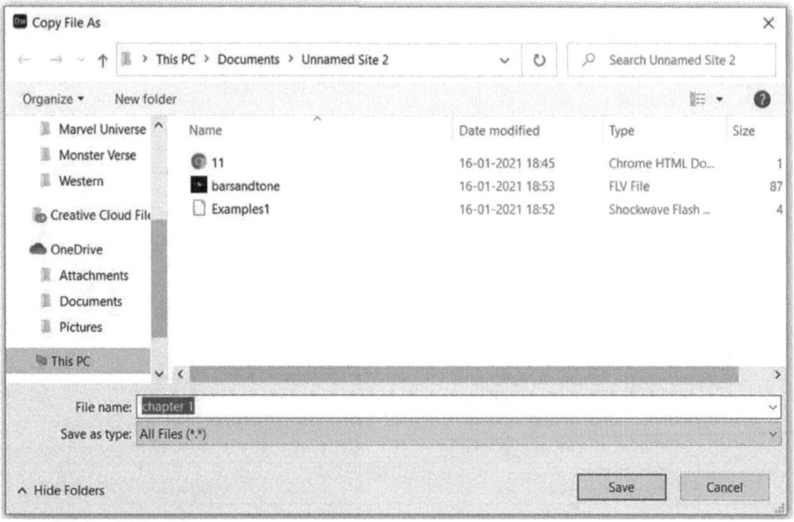

Figure 4.34: Copy File As dialog box

12. Click on **Save** button.

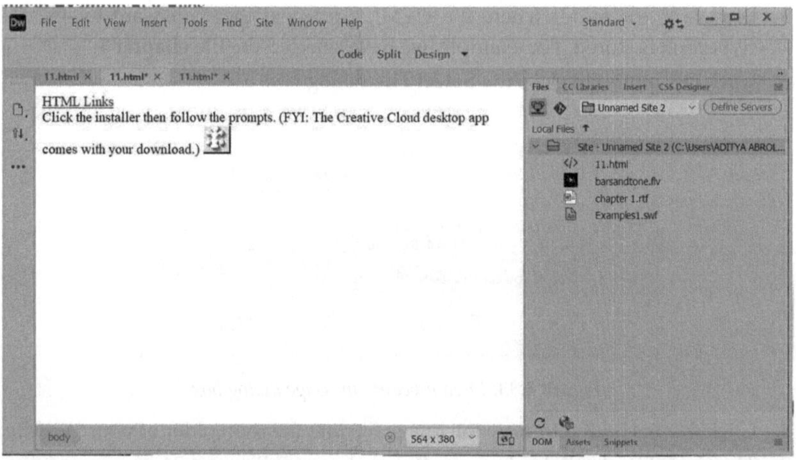

Figure 4.35: The selected text gets changed to a hyperlink

16. Select the **File** menu and choose save option or press the Ctrl+S keys together from the keyboard shortcut to save the HTML document.

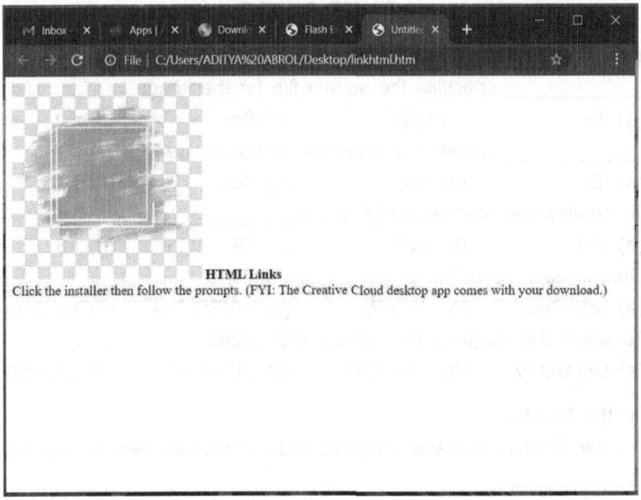

Figure 4.36: *Preview the HTML document in the Internet Explorer*

17. Click the hyperlink in the Web page.
18. The linked Web page is opened in Internet Explorer.

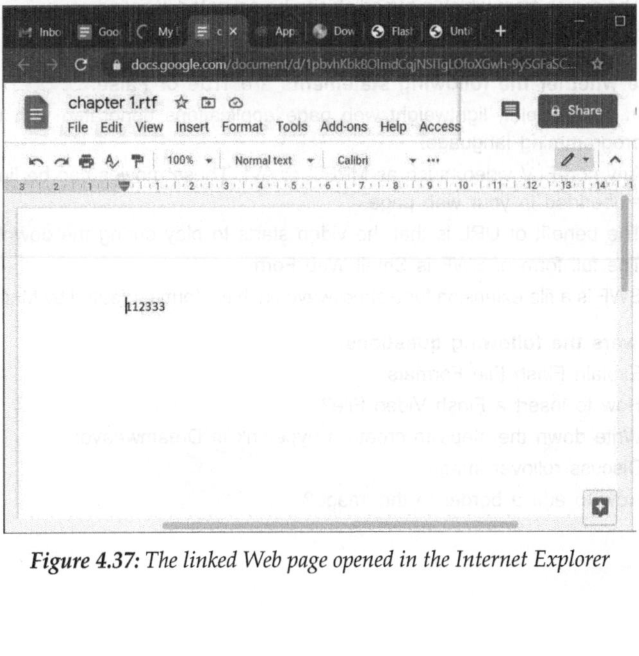

Figure 4.37: *The linked Web page opened in the Internet Explorer*

EXERCISES

A. Multiple Choice Questions.

1. ____________ specifies the source file for the image.
   (a) ID (b) Link (c) Scr (d) Alt
2. ____________ specifies a hyperlink for the image.
   (a) ID (b) Link (c) Scr (d) Alt
3. To preview the rollover image, press ____________.
   (a) F11 (b) F12 (c) F9 (d) F8
4. Dreamweaver is not a ____________ editor.
   (a) NotePad (b) WordPad (c) WYSIWYG (d) All of these
5. To select the image in the insert panel, press ____________.
   (a) Ctrl+Alt+V (b) Ctrl+Alt+I (c) Ctrl+Alt+F (d) Ctrl+Alt+X

B. Fill in the blanks.

1. A video file that contains encoded audio and video data for delivery through ____________.
2. In ____________, Adds or subtracts pixels from a resized JPEG and GIF image files to match the appearance of the original image as closely as possible.
3. The full form of URL is ____________.
4. The region from which a hyperlink can be activated is called as ____________.
5. The destination page of the hyperlink is called as ____________.

C. State whether the following statements are True or False.

1. In Java applet, lightweight web page applications generated with the Java programming language.
2. Any non-FLV video, such as MPEG or AVI. These movies can be linked toor embedded in your web page.
3. The benefit of URL is that the video starts to play during the download.
4. The full form of SWF is Small Web Form.
5. SWF is a file extension for a shockwave flash file format created by Macromedia.

D. Answers the following questions.

1. Explain Flash File Formats.
2. How to insert a Flash Video File?
3. Write down the steps to create a hyperlink in Dreamweaver.
4. Discuss rollover image.
5. How to add a border to the image?

5 Working with Framesets and Frames

Learning Objectives

After studying this chapter, you should be able to do:

- Explain forms • Discuss how to add forms • Know about how to insert text field, textarea, radio button, drop-down list, check box and button • Identify how to create form validation • Discuss how to create a jump menu

Framesets are basically a set of frames. It may comprise of the various sets of frames which will be required while rendering a page. If we talk about Frames, they hold a particular document. So, in other words, a Frame holds only one document or page but a Frameset has many numbers of frames holding different documents/ pages. Working with frames is a task of professionals. Using framesets and frames, a website is well managed and sophistically moving and rendering. Each frame has a unique document for rendering. It will have all of the information for it. While framesets have to maintain information of different frames altogether.

Definition: A frame is a region in a browser window that can display an HTML document independent of what is being displayed in the rest of the browser window.

Forms in Dreamweaver

Whenever you are visiting any website, you seldom come through 'Forms'. Forms are used to capture information that is entered by the user in the website. Similarly 'Form' in Dreamweaver is a utility tool which you create using different components like- text box, check box, radio button, input button etc. to capture the required data from the user. Forms can be validated and used according to your purpose. Forms are created to serve a motive/purpose. It is made with simple UI features so that the user finds it easy and friendly to use. If the user will find it difficult to use and fill, then the purpose will not be served. Since you have to gather information you need to be clear and easy with the form language and form design.

Memorize

A dynamic form element is a form object that gets its initial value by the web server where the web site is stored.

Inserting a Form

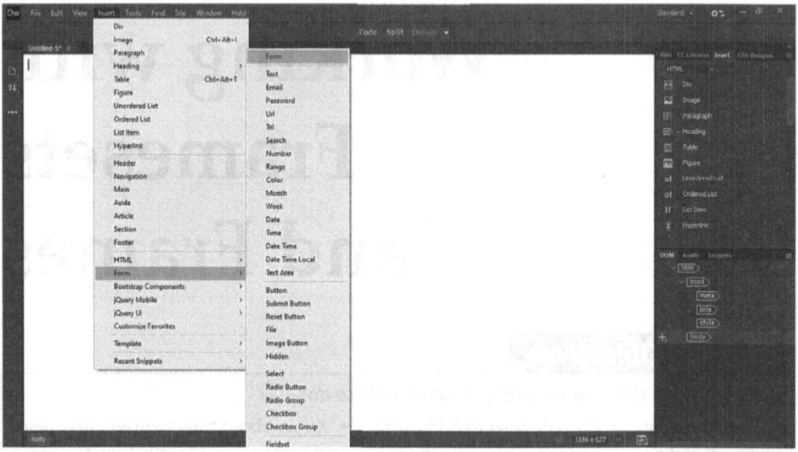

Figure 5.1: Insert Form

You will start by inserting a form to the design pane. This is the Dreamweaver home screen, where you will have plenty of options and you will start by creating a form. Firstly, you will go to the insert menu and then you will browse to the 'Form' option and then further you will select 'Form' from the sub menu as shown in the image above. Form is basically used to fetch data from users and post it to our database. A form generally asks a user to input the details asked in the form and then submit it. This is a typical use and functioning of the form. There are various types and situations where forms are used and required to capture data from users.

Figure 5.2: Inserting Form in Dreamweaver

Inserting a Text field

Let us talk about the Text Field. A Text Field is an area which is assigned to take a single line of text input. It is interesting to note that the text field is an editable component of the form. Here, you will be talking about the insertion of Text Field in your form. First you will go to the Insert menu from the above menu options. Then you will browse to Form to see all the available form components. Then you will go for the Text option in the sub menu. Following the above steps, you can successfully add a text field into your form and hence start using it. All other components can be inserted in a similar way. This is how you add Text field.

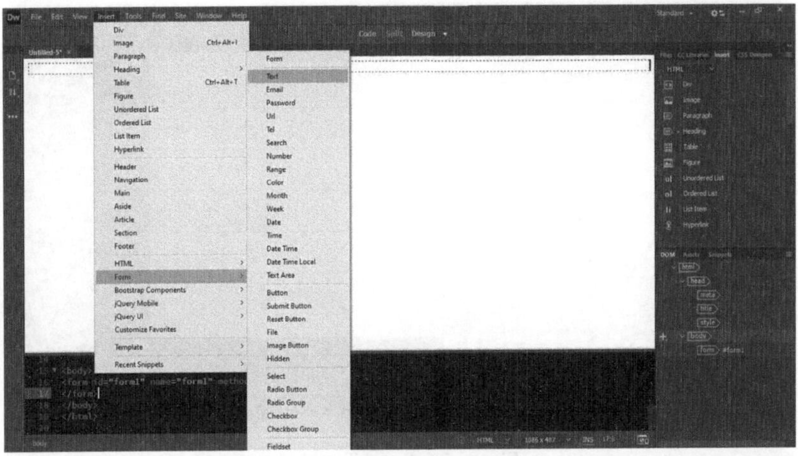

Figure 5.3: Insert Text

Extra Byte

The user clicks inside the textbox, and types the information required.

Inserting a Text Area

Now let us talk about the Text Area. A Text Area is an area which is assigned to take a multi line of text input. It is interesting to note that the Text Area is an editable component of the form. Here, you will be talking about the insertion of Text Area in your form. First you will go to the Insert menu from the above provided menu bar. Then you will browse to Form to see all the available form components. Then you will go for the Text Area option in the sub menu. Following the above steps, you can successfully add a Text Area into your form and hence start using it. All other components can be inserted in a similar way. This is how you add Text Area.

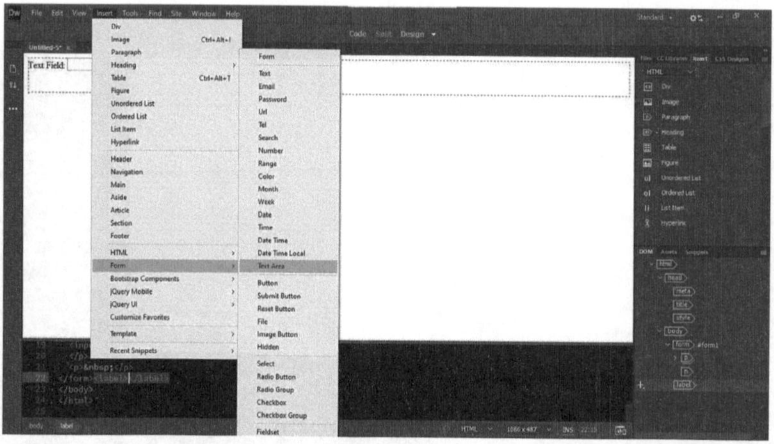

***Figure 5.4:** Insert Text Area*

***Figure 5.5:** Inserted Text Area*

Memorize

The textarea object is similar to the text field object set to multiline data from the user using the text area element in a form.

Inserting a Radio Button

Now you will discuss about the Radio Button. A Radio Button is a type of button which allows the user to select a single option from a number of given options. It is interesting to note that the Radio Button is a type of component of the form which is generally used whenever you have to choose from a variety of options. Here, you will be talking about the insertion of Radio Button in our form. First you will go to the Insert menu from the above provided menu bar. Then you will browse to Form to see all the available form components. Radio button denotes choice or decision. Then you will go for the Radio Button option in the sub menu. Following the above steps, you can successfully add a Radio Button into your form and hence start using it. All other components can be inserted in a similar way. This is how you add Radio Button.

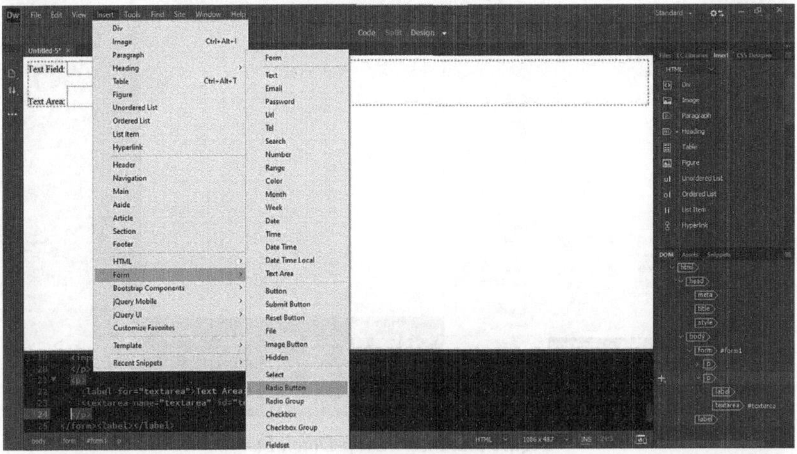

Figure 5.6: *Insert Radio Button*

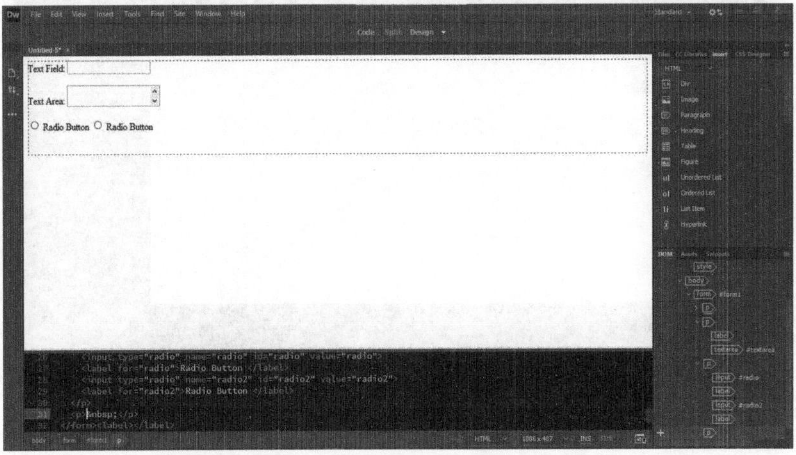

Figure 5.7: *Inserted Radio Button in Dreamweaver*

Inserting a Drop-Down List

Now we will talk about the Drop-Down List. A Drop-Down List is a type of list which allows the user to select a single option from a number of given options. It is interesting to note that the Drop-Down List is a type of component of the form which is generally used whenever you have to select from a variety of options. Here, you will be talking about the insertion of Drop-Down List in your form. First you will go to the Insert menu from the above provided menu bar. Then you will browse to Form to see all the available form components. Drop-Down List allows you to select an option. Then you will go for the Drop-Down List option in the sub menu. Following the above steps, you can successfully add a Drop-Down List into your form and hence start using it. This is how you add Drop-Down List.

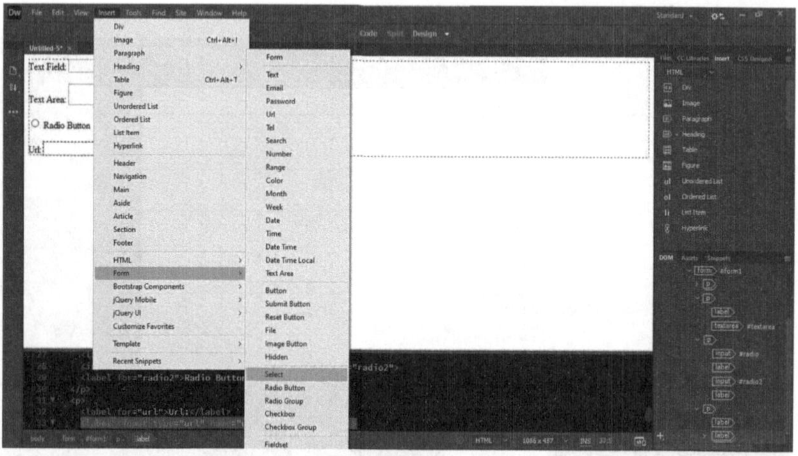

Figure 5.8: Insert Drop-Down List

Figure 5.9: Inserted Drop-Down List

Inserting a Check Box

Now let us talk about the Check Box. A Check Box is a tickable box which is used to confirm or agree to the asked question. It is interesting to note that the Check Box is an editable component of the form. Here, you will be talking about the insertion of Check Box in your form. First you will go to the Insert menu from the above provided menu bar. Then you will browse to Form to see all the available form components. Then you will go for the Check Box option in the sub menu. Following the above steps, you can successfully add a Check Box into your form and hence start using it. All other components can be inserted in a similar way. This is how you add Check Box.

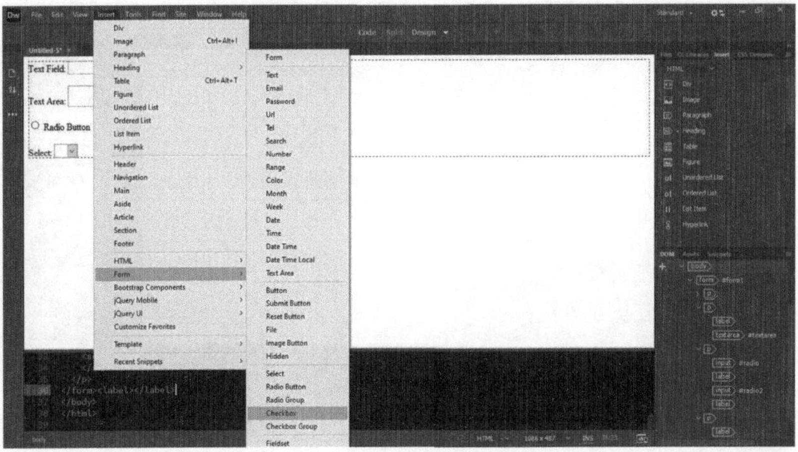

Figure 5.10: *Insert Check Box*

Figure 5.11: *Inserted Check Box*

Inserting a Button

Now you will talk about the Button. A Button is a type of form component, which is used to perform some kind of operation on the click of it. There are a few types of buttons that you can use, some of them are namely- Button, Submit button, and Reset button. Here, you will be talking about the insertion of a Button in your form. First you will go to the Insert menu from the above provided menu bar. Then you will browse to Form to see all the available form components. Then you will go for the Button option in the sub menu. Following the above steps, you can successfully add a Button into your form and hence start using it. All other components can be inserted in a similar way. This is how you add a Button.

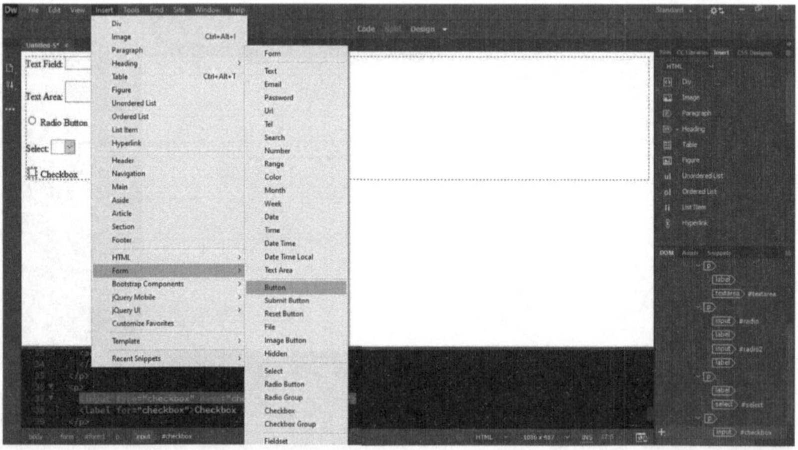

Figure 5.12: Insert Button

Figure 5.13: Inserted Button

Validating the Form

Now you will talk about validating the form. Till now you have added all of the components of the form in the above described manner. What validating a form will do is, it will ensure the correctness of the data that is provided by the user while filling the form. Now you will have to validate each of the fields using the different types of validators that are offered by the HTML. Using the validations provided by the HTML for the form, you can successfully validate your form and hence start using it. All other components will contribute altogether for the proper functioning of the form with the validations. Below shown are the different types of validations that you have added to our form. Some are text related, some are required fields etc. This is how you add validations to your form.

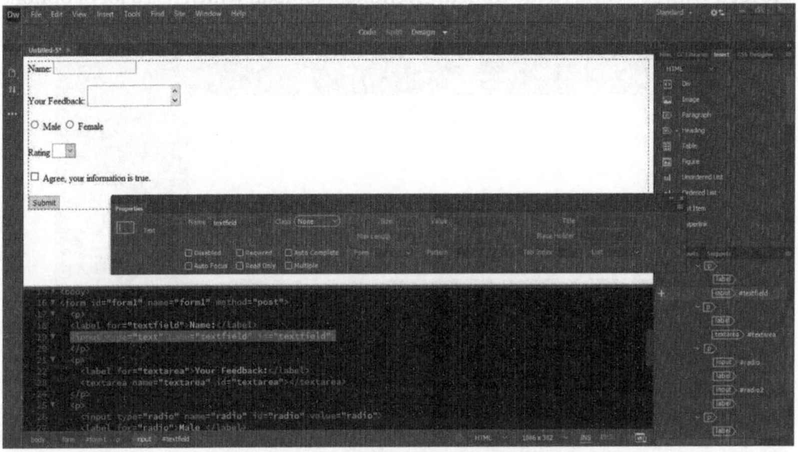

Figure 5.14: *Properties Dialog Box*

Using Dreamweaver you can set the validations for your form in the above shown way, which are offered by the Dreamweaver itself. These are the features of the product.

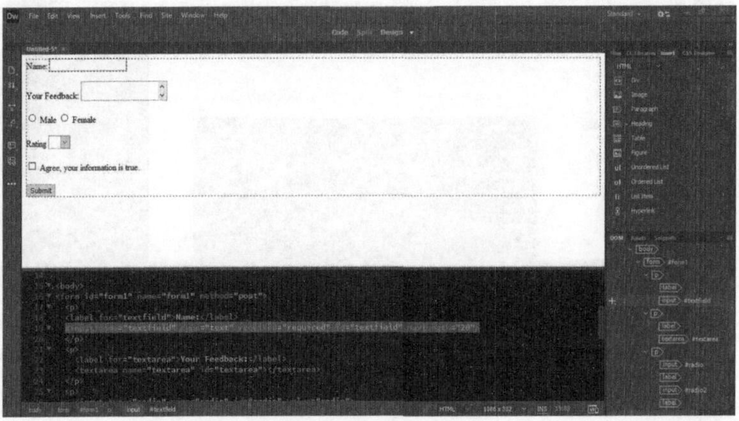

Figure 5.15: *Validate Form*

As you can see in the above image, you have highlighted the validation code which is added to your form on the selection of various validations.

Extra Byte

The validate form action checks the content of specified text fields to ensure that the user has entered the correct type of data.

Creating a Jump Menu

If you wish to create a jump menu, you will simply follow the below given steps, to successfully implement it.

First you will start by inserting a Form from the top most menu bar. Then you will proceed with selecting Aside from the rightmost toolbar, which has a lot of options to choose from.

***Figure 5.16:** Insert Form*

Then a pop-up menu will open and you will select the category and provide the link to the list items. You can additionally select some css style rules if we wish to apply some.

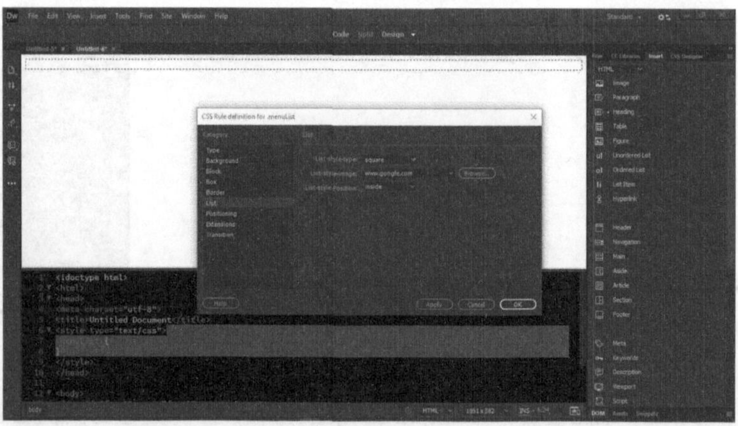

***Figure 5.17:** CSS Rue definition for menuList*

Then after the selection of preferred choices, we will then see the design pane and code pane similar to what is shown below.

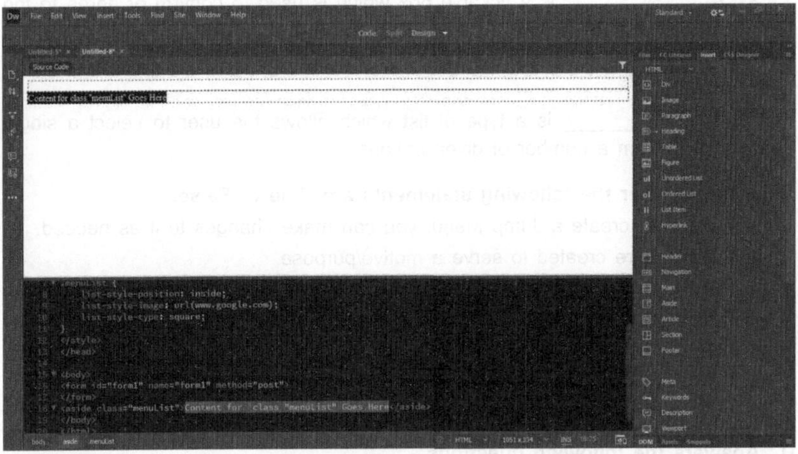

Figure 5.18: *Source code page*

Note: After you create a Jump Menu, you can make changes to it as needed.

In this way code will be added to the code pane automatically according to the settings which you have selected. In the similar way, you can create the jump menu.

EXERCISES

A. Multiple Choice Questions.

1. A ____________ is a region in a browser window that can display an HTML document independent of what is being displayed in the rest of the browser window.
   (a) Frame (b) Form (c) Jump (d) Validate
2. A ____________ is a type of form component, which is used to perform some kind of operation on the click of it.
   (a) Frame (b) Form (c) Jump (d) Button
3. ____________ is basically used to fetch data from users and post it to our database.
   (a) Frame (b) Form (c) Jump (d) Validate
4. ____________ allows you to select an option.
   (a) Drop-Down List (b) Form
   (c) Jump (d) Button
5. A ____________ is an area which is assigned to take a multi line of text input.
   (a) Button (b) Text Area (c) Jump (d) Form

B. Fill in the blanks.

1. A ____________ is an area which is assigned to take a single line of text input.

2. A ____________ element is a form object that gets its initial value by the web server where the web site is stored.
3. A ____________ is a tickable box which is used to confirm or agree to the asked question.
4. ____________ is basically used to fetch data from users and post it to our database.
5. A ____________ is a type of list which allows the user to select a single option from a number of given options.

C. State whether the following statements are True or False.

1. After you create a Jump Menu, you can make changes to it as needed.
2. Frames are created to serve a motive/purpose.
3. The textarea object is similar to the text field object set to multiline data from the user using the text area element in a form.
4. Frames are available in Edit menu.
5. There are a few types of buttons that you can use, some of them are namely- Button, Submit button, and Reset button.

D. Answers the following questions.

1. How to insert a text area in a web page?
2. What is the difference between textarea and text field?
3. Write down the steps for form validation.
4. How to create jump menu?

6 Using HTML to Create Web Pages

Learning Objectives

After studying this chapter, you should be able to do:

• Explain HTML and its History • Discuss how to create and view HTML document • Identify empty and container tag • Explain Background, Bgcolor, text, setting margins, font elemnts, HR rule, heading elements, <p> tag, style tag, ordered list, unordered list and IMG elements • Discuss HTML table and its attributes • Discuss the working with forms in HTML

Introduction

HyperText Markup Language (**HTML**) is a language understood by your Web browser like Internet Explorer or Netscape Navigator. All the documents available on the **World Wide Web** (**WWW**) are written in HTML, that run on any type of computer having a Web browser. It has a collection of styles (indicated by tags) that define the various components of a World Wide Web document. An HTML document can be opened in any operating system or any hardware such as PC (**Personal Computer**), **Macintosh** or **UNIX operated machine**.

HTML History

HTML was invented for the Internet by **Tim Berners-Lee** while at CERN, the European Laboratory for Particle Physics (CERN) in **Geneva**. HTML documents are created as plain-text (**ASCII** or **American Standard Code for Information Interchange**) files using a text editor (e.g., Notepad on a Windows machine). However, one can also use a word processing software which saves the document as "text only with line breaks." After creating a text file, give it the extension as **.HTML** or **.HTM** and run it using a Web browser, such as Internet Explorer.

Creating HTML Document in Text Editor (Notepad)

If you are using a word processing software or Notepad to create an HTML document, type the document and save it with a file name with an extension .htm or .html.

1. Click the **Start** button and click ok **Notepad.**
2. The **Notepad** window appears. Type the HTML code as shown in Figure 6.1.

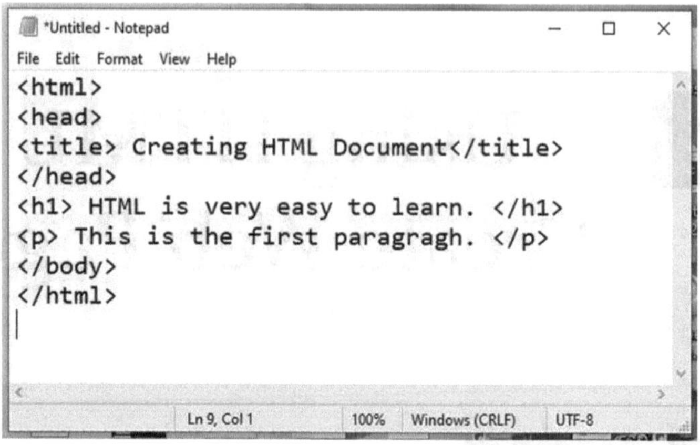

Figure 6.1: Notepad window opens

3. To save the document, click File menu and choose Save As.
4. The Save As dialog box appears as shown in Figure 6.2. In the File name: list box type the name of the file and put .HTML after it.
5. And then click the Save button.

History time

HTML was invented in 1990 by a scientist called Tim Berners-Lee.

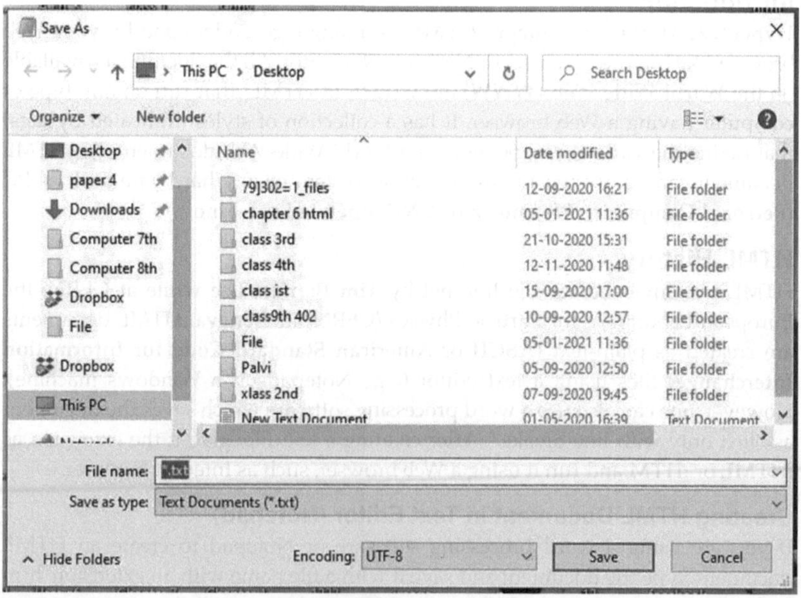

Figure 6.2: Save As dialog box

Shortcut key

For open a New document, press Ctrl+N.

Viewing an HTML Document

Perform the following steps to view your HTML document in Internet Explorer/ Google Chrome:

1. Open Internet Explorer/Google Chrome by clicking its icon on the desktop. The Google Chrome window appears.
2. Press Ctrl + O. The Open dialog box will appear.
3. Find and select your saved HTML document which you want to open.
4. Click the Open button.
5. Google Chrome will display the web page you had created using the Notepad program.

Memorize

You can double click on the icon of your saved HTML file and open it in a web browser.

Types of HTML Elements

HTML elements can be categorized as:

(a) Container elements (b) Empty elements

Container Elements

This type of HTML elements require pair tags, i.e., a starting as well as an ending tag, for example, `<title> .... </title>` `<B>....</B>`, etc. The end tag or *off* tag `</Tag>` is just like the start tag or ON tag `<Tag>`, except that it has a slash `(/)` in it. In HTML, elements that include both an *ON* and an *OFF* tag are called *container* elements. These tags affect everything that comes between their starting and ending tags.

Empty Elements

This type of HTML elements require just a starting tag and not an ending tag. For example, `<BR>`, `<HR>,` etc. For example, `<Br>` breaks a line and `<HR>` inserts a horizontal rule. Some elements have only an ON tag, but they do not have a corresponding end or OFF tag. These elements are called empty elements. Empty elements carry out their specific jobs and do not act on blocks of text.

Extra Byte

The following points must be kept in mind while writing HTML code.

1. Each tag should be enclosed within a left bracket (<) and a right bracket (>).
2. Opening tag is denoted by < > and closing tag is denoted by </>.
3. Tag names are not case sensitive. Normally tag names are written in Upper Case so that they can be distinguish from the normal text.

HTML Document

Every HTML document should contain certain standard HTML tags. A tag is a coded HTML command that indicates how a part of Web page should be displayed. Each document consists of head and body tags. The head contains the title and the body contains the actual text that is made up of paragraphs, lists and other elements. Web browsers expect specific information because they are programmed according to HTML specifications. A sample HTML document is given in Example 1.

Example 1:

```
<html>
<head>
<TITLE> A Simple HTML Example</TITLE>
</head>
<body>
<H1>HTML is very EASY to Learn </H1>
<P>Welcome to the world of HTML.</P>
<P>This is the first paragraph. However short it is still a
paragraph!
</P>
<p>And this is the second paragraph. </p>
</body>
</html>
```

Figure 6.3 show the output when this document is read using the Internet Explorer.

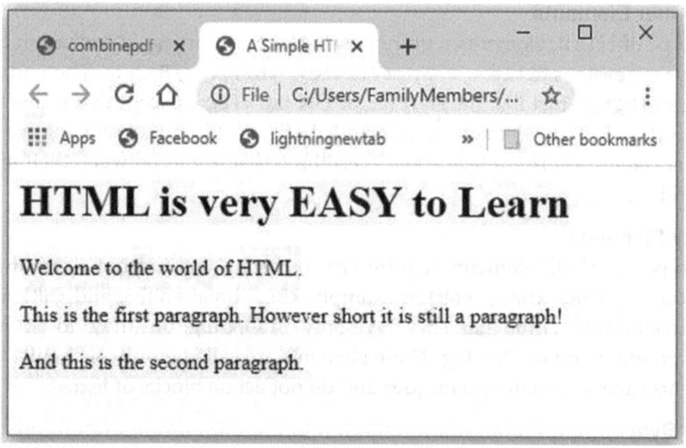

Figure 6.3: Result of Example 1 using the Internet Explorer

The required elements are the **<html>**, **<head>**, **<title>**, and **<body>** tags (and their corresponding terminating end tags). It is better to include end tags because you are not aware about the type of Internet browser that a Web surfer may be using.

HTML Page Structure

An HTML page consists of the following tags:

<HTML>: This tag specifies the document as an HTML document.

<HEAD>: This tag contains information about the document, including its title, scripts used, style definitions and document descriptions.

<TITLE>: This tag contains the document title. The title specified inside **<Title>** tag appears on the browser's title bar. You should be very careful while choosing the title because a title is also used to identify a Web page for search engines.

<BODY>: This forms the largest part of the HTML document. The **<Body>** tag encloses all the tags, attributes and information to be displayed in the Web page. The information written within the body tag is displayed in the browser window.

Background

This attribute is used to specify a URL (Uniform Resource Locator), which is pointing to an image. It specifies the name of the **GIF** file (image) that will be used as the background of the document. The GIF tiles up across the page to give a background.

Syntax:

```
<Body background="filename.gif">
```

Example 2:

```
<html>
<head>
<TITLE>Simple Background Image</TITLE>
</head>
<body background="Mountain.jpg">
<H1>HTML is very EASY to Learn </H1>
<P>Welcome to the world of HTML.</P>
</body>
</html>
```

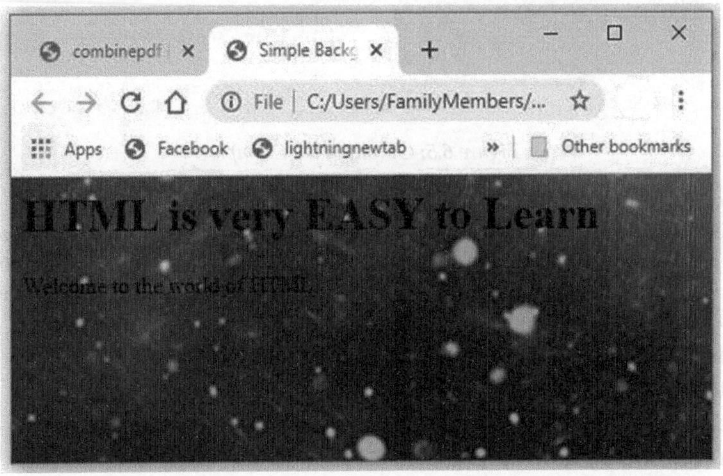

Figure 6.4: Displaying background coded in Example 2

BGCOLOR

BGCOLOR changes the default background color as per the specified color. The program coded in example 3 gives the background as Grey but text displayed in Yellow. This is possible by giving the body attribute **BGCOLOR = GREY** and **TEXT = YELLOW**.

Example 3:

```
<html>
<head>
<TITLE>A Simple HTML Example</TITLE>
</head>
<body bgcolor = Grey Text=Yellow>
<H1>HTML is very EASY to Learn </H1>
<P>Welcome to the World of HTML.</P>
</body>
</html>
```

The output of the Example 3 is shown in Figure 6.5.

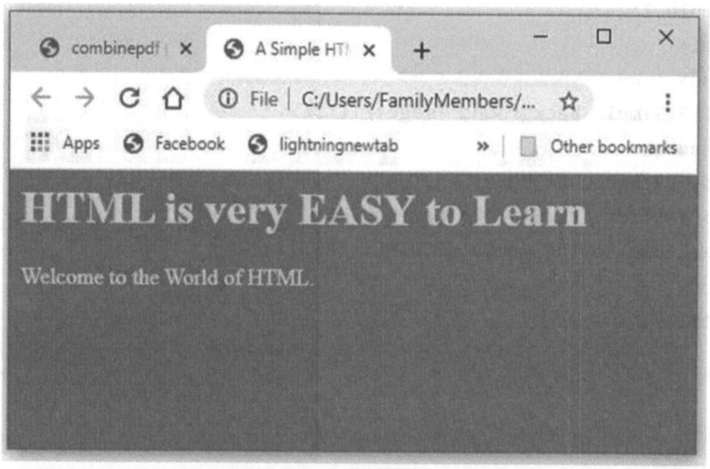

Figure 6.5: Output of the Example 3

Text

This command changes the body text color from its default value to the color specified with this attribute. A sample HTML document containing **<BODY>** attributes is shown in Figure 6.6. This HTML document contains various elements described so far.

Example 4:

```
<html>
<head>
<TITLE> A Simple HTML Example</TITLE>
</head>
```

```
<body TEXT = BLUE>
<H1>HTML is very EASY to Learn </H1>
<P>Welcome to the world of HTML.</P>
</body>
</html>
```

The output of the Example 4 is shown in Figure 8.8.

Figure 6.6: Result of the Example 4

Setting Margins

You can use **LEFTMARGIN** and **TOPMARGIN** tags to specify how much space you would like to have on both left and right hand sides.

Left Margin

The **LEFTMARGIN** attribute of **<Body>** tag is used to specify the distance between the left side of the document and the left edge of the browser window.

Syntax:

```
<Body leftmargin=value> </body>
```

Example 5:

```
<html>
<head>
<TITLE>LEFT MARGIN ATTRIBUTE</TITLE>
</head>
<Body Leftmargin="90" TEXT="RED">
<H1>This is Left Margin</H1>
</body>
</html>
```

TThe output of the Example 5 is shown in Figure 6.9. The text between the <Body> element will be indented 90 pixels away from the left hand side of the page.

Figure 6.7: Result of Example 5 as read by the Internet Explorer

Top Margin

The **TOPMARGIN** attribute of **<Body>** tag is used to specify the distance between the Top of the document and the Top of the browser window.

Example 6:

```
<html>
<head>
<TITLE>TOP MARGIN ATTRIBUTE</TITLE>
</head>
<Body Leftmargin="80" Topmargin="160" TEXT="RED">
<H1>HTML is very EASY to Learn </H1>
<P>Welcome to the world of HTML.</P>
</body>
</html>
```

TThe output of Example 6 as shown in Figure 8.10. The text between the <Body> element will be indented 80 pixels away from the left side and then 160 pixels away from the Top of the page.

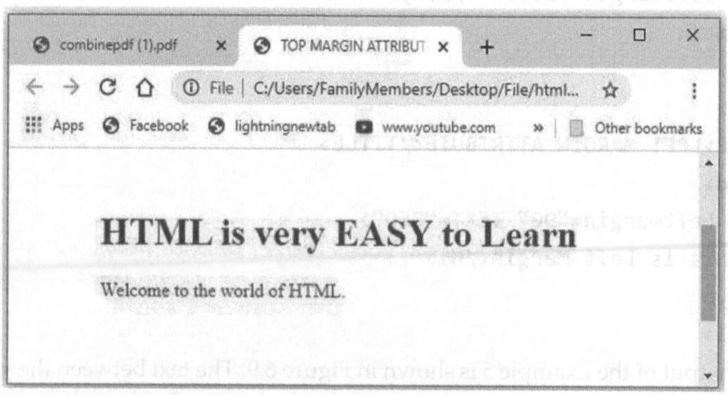

Figure 6.8: Result of the Example 6

Font Element

The font element **<FONT> </FONT>** is used to format the size, type face and color of the enclosed text. This element will change the appearance of the text of the body for visual markup of the contents.

The **<FONT>** tag has three attributes namely **SIZE**, **FACE** and **COLOR**. All text specified within the tags **<FONT> </FONT>** will appear in the font, size and color as specified by the attributes of the tag **<FONT>**.

Font Size

To set the relative size of the text by setting the SIZE attribute at the **<FONT>** element. The **SIZE** attribute is represented as **<FONT SIZE = Value>**. The **SIZE** attribute can be specified in absolute or relative values ranging from **1** (smallest) to **7** (largest). Using a relative font size (putting a plus or a minus sign before the number) will change the font size relative to the **BASEFONT** tag or the default font size. For example, **<FONT SIZE = "+12">**.

Example 7:

```
<html>
<head>
<TITLE>A Simple HTML Example</TITLE>
</head>
<Body Bgcolor="Aqua" TEXT="Black">
<Font size="7">
<p>This font is largest size</P> <BR>
<Font Size="3">
This font is Smallest size.<BR>
<font size="+12">This font size is larger than font size 7.
</body>
</html>
```

The HTML code given in Example 7 will display the text in the largest and smallest font size. The output of Example 7 is shown in Figure 6.8.

***Figure 6.9:** Result of Example 8*

Font Face

The **FACE** attribute specifies a typeface that you would like to use for the text enclosed by the font element. You can use a single typeface (such as Arial, Courier and Verdana) or you can give a list of typefaces sepearated by commas (,) The **FACE** attribute is represented as:

```
<FONT FACE = "Font Name">
```

Example 8:

```
<html>
<head>
<TITLE>A Simple HTML Example</TITLE>
</head>
<Body Bgcolor="Aqua" TEXT="Black">
<p><Font face="Arial" font size = "5">This text is displayed in Arial</p> <BR>
<p><Font face="Courier, Verdana">This text is displayed in either Courier or Verdana</p>
</body>
</html>
```

The code given in Example 8 will display the text in different faces as shown in Figure 8.12.

Font Color

The **COLOR** attribute is used to specify the color of the text to be shown on the screen.

The color can be set by giving the name of the color supported by the browser or by giving the value as **#RRGGBB**, the hexadecimal color value.

The **COLOR** attribute is represented as:

```
<FONT COLOR = "Aqua">
```

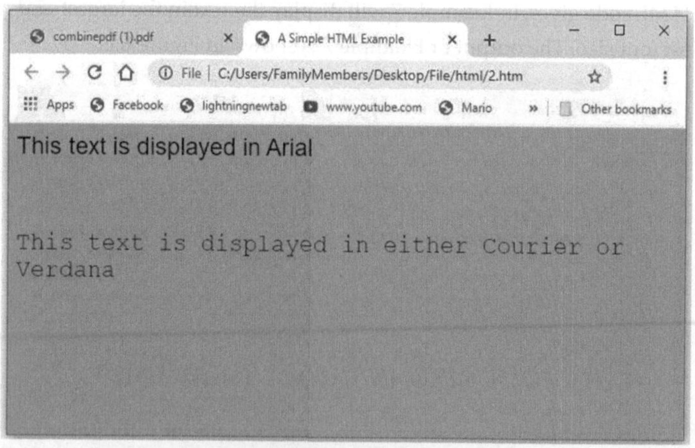

Figure 6.10: Result of the Example 8

Example 9:

```
<html>
<head>
<TITLE>A Simple HTML Example</TITLE>
</head>
<Body Bgcolor=”Aqua”>
<p><Font color=”Red” font size = “5”>This text is displayed in color red and size is 5</p></font> <BR>
<p><Font color=”#808000” Font face = “Calibri” font size=”8”>This text is displayed in color Maroon and font face is Calibri</p>
</body>
</html>
```

The Example 9 will display the text in different faces as shown in Figure 6.11.

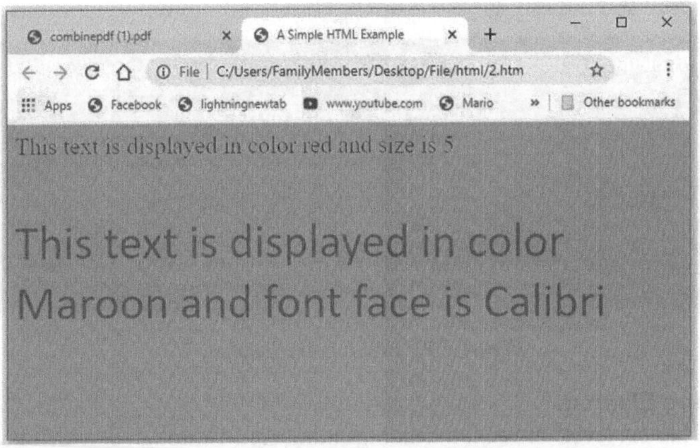

Figure 6.11: Result of the Example 10

Horizontal Rule (HR) Element

The HR element is used to draw a horizontal line. The attributes of the **<HR>** tag are explained below:

Align: Aligns the line on the screen.
ALIGN = LEFT (aligns the line to the left of the screen) ALIGN = RIGHT (aligns the line to the right of the screen) ALIGN = CENTER (aligns the line in the centre of the screen)

Size: Changes the size of the line.

Width: Sets the width of the rule.

No Shade: Renders the line as an unshaded gray line without the hollow and slightly three dimensional appearance that most browsers give to thicker lines.

Example 10:

```
<HTML>
<HEAD>
```

```
<TITLE> A Simple HTML Example </TITLE>
</HEAD>
<body BGCOLOR=BLUE TEXT=WHITE>
<p>The HR element is used to draw a Horizontal line</p>
<p ALIGN=CENTER> Welcome to the World of HTML
<HR WIDTH=200 SIZE=2 NOSHADE COLOR=GREEN></P>
</body>
</HTML>
```

The Example 10 will display the output as shown in Figure 6.12.

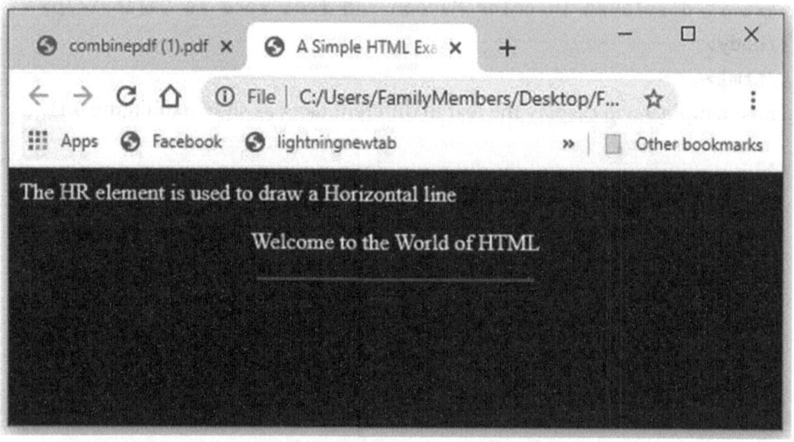

Figure 6.12: Result of the Example 10

Heading Element

HTML has six levels of Section headings numbered 1 through 6, with 1 being the most prominent Section. Text with heading tags is displayed in larger and/or bolder fonts than the normal body text by a Web browser. The first heading in each document should be tagged as <H1>.

Syntax:

```
<Hy>Text of heading </Hy>
```

where `y` is a number between `1` and `6` specifying the level of the heading.

Example 11:

```
<HTML>
<HEAD>
<TITLE>A Simple HTML Example</TITLE>
</HEAD>
<body BGCOLOR=BLUE TEXT=WHITE>
<H1>This is heading 1<H1>
<H2>This is heading 2<H2>
<H3>This is heading 3<H3>
```

```
<H4>This is heading 4<H4>
<H5>This is heading 5<H5>
<H6>This is heading 6<H5>
</body>
</HTML>
```

The Example 11 will display the output as shown in Figure 6.13.

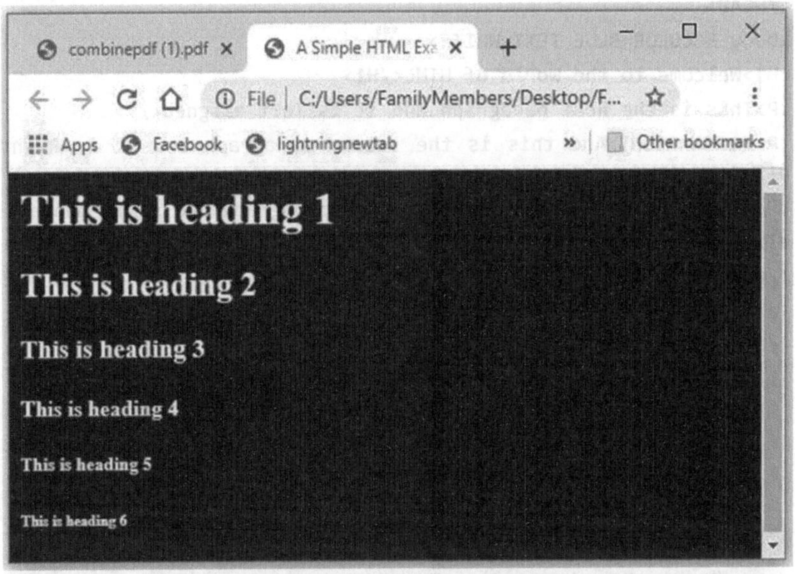

Figure 6.13: Result of the Example 11

By default, headings are left-aligned, but using the **ALIGN** attribute, the text may be aligned to left, right or centre of the screen.

Note: Heading tags are used by search engines to identify words which are more important than the rest of the page text.

Paragraph <P> Tag

In the source file, there may be line breaks between sentences. A Web browser ignores the line breaks and starts a new paragraph only when it encounters another **<P>** tag. The Paragraph can be aligned left, right or centre by using the **ALIGN** attribute.

A sample HTML document contains the left alignment. Here the line Welcome to the World of HTML would be shown to the left of the page when browsed by IE.

To preserve readability in HTML files, you should put headings on separate lines. Use a blank line to identify the start of a new section and separate paragraphs with blank lines (in addition to the <P> tags). These extra spaces are needed to help you when you edit files. Note that the browser ignores the extra spaces because it has its own set of rules on spacing that do not depend on the spaces you put in your source file.

Using the `<P>` and `</P>` as a paragraph container means that you can centre a paragraph by including the **`ALIGN = alignment attribute`** in source file.

Example 12:

```
<HTML>
<HEAD>
<TITLE>A Simple HTML Example of Paragraph</TITLE>
</HEAD>
<body BGCOLOR=BLUE TEXT=WHITE>
<H1>Welcome to the World of HTML</H1>
<P>This is the first paragraph and it is left aligned</P>
<P ALIGN=RIGHT>And this is the second paragraph and it is Right
aligned.</P>
<P ALIGN=CENTER>And this is the Third paragraph and it is center
aligned</P>
</body>
<address>Created by Jain</address>
</HTML>
```

The Example 12 will display the output as shown in Figure 6.14.

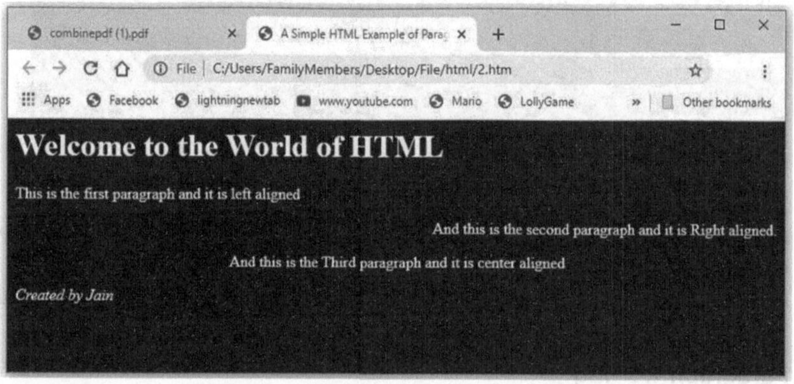

Figure 6.14: Result of the Example 12

Extra Byte

Align attribute ***can also be given with Heading tag, Font tag or Paragraph tag.***

Style Tags

Tags for the text styles add the distinction to certain characters of the text.

Boldface

The boldface tag `<B> </B>` is used to make the text you want to show in Boldface style.

Italics

The italics tag `<I> </I>` is used to mark the text you want to display in *Italics* face style.

Underline

The tag **<U> </U>** is used to make the text you want to display the text as Underlined.

Example 13:

```
<HTML>
<HEAD>
<TITLE>A Simple HTML Styles tags</TITLE>
</HEAD>
<body BGCOLOR=BLUE TEXT=WHITE>
<H1>Welcome to the World of HTML</H1>
<P><b>This text is displayed in Boldface</b></P>
<P><I>This text is displayed in Italics</I></P>
<P><U>This text is displayed in Underlined</U></P>
</body>
<address>Created by Jain</address>
</HTML>
```

The Example 13 will display the output as shown in Figure 6.15.

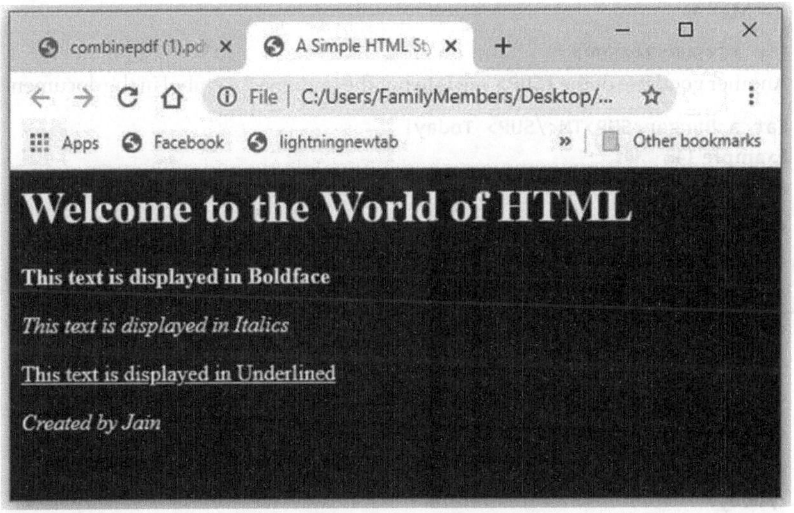

Figure 6.15: Result of the Example 13

<EM> </EM>

The Emphasis element indicates typographic emphasis and is typically rendered in an italic font. For example,

```
There is a great difference between <EM>knowing</EM> a thing and <EM>understanding</EM> it.
```

The output of the above example is:

There is a great difference between *knowing* a thing and *understanding* it.

Preformat Element <PRE> </PRE>

The **<PRE>** tag stands for preformatted text. It allows you to include preformatted text in HTML document (including spaces and lines). The text contained in this tag is rendered in a fixed pitch font like the Courier font. Most browsers follow the HTML standard for block level elements and create a paragraph break before the **<PRE>** start tag and after the **</PRE>** closing tag.

Subscript Element

The subscript element coded by **_{** and **}** tags puts the enclosed text in subscript (a bit lower than regular text). This element is useful for mathematical formulas.

For example, the following line of HTML code contains the chemical formula for water (H2O):

We all need **H₂O**.

Superscript Element

The superscript element **** renders the enclosed text in superscript (a bit higher than regular text) as shown in Figure 8.18. This element is also useful for mathematical formulas. For example, the following is the HTML code for Einstein's famous equation

$E = MC^2$ as:

```
E = MC<SUP>2</SUP>
```

Another good use of the **<SUP>** tag is to put the trademark symbol in the document.

```
Eat a Burger<SUP>TM</SUP> Today!
```

Example 14:

```
<html>
<head>
<TITLE> A Simple Inline Element Example</TITLE>
</head>
<body>
<H1>HTML Sub and Sup elements</H1>
<P>We all need H <SUB>2</SUB>O.</P>
<P>E = MC<SUP>2</SUP></P>
<P>Eat a Burger<SUP>TM</SUP> Today!</P>
</body>
</html>
```

The Example 14 will display the output as shown in Figure 6.16.

Ordered List <ol>

Ordered List is a list with numbers in an order ascending or descending. In this, each item (paragraph) is prefaced with a number. The tags used for this are **<OL> </OL>**. The browser applies the appropriate number to each line when it opens the page.

Ordered lists have additional attributes that you can use to specify the first number of the list, as well as to create hierarchical information. First you can start a numbered list with a value other than 1 (or A, a, I or i).

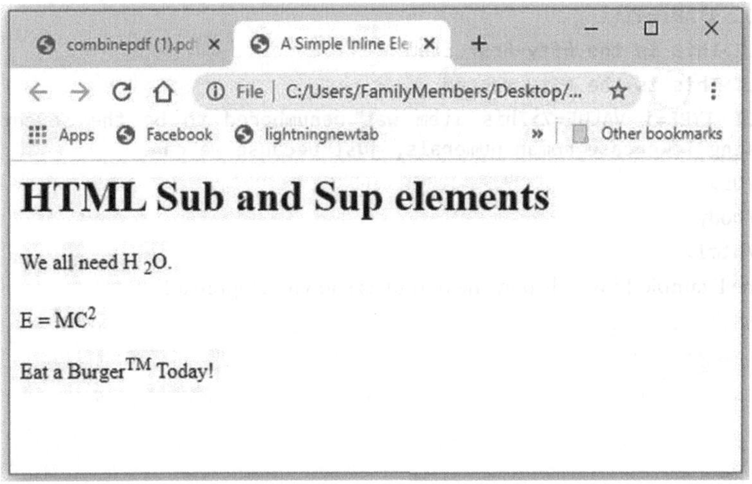

Figure 6.16: Result of the Example 14

A Specifies a sequence of upppercase letters.

a–Specifies a sequence of lowercase letters.

I–Specifies a sequence of uppercase Roman numerals.

i–Specifies a sequence of lowercase Roman numerals.

Simply include the **START = attribute** in the initial **<OL>** tag, as in **<OL START = 51>**. Or, you can even change specific numbers within a list by using the **VALUE = attribute** in the **<L1>** tag, as in **<L1 VALUE = 7>**. To use these attributes, include them in the **<OL>** tag.

Example 15:

```
<html>
<head>
<TITLE> A Simple HTML Example</TITLE>
</head>
<body BGCOLOR = YELLOW>
<H1 ALIGN=LEFT>Sample Lists</H1>
<OL>
<LI>Lions
<LI>Tigers
<LI>Bears
<LI>Oh, My!
</OL>
<OL TYPE=A>
```

```
<LI>Outlines use sequential lists with letters.
<LI>So do some (unpopular) numbering schemes for documentation.
</OL>
<OL START=51>
<LI>This is the fifty-first item.
<LI>This is the fifty second.
<LI TYPE=i VALUE=7>This item was renumbered to be the seventh,
using lowercase roman numerals, just because we can.
</OL>
</body>
</html>
```

The Example 15 will display the output as shown in Figure 6.17.

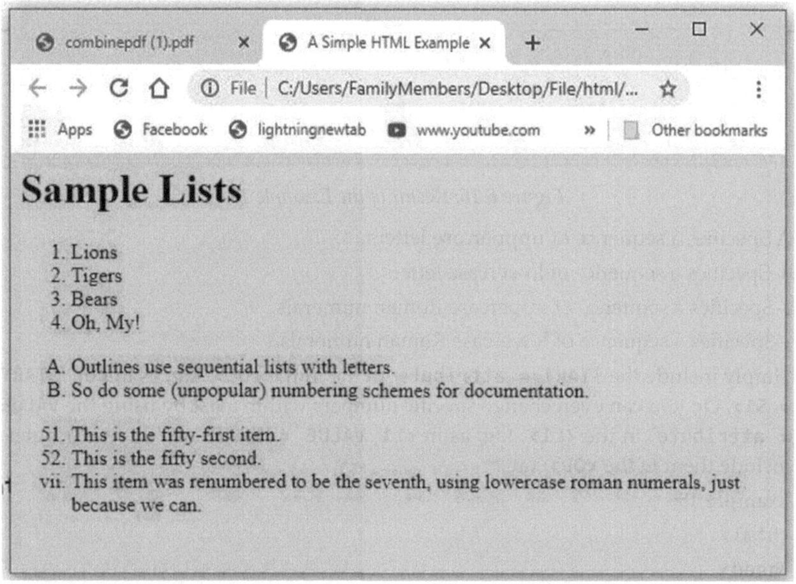

Figure 6.17: *Result of the Example 15*

Unordered List <Ul>

This is an unordered list. In this, each item (paragraph) is prefaced with a bullet. The tags used for this are **<UL>** and **</UL>**.

The basic bulleted list has a default progression of bullet types that changes as you move through indented levels. The **TYPE** attribute can be used in the **<UL>** element so that no matter what the indent level the bullet type can be specified thus:

- **TYPE = disc**
- **TYPE = circle**
- **TYPE = square**

Example 16:

```
<html>
```

```
<head>
<TITLE> A Simple HTML Example</TITLE>
</head>
<body BGCOLOR = YELLOW>
<H3>CHAPTER I</H3>
<P><UL>
<LI>Section 1 </LI>
<LI>Section 2 </LI>
<LI>Section 3 </LI>
</UL></P>
</body>
</html>
```

The Example 16 will display the output as shown in Figure 6.18.

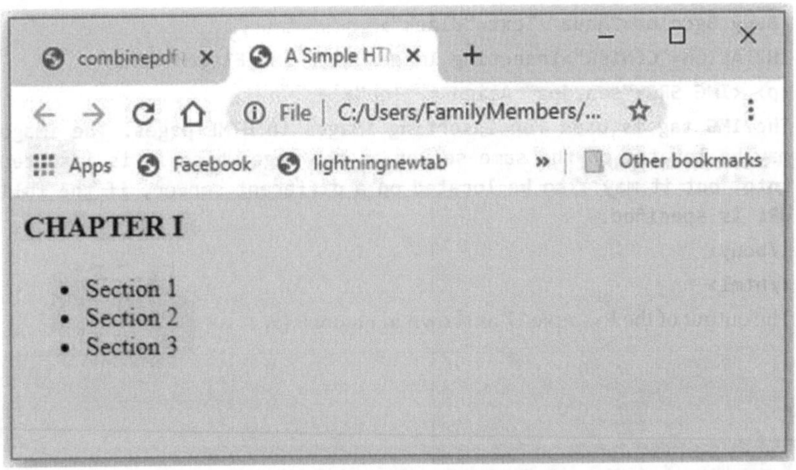

Figure 6.18: Result of the Example 16

IMG (Image Element)

An image can be inserted into a Web page using the tag **<IMG> </IMG>**. This tag takes the name of the image file (filename.gif) as an attribute. In addition, HTML also allows control of the height, width, border, etc., of every image placed on Web page. The attributes are associated with **<IMG>** tag.

The **IMG** element is empty, meaning there is no closing **</IMG>**. It has several attributes:

SRC = "image_url"

SRC gives the URL of the image document. The URL points the location where the image is stored.

Aligning Image in Web Page

ALIGN tells the browser how to align the image with the text. There are different types of alignments these are:

Top align: It aligns the Top of the image with the top margin of the item in the line **Align="TOP"**.

Bottom align: It aligns the Bottom of the image with the baseline of the text **Align="BOTTOM"**.

Middle align: It aligns the Middle of the image with the baseline of the text **Align="MIDDLE"**.

Left and Right align: It supports left and right-aligned images. The image floats to the left or right margins, with the text following the image element flowing around the image, for example, **Align="Left"** and **Align="Right"**.

Example 17:

```
<html>
<head>
<TITLE>Image at the Top of the Image</TITLE>
</head>
<Body Bgcolor="Aqua" Text="Black">
<H2 ALIGN="CENTER">Inserting Images with IMG Element</H2>
<p> <IMG SRC="sea.jpg" Align = "Top">
The IMG tag is used for inserting images in HTML pages. The image may be located on the same server as the page which it is inserted into, but it may also be located on a different server, if the full URL is specified.
</body>
</html>
```

The output of the Example 17 as shown in Figure 6.19.

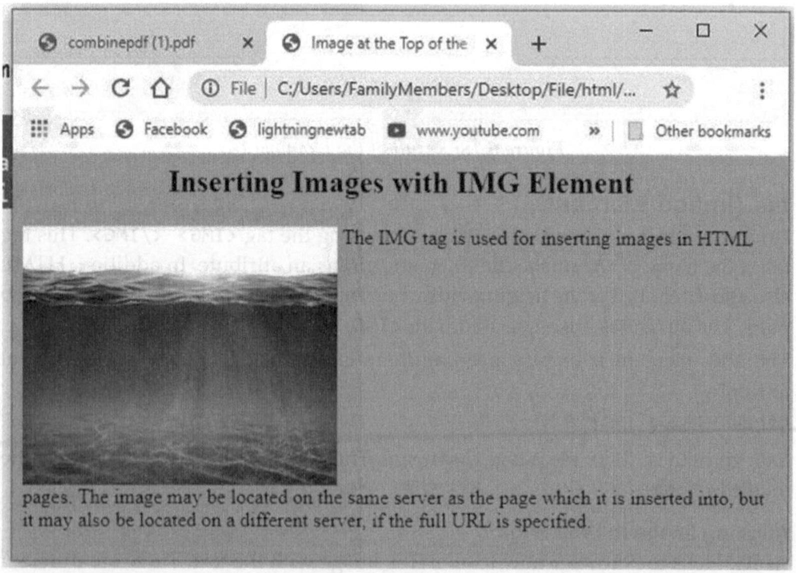

***Figure 6.19:** Viewing the image which is the result of Example 17*

Memorize

In the src attribute, specify the exact path/ location of an image where it is stored. If it does not exist, a Crossmark will appear in a box in place of that image.

Resizing an Image

Images can be loaded faster by specifying the height and width of an image. As the browser loads the page, it notes the height and width attributes and leaves that much space for the image.

To specify image height and width, add the **HEIGHT=** and **WIDTH=** attributes in the **<IMG>** tag as shown below:

```
<img scr=”Mount.jpg” width=”100” height=”50”>
```

Example 18:

```
<html>
<head>
<TITLE>Resizing an Image</TITLE>
</head>
<Body Bgcolor=”Aqua” Text=”Black”>
<H2 ALIGN=”CENTER”>Using the Height and Width attributes</H2>
<IMG SRC=”Mount.jpg” Align = “Left” Alt = “Beautiful Mountain”
Height=”180” Width=”250”>
<p>
The IMG tag is used for inserting images in HTML pages. The image
may be located on the same server as the page which it is inserted
into, but it may also be one located on a different server, if the
full URL is specified.</p>
</body>
</html>
```

The output of the Example 18 is shown in Figure 6.20.

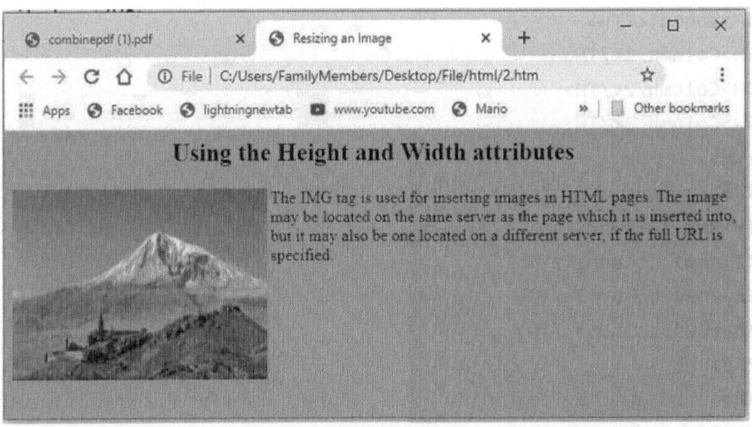

***Figure 6.20:** Viewing the file which is the result of Example 18*

HTML Tables

HTML Tables are contained within a **TABLE** element. The **TABLE** element denotes the range of the table, and uses attribute to define properties of it.

Basic Table Tags

The **Table** element in HTML is **<Table> </Table>**. Everything within a table is enclosed between these two "tags", and which both are required.

```
<Table>
.......
.......
</Table>
```

There are a number of optional attributes we can specify in the **<TABLE>** tag, but these are discussed after the creation of a simple table.

After the **<TABLE>**, the next thing we need is the **<TR>** tag. **<TR>** creates a table row, which contains one or more cells of information. To create these individual cells, we use the **<TD>** tag. **<TD>** stands for table data. We place the table information within the **<TD>** and **</TD>** tags. Within the Table element, we use **<TH>** for table headers and the **CAPTION** element for the table's caption.

Creating a Table

To create the simple Table in the HTML document.

Example 19:

```
<HTML>
<HEAD>
<Title>An Example of Table Format</Title>
</head>
<body>
<table>
<caption>This is the caption of Table</caption>
<TR>
<TH> </TH>
<TH>Column 1</TH>
<TH>Column 2</TH>
<TH>Column 3</TH>
</TR>
<TR>
<TH>ROW 1</TH>
<TD>row1 column1</TD>
<TD>row1 column2</TD>
<TD>row1 column3</TD>
</TR>
<TR>
<TH>ROW 2</TH>
```

```
<TD>row2 column1</TD>
<TD>row2 column2</TD>
<TD>row2 column3</TD>
</TR>
<TR>
<TH>ROW 3</TH>
<TD>row 1 column1</TD>
<TD>row 2 column2</TD>
<TD>row 3 column3</TD>
</TR>
</TABLE>
</Body>
</HTML>
```

The output of the Example 19 is shown in Figure 6.21.

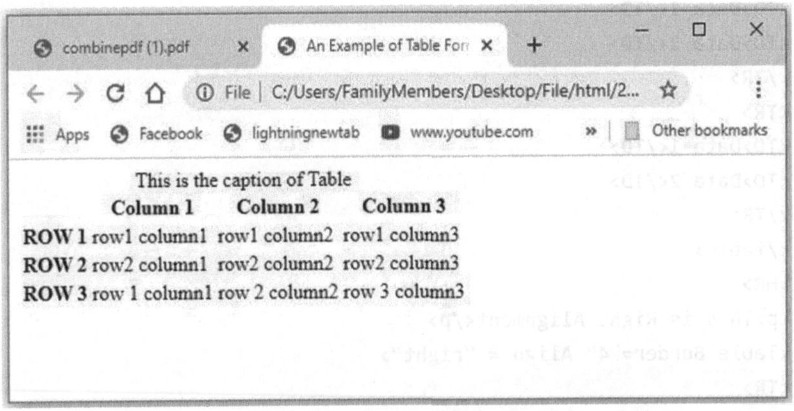

Figure 6.21: Previewing the table which is the result Example 19

Table Attributes

Align

To align table, **ALIGN** attribute of **<TABLE>** tag may be used. This can have values left, right and center indicating that the table should be placed.

Left align: Aligned at the left window border.

Right align: Left-align table Center align: Center-align table Right align: Right-align table Example 20:

```
<Html>
<Head>
<Title>Table Alignment</Title>
</head>
<body>
<p> This is Left Alignment</p>
```

```
<Table Border="4" Align = "left">
<TR>
<TD>Data 1</TD>
<TD>Data 2</TD>
</TR>
<TR>
<TD>Data 1</TD>
<TD>Data 2</TD>
</TR>
</table>
<HR>
<p Align="Center">This is Center Alignment</p>
<Table Border="4" Align = "center">
<TR>
<TD>Data 1</TD>
<TD>Data 2</TD>
</TR>
<TR>
<TD>Data 1</TD>
<TD>Data 2</TD>
</TR>
</table>
<HR>
<p>This is Right Alignment</p>
<Table Border="4" Align = "right">
<TR>
<TD>Data 1</TD>
<TD>Data 2</TD>
</TR>
<TR>
<TD>Data 1</TD>
<TD>Data 2</TD>
</TR>
</table>
</Body>
</Html>
```

The output of Example 20 is shown in Figure 6.22.

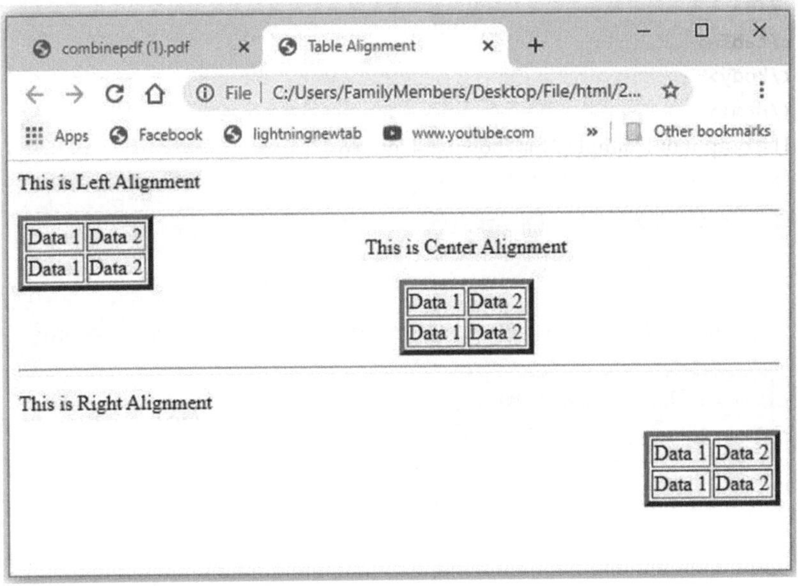

Figure 6.22: Previewing the Table attributes which is the result of Example 20

Table's Border Color

`BORDERCOLOR` attribute is used to specify the color of table's border. The attribute of `BORDERCOLOR` is `BORDERCOLOR="colorname"`.

Example 21:

```
<Html>
<Head>
<Title>Add Border and Border color to the table</Title>
</head>
<body>
<table BORDER="3" BORDERCOLOR="Brown">
<TR>
<TD>Data 1</TD>
<TD>Data 2</TD>
<TD>Data 3</TD>
<TD>Data 4</TD>
</TR>
<TR>
<TD>Data 1</TD>
<TD>Data 2</TD>
<TD>Data 3</TD>
<TD>Data 4</TD>
```

```
</TR>
</table>
</body>
</Html>
```

The output of Example 21 is shown in Figure 6.23.

Figure 6.23: Result of Example 21 showing the table border

Working with Forms

Forms are such HTML tools which allow readers to communicate with one another via the Web. It is a collections of markup tags that work with Web servers to produce a means of obtaining whatever information we need from visitors of our Website.

`<FORM>` Tag

A **FORM** tag is used in an HTML document just like any other element. It has a start tag, **<FORM>** and an end tag **</FORM>**, The form itself contains regular text, other HTML elements, such as tables and form elements, such as check boxes, pull-down menus and text fields. Forms cannot be nested, i.e., you cannot put one into another. Forms can include other elements, such as list or **<PRE>**. FORM attributes are mentioned in the following paragraphs. For example,

```
<FORM ACTION = "HTTP://WWW.GOOGLE.COM\HTML\ FORMS.HTML"METHOD = "POST">
```

Different attributes of the forms are as follows:

(a) **Action attribute** (b) **Method attribute** (c) **Enctype attribute**

Action Attribute

It specifies the Uniform Resource Locator (URL) of the program or script that accepts the contents of the form for processing. If this attribute is absent, the base URL (URL where the form is located on the server) of the form is automatically used.

Method Attribute

Method attribute specifies which method type will be used to submit the form data. The method we use depends on how our particular server works. The possible values are:

(a) **get** (b) **post**

These are the HTTP methods that a browser uses to talk to a server. **GET** is the default method for browsers to submit information. HTML pages are generally retrieved by requesting a single URL from a Web server using the **GET** method. For example, when we write

HTTP://WWW.GOOGLE.COM\HTML\FORMS.HTML

The above URL is translated into a valid HTTP **GET** request like the following:

GET HTML/FORMS.HTML

The **GET** method is not very secure, since that data input appears in the URL. Furthermore, it is impossible to append a large amount of data with the **GET** method. Another problem is that it is not suitable for foreign languages other than English.

Enctype Attribute

ENCTYPE specifies the encoding for the fill-out form contents. It only applies if **METHOD** is set to **POST**. It identifies the media type. This media type is used for encoding the name/value pairs of the form's data.

Form's Elements

The Form element consists of the following parts:

(a) **SELECT** (b) **OPTION** (c) **TEXTAREA** (d) **INPUT Option**

SELECT

Inside **<FORM> ... </FORM>** tag, any number of **SELECT** tags are permitted freely intermixed with other HTML elements and text. This tag allows a user to choose one of the set of alternatives. **SELECT** element is used for query. The **SELECT** element is specialized for creating drop-down or scrollable lists of menus only.

The basic structure of a **SELECT** element is mentioned as follows:

```
<SELECT Name="select-menu">
<OPTION> View the product?
<OPTION> Call for help?
<OPTION> Request a catalogue?
<OPTION> Exit from this form?
</SELECT>
```

The attributes to **SELECT** tags are as follows:

Name: This attribute is used to create a label for the **SELECT** data structure like ("select-menu") in the above example. Functionally, this is equivalent to the radio button possibility with the **INPUT** element of **Type = "radio"**, where one, and only one, of a set of options can be made.

Size: It determines that how many options are visible at a time. The default value of size is 1. If **SIZE** is 2 or more, the **SELECT** will be represented as a scrolled list.

Multiple/Single: Because the default value of choosing options is **SINGLE**, therefore, user can choose only **SINGLE**. In both of the above examples of **SELECT** statements, the user can make one, and only one, choice. By adding the attribute **MULTIPLE**, the user will be able to choose more than one among several options.

OPTION

This tag occurs only within the **SELECT** element (described previously) and is used to represent each choice of the **SELECT**. The attributes of **OPTION** are:

Selected: It indicates that this option initially is selected.

Value: If present, this is the value returned by **SELECT** if this option is chosen; otherwise, the value returned is that set by the **OPTION** element.

TEXTAREA

TEXTAREA element is used to ask the user to enter several lines of text (as opposed to the single line with an **INPUT** element of **Type="text"**). A sample **TEXTAREA** tag is as follows:

```
<TEXTAREA NAME="comments" ROWS=4 COLS=30></TEXTAREA>
```

This allows the user to enter any amount of text, with only four rows and 30 columns visible. The attributes associated with **TEXTAREA** are as follows:

Cols: The number of columns that will be displayed (the user can use the scrollbar to move through more columns if necessary).

Name: The logical name associated with the returned text.

Rows: The number of rows that will be displayed (note that the user can use more rows and scroll down to them).

INPUT

INPUT element is the basic way to get input from the user in a variety of situations. The reason is that an **INPUT** element can define many types of graphical user interface features. These are as follows:

(a) **Pull-down menus** (b) **Radio buttons** (c) **Text input boxes**
(d) **Text fields** (e) **Check boxes**

A sample **INPUT** tag that queries the user for a name (using **"text"** as the value of the attribute Type) is given below:

```
<INPUT Type = "text" Size = 40 Name = "user-name">
```

Type identifies the **text** value of the attribute that will be displayed as 40 characters.

The **Name** attribute of the **INPUT** element designates the variable name that will be used in the data structure sent to the query program. This name is used to identify the value of the user's response from this **INPUT** element.

The **INPUT** tag is very versatile and can be used to create many kinds of user interface features.

The **INPUT** element has the following attributes:

Align: Used only with the image Type. Possible values are top, middle, and bottom, and they define the relationship of the image to the text following it.

Checked: **CHECKED** (no value needed) specifies that this checkbox or radio button is checked by default. This is only appropriate for checkboxes and radio buttons.

Maxlength: **MAXLENGTH** is the maximum number of characters that are accepted as input. This is only appropriate for text entry fields and password entry fields (and only for single-line text entry fields at that). If this is not present, the default will be unlimited.

Name: Specifies a symbolic name used in transferring and identifying the output from this element of the form.

Size: **SIZE** is the physical size of the input field in characters. This is only appropriate for text entry fields and password entry fields. If this is not present, the default is **20**. Multiline text entry fields can be specified as follows:

SIZE = WIDTH, HEIGHT

Src: Defines the source file for the image when the attribute **Type** is set to image.

Text: A single-line, text-entry area (the **TEXTAREA** element is used for multiline text input). If the only element in the form has attribute **Text**, the user can submit the form by pressing key on the keyboard.

Type: Defines what kind of input field is presented to the user.

Value: **VALUE** can be used to specify the default contents of the field. For a checkbox or a radio button, **VALUE** specifies the value of the button when it is checked.

HTML Form Program

Example 22 gives an HTML program for a form design. The corresponding output is shown in Figure 8.26.

Example 22:

```
<HTML>.
<HEAD>
<TITLE>FORM FOR THE JOB</TITLE>
</HEAD>
<BODY>
<H1 align= "center">EXECUTIVE FORM</H1>
<HR>
<FORM METHOD="POST" ACTION="http://www.mcp.com
/cgi-bin/post-query">
<P><strong>Name: </STRONG><input TYPE="TEXT" NAME="theName"></P>
<P><strong>Father's/Husband Name: </STRONG>
<input TYPE="TEXT"</P>
<P><strong>E-mail id: </STRONG><input TYPE="TEXT"</P>
<P><STRONG>Sex: </STRONG>
<input checked TYPE="radio" NAME="theSex" VALUE="male">Male
<input TYPE="radio" NAME="theSex" VALUE="female"> Female
</P>
<P><STRONG>Educational Qualification: </STRONG>
```

```
<SELECT Name="select-menu">
<OPTION SELECTED> None
<OPTION>Graduate
<OPTION>Undergraduation
<OPTION>Post Graduate
<OPTION>10+2
</SELECT>
<P><STRONG>Which type of job you want: </STRONG>
<INPUT Type="checkbox" Name="per">Permanent
<INPUT Type="checkbox" Name="adhoc">Adhoc
<P><input TYPE="SUBMIT" VALUE="Submit">
<input TYPE="RESET" VALUE="Clear Form"></P>
</FORM>
<HR>
</BODY>
</HTML>
```

The output of Example 22 is shown in Figure 6.24.

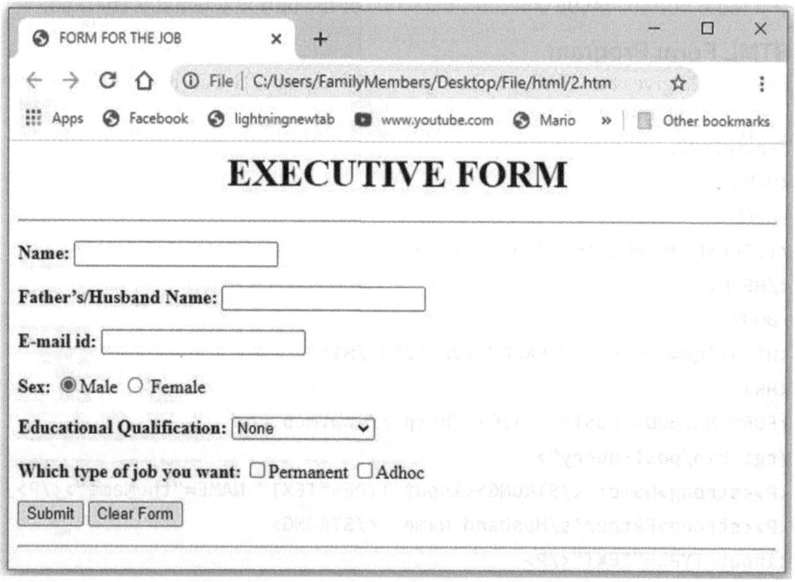

Figure 6.24: Result of Example 22 which is a sample of Form filling

EXERCISES

A. Multiple Choice Questions.

1. What does HTML stand for?
   (a) HyperText Markup Language
   (b) Home Tool Markup Language
   (c) Hyperlinks and Text Markup Language
   (d) None of these
2. Which is the correct HTML tag for the largest heading?
   (a) <Heading> (b) <H1> (c) <Head> (d) <H6>
3. A comment must start with and end with:
   (a) <!— and —> (b) ** and /** (c) <C>and</C> (d) None of these
4. What is the file extension used for HTML file?
   (a) .webpage (b) .shtml (c) .html (d) .doc
5. Between which set of tags does most of the content of your web page need to be placed?
   (a) <text></text> (b) <body></body>
   (c) <title></title> (d) <head></head>

B. Fill in the blanks.

1. HTML stands for ___________.
2. The lowest level of heading is ___________.
3. ___________ and ___________ are two types of tags.
4. ___________ is the inventor of HTML language.
5. WYSIWYG stands for What You See Is What You Get.

C. State whether the following statements are True or False.

1. HTML is a case sensitive.
2. Empty tags are not required to be closed.
3. <TITLE> tag specifies the title of the document.
4. HTML stands for HyperText Markup Language.
5. HTML requires only a text editor and web browser.

D. Answers the following questions.

1. What is HTML? Explain its features.
2. How to view the HTML document?
3. Differentiate between Container and Empty elements.
4. What is the use of <B>, <I> and <U> tags?
5. What is the use of 'scr' attribute of <IMG> tag?

7 Photoshop CS6

Learning Objectives

After studying this chapter, you should be able to do:

• Understanding Computer Graphics • Starting Photoshop • Components of Photoshop • Creating a new document • Saving a document • Making selection technique • Transforming selection • Art history brush • Layers palette • Creating a new layer • Understanding layer and vector

Students, you must have noticed the photographs in marriage albums, in any catalogue, posters, etc. Such photographs are so much different from the common pictures. Have you ever imagined how these pictures look so good? This can be made possible with the help of Adobe Photoshop software.

Adobe Photoshop is a graphics editing software program, used to edit or modify as well as create new images. Photoshop is developed by **Adobe Systems**. It is widely used by lots of photographers, artists and the people who handle graphics.

Uses of Photoshop

- It is used for image editing, color correction, touch ups, painting and drawing.
- It is used used in multimedia presentations, webpages, and animation projects.
- Photoshop is generally used to create and edit the magazine covers, book covers, albums, brochures, etc.

FACT

The Photoshop was created in 1988 by Thomas and John Knoll.

Understanding Computer Graphics

The computer graphics or digital images can be divided into the two categories:

a. **Bitmap Graphics:** Bitmap (or raster) images are stored as a series of tiny dots called Pixels. Each pixel is actually a very small square that is assigned a color and arranged in a pattern to form the image.

b. **Vector Graphics:** A Vector image is made up of various 'objects', a term which essentially means lines and shapes. These objects are defined mathematically by a set of algorithms or formulas, which allow them to be redrawn over and over. Most forms of 'ClipArt' are vector-based.

Features of CS6

The features of CS6 are as follows:

- User friendly interface.
- Retouching and transforming of photos are easily possible.
- You can open and save JPEG files upto 65, 535 pixels in width or height in the Photoshop CS6.
- Photos hop contains many new 3D features in CS6.
- Photoshop CS6 now supports high resolution displays as documents can be viewed at 200%.
- You can add as many layers as you need. You can use the properties panel to quickly modify the layer components selected in the Layers panel.
- Create graphics for web based applications with reduced file size, thereby helps in faster loading of the website.

Starting Photoshop

To start Photoshop, follow the given steps:

1. Click on the **Start** button.
2. Click on **Adobe Photoshop CS6** option.

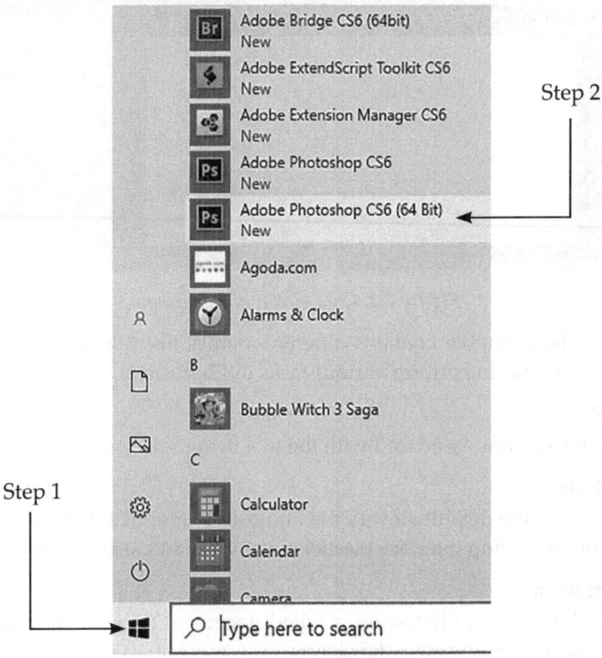

***Figure 7.1:** Launch Photoshop*

The Photoshop Window opens.

Components of Photoshop

The components of Photoshop window are as follows:

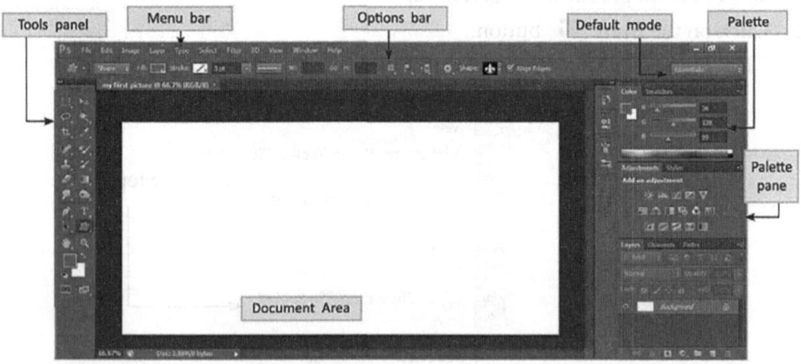

Figure 7.2: Component of Photoshop

Menu Bar: The menu bar contains different menus, like File, Edit, Image, Layer, Select, Window, etc. to perform various tasks in Photoshop.

Options Bar

It displays the options associated with the tool being selected.

Default Mode

The Essentials is the default view of the Photoshop interface. You can also change the mode of Photoshop interface by clicking any one mode available in this box.

Document Area

The large white area in Photoshop is called document area. In this area, you can perform various operations on the objects.

Tools Panel

The tools panel is present by default on the left side of Photoshop Window.

There are following five kinds of tools in the Photoshop tools panel.

- **Selection Tools:** It consists of various selection tools like Magic Wand, Marquee, Move, Lasso and Crop tools.
- **Paint and Retouching Tools:** It consists of Healing Brush, Brush, Eraser, Clone, Fill, Blur, Stamp, Dodge, Burn, Gradient and Sponge tools.
- **Text and Drawing Tools:** It consists of Text tool, Shape tool, Pen tool, etc. They are used for drawing and typing text.
- **View Tools:** Hand and Zoom tools are the main view tools. They are used for viewing the objects.
- **Other Tools:** There are many other tools that help us in various ways while working with images. For example, Foreground color, Background color, Switch and Default colors.

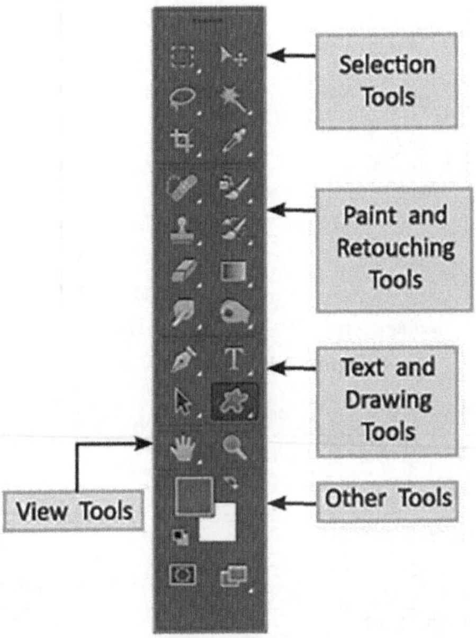

Figure 7.3: *Tools Panel*

Palettes

Palettes are floating windows that are placed one after the other with different options that you use for editing the images. These are present on the right side of the Photoshop window.

To move the palette, follow the given steps:

- Click on the top of the palette.
- Hold the left mouse button pressed and drag the palette.
- To close or expand the palette, click the double arrow.

Creating an Image/New Canvas/Window

To create a new Canvas/Image, follow the given steps:

1. Select File → New (or press Ctrl + N)

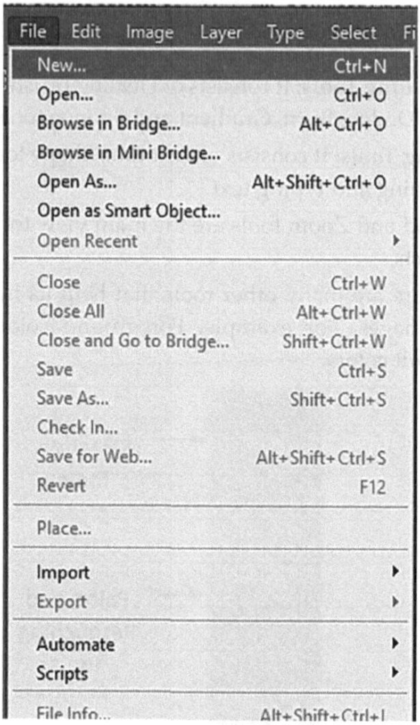

Figure 7.4: File Menu

2. A dialog box appears.

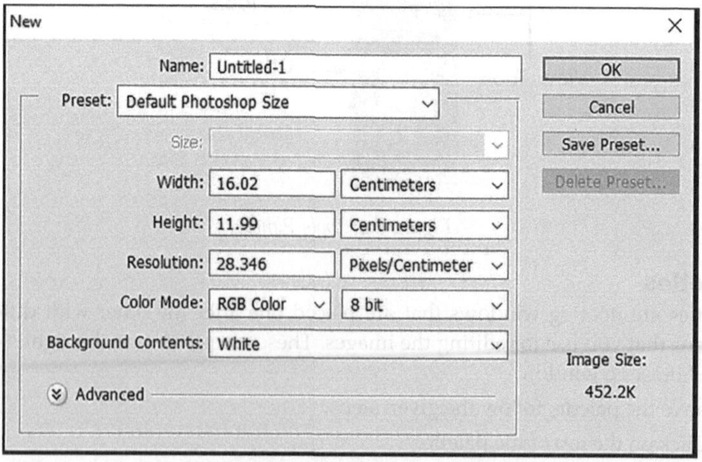

Figure 7.5: New Dialog box

3. Type a name for the new file.
4. Select a preset image category from the Preset pop-up menu.
5. Enter the resolution for the new document.
6. From the Color Mode drop-down list, select a **color** mode.
7. Select your desired color depth for your document.
8. In the Background Contents drop-down list, select an option for how you want the background layer to be filled.
9. Click the **Advanced** button to display a couple of additional options:
10. Click **OK** when you finish entering your options.

Extra Byte

A resolution of 72 ppi (pixels per inch) is generally used for Internet images.

To Open a Pre-existing Image

To open a Pre-existing Image, follow the given steps :

1. Click the **File** menu.
2. Click **Open** option.

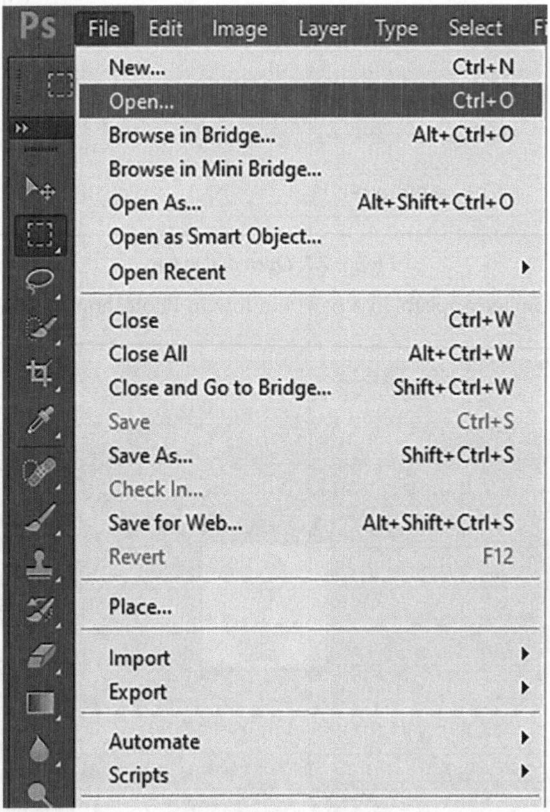

***Figure 7.6:** File menu*

3. In Open dialog box, select the location of the image. And select the image file name.
4. Click **Open** button.

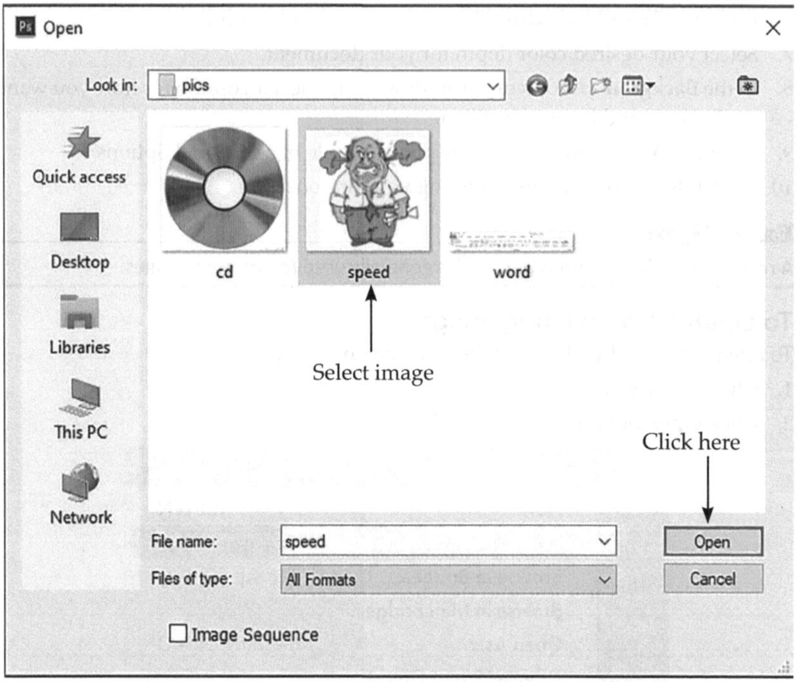

Figure 7.7: *Open dialog box*

The selected image appears in a new window in Photoshop. A sample is shown here:

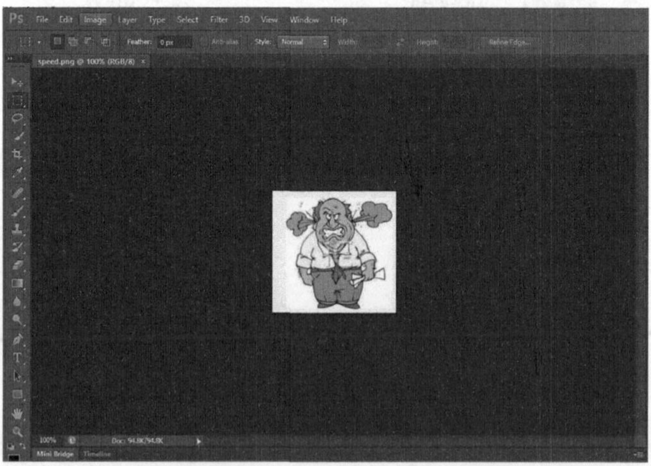

Figure 7.8: *Opening a pre-existing image*

Saving a File

After creating or editing the image, you must save the file. To save a file in Photoshop, follow the given steps:

1. Click on the **File > Save As** option. The Save As dialog box opens.
2. Type the name of file in **File Name box** and click on the **Save** button.

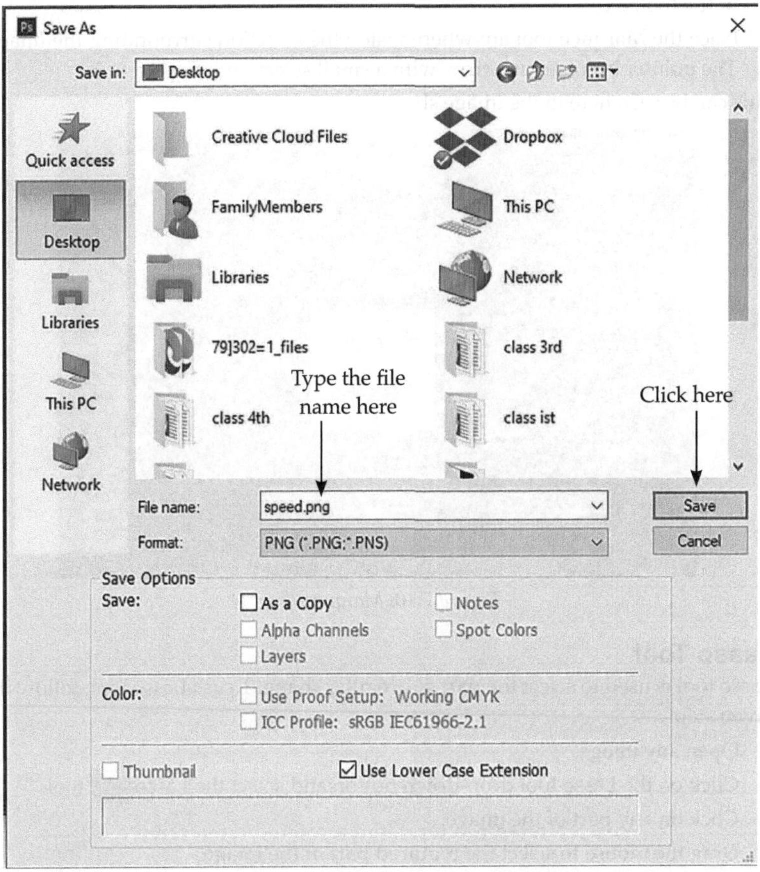

Figure 7.9: Save As dialog box

Memorize

A Photoshop file is saved with an extension .psd.

Using Selection tools in Photoshop

A selection defines the editable area in a photo. Photoshop has multiple selection tools to accommodate the different types of selections.

Marquee Tools

Marquee tools help make rectangular, elliptical, and single row or single column selections. The Marquee tools are found in the uppermost left corner of the Toolbox.

The Rectangular Marquee tool draws square or rectangular selection borders, and the Elliptical Marquee tool draws round or elliptical selection borders. The steps to use the selection tools are:

1. Open the image you wish to make changes in.
2. Select the Selection Tool from the toolbox. Click the rectangle marquee tool  in the toolbox.
3. Place the Marquee tool anywhere inside the selection surrounding the image. The pointer becomes an arrow with a small selection icon next to it.

This can be seen here in the image shown:

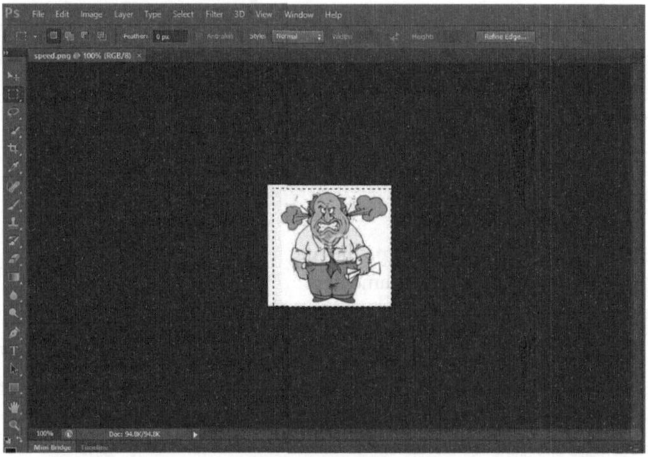

Figure 7.10: *Marquee Tools*

Lasso Tool

Lasso tool is used to select the part of irregular shape. To use Lasso tool, follow the given steps:

1. Open any image.
2. Click on the Lasso tool drop-down button and select the Lasso  tool.
3. Click on any part of the image.
4. Drag the mouse to select the required part of the image.
5. Release the mouse at end.

Figure 7.11: *Lasso Tool*

Polygonal Lasso Tool

Similar to the Lasso tool, except that instead of holding your mouse button down to draw, left-click on various points to create a selection with a series of straight edges. You can also hold down the Alt key to draw freehand sections.

To use Polygonal Lasso tool, follow the given steps:

1. Open any image.
2. Click on the Lasso tool drop-down button and select the Polygonal Lasso tool.
3. Click on any part of the image to select it.
4. Drag the mouse over the part and you will see a line follow your Polygon Lasso tool.
5. Click again to draw the first line between the two mouse clicks.
6. Move the mouse pointer on the part to be selected and another line indicates your selection.
7. Continue this process till you reach the starting point.

Figure 7.12: Polygonal Lasso Tool

Magnetic Lasso Tool

This is a very handy tool for selecting areas which have reasonably well-defined edges. Left-click at the starting point of your selection and simply move the mouse along the edge.

To use Magnetic Lasso tool, follow the given steps:

1. Open any image.
2. Click on the Lasso tool drop-down button and select the Magnetic Lasso tool.
3. Click on any part of the image to be selected.
4. Drag the mouse over the object to select it. You will see the dashed border along the edges.
5. Double-click at the ending point.

Figure 7.13: Magnetic Lasso Tool

Magic Wand Tool

The Magic Wand tool allows you to select an area of an image based on its colour. When you click an area in an image with the magic wand, all areas which are a similar colour are selected. You can specify various options to determine the exact selection. To do selection using Magic Wand Tool, follow these steps:

1. Open the image.
2. Select the Magic Wand from the toolbox.
3. Click anywhere on the image and drag mouse to make a freehand selection border around the part of the image to be selected.
4. Release the mouse to close the selection.

Figure 7.14: Magic Wand Tool

Cropping the Image

The Crop tool in Photoshop allows you to remove portions of an image and focus on the remaining components within an image. The steps to use this tool are:

1. Open any image.
2. Select the Crop tool.

3. Click and drag the mouse over the part of the image you would like to keep.
4. Release the mouse button.

A dotted line appears around your selection and the rest of the image becomes dim.

Before cropping After cropping

***Figure 7.15:** Cropping an image*

Moving a Selection

The Move tool allows us to move a selection by dragging it with the mouse or using the keyboard arrows keys.

To move an image or a part of the image, follow these steps:

1. Open the image you wish to crop.
2. Select the Selection tool from the toolbox and make selection.
3. Select the Move tool.
4. Place the Mouse over the selected part and drag it to a new location. The selected part of the image is removed from its original position.

***Figure 7.16:** Moving a Selection*

Extra Byte

The selected part of the image within your selection is known as Cropping Marquee.

Shortcut key

- To use Lasso tool, press L key.
- To use Magic Wand tool, press W key.
- To use Crop tool, press C key.

Rotate

You can rotate the selected part of an image with the help of the Transformation handlers.

To rotate image, do this:

1. Open an image.
2. Make sure that some portion of image is selected.
3. Click **Edit** menu and choose **Free Transformation** command which is to be applied to the portion.
4. Click the right mouse button. A shortcut menu appears. Select the Rotate command as shown in Figure 7.17.

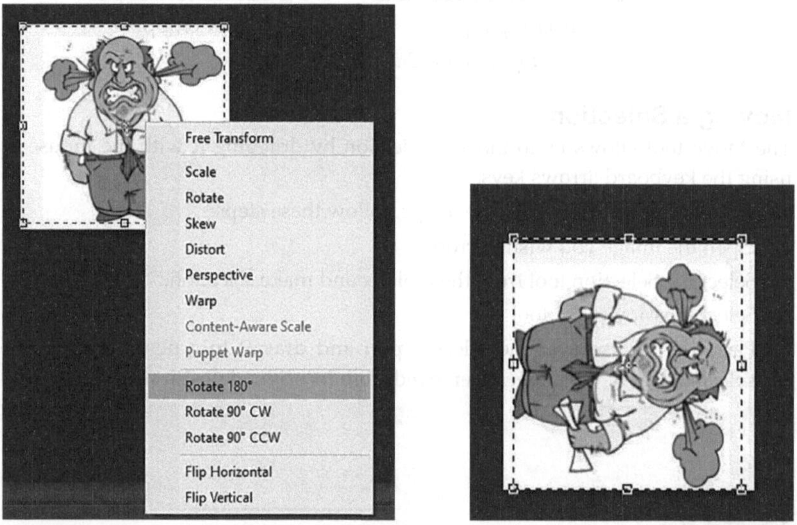

Before rotation After Rotation

Figure 7.17: *Rotating an image*

Closing an Image

You can close a Photoshop document by performing the following steps:

1. Click the **File** menu.
2. Choose the **Close** option.

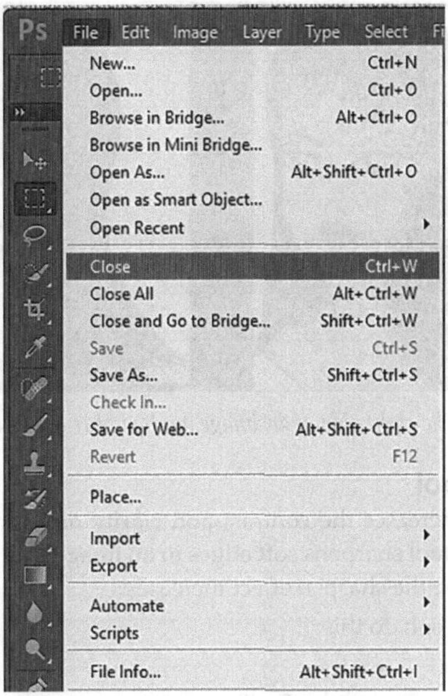

Figure 7.26: Closing an image

Image Editing Tools

The Blur Tool

The Blur Tool softens hard edges in an image. You can use Blur Tool to remove minor imperfections and smooth out wrinkles. You can use the Lighten and Darken Blending Modes with Blur Tool to avoid over blurring the image.

1. Open the image.
2. Click on the **Blur Tool** in the **Toolbox.**
3. Click the drop-down list and select the **Brush:** size in the pop-up palette.
4. Click the drop-down list to select the **Mode:** to set painting in the image.
5. Click the **Strength:** drop-down list to set the strength of stroke for painting.
6. If you select the **All Layers** option, then it is used for image, which consists of more than one layer, if the blur effect is to be applied to all layers.
7. Place the mouse pointer on the image and drag it to blur the pixels.
8. After applying blur effect, release the mouse button. Figure 9.18 shows the original image and the blurred image after applying Blur effect. The Blur Tool is useful to improve the appearance of images with jagged and rough edges.

Figure 9.18: The right side of an image applied blur effect using Blur Tool

The Sharpen Tool

The Sharpen Tool increases the contrast and clarity of blurred images with soft edges. The Sharpen tool sharpens soft edges in an image. The more you paint over an area with the Tool, the sharpen effect increases.

To use the sharpen Tool, do this:

1. Open the image.
2. Click the Sharpen Tool in the Toolbox.
3. Click the drop-down list and select the Brush: size in the pop-up palette.
4. Click the drop-down list to select the Mode: to set painting in the image.
5. Click the Strength: drop-down list to set the strength of stroke for painting.
6. Click and Drag the mouse pointer over the image. As you drag over an area, the pixels randomly change color. The more you drag, the more diverse the colors of the adjacent pixels become (See Figure 9.19).

The Smudge Tool

The Smudge Tool creates the effect of smudging wet paint with a finger. The tool picks up color where the stroke begins and pushes it in the direction you drag.

To use the Smudge effects in an image, do this:

1. Open the image.
2. Click the Smudge Tool from the Toolbox.
3. Choose a Brush Size and Blending Mode in the Options bar.

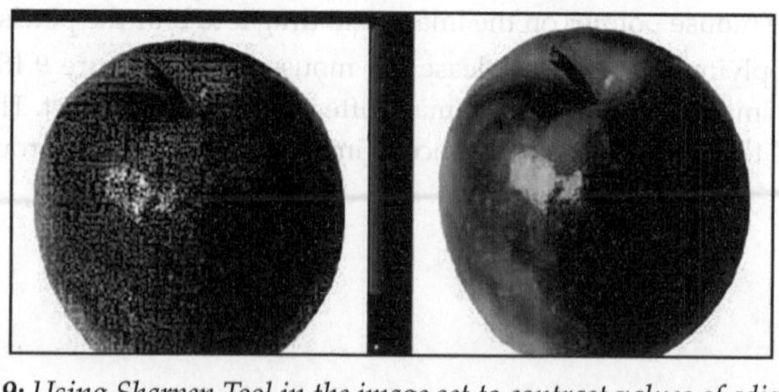

Figure 9.19: Using Sharpen Tool in the image set to contrast values of adjacent pixels

4. Click the Strength: drop-down list to set the strength of stroke for painting.
5. If you check the Finger Painting box in the Options bar to smudge the foreground color at the beginning of each stroke. If this is deselected, the Smudge Tool uses the color under the pointer at the beginning of each stroke.
6. Place the mouse pointer on the image and drag to smudge an area as you move them. Figure 9.20 shows the effect of rose using the Smudge Tool on a colored stroke created with the brush.

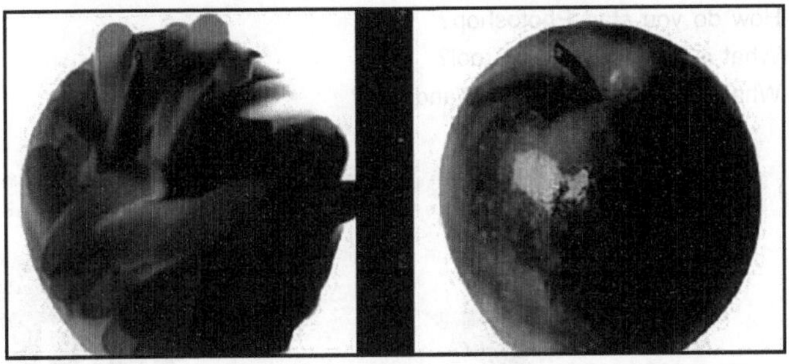

Figure 9.20: *The Left side of image using Smudge Tool smudges color*

EXERCISES

A. Multiple Choice Questions.

1. What is the extension of files saved in Photoshop?
   (a) .ppt (b) .psd (c) .pptx (d) None of these
2. In what year was Photoshop created?
   (a) 1998 (b) 1988 (c) 1898 (d) None of these
3. One of the co-creator of Photoshop is:
   (a) John Bush (b) John Knoll (c) John Lord (d) John Ibraham
4. Photoshop is a graphics editor software developed and published by:
   (a) Microsoft (b) Google (c) Adobe (d) None of these
5. A vector image is made up of–
   (a) Lines (b) Curves (c) Both (a) and (b) (d) None of these

B. Fill in the blanks.

1. The first version of Photoshop software was named as ____________.
2. Images are made up of ____________
3. The shortcut key to use crop tool is ____________
4. The Photoshop files are saved with ____________ extension.
5. The Photoshop tools panel is present in ____________ side of its window.

C. State whether the following statements are True or False.

1. The Open dialog box is used to select the image to be opened.
2. The Magic Wand tool is unlike the rest of the selection tools, as it selects areas based on colour.

3. The Move tool allows us to move a selection by dragging it with the mouse or using the keyboard arrows keys.
4. Magic Wand helps to make freehand selections of irregularly shaped areas.
5. The Rectangular Marquee tool is used to make a free selection as you go.

D. Answers the following questions.

1. Write a short note on Bitmap Vs Vector Graphics.
2. Write the steps to save and open a Photoshop file.
3. How do you start Photoshop?
4. What is the use of Crop tool?
5. What is the use of Magic Wand tool?

8 Flash Animation

Learning Objectives

After studying this chapter, you should be able to do:

• Creating Graphics in Flash Professional • Selecting Objects • Draw Rectangles and Ovals • Create Instances • Working with Timeline • Animation Basics • Understanding Motion Tweens • Shape Tweening • Understanding Actions • Add a code snippet to an object or Timeline frame • Add new snippets to the Code Snippets panel

Introduction

Adobe® Flash® Professional provides a complete interactive authoring environment for creating digital animation and interactive Websites. It is basically used to create rich interactive applications using video, sound, graphics and animation.

FACT

The first prominent use of the Adobe Flash animation format was by Ren & Stimpy creator John Kricfalusi.

Creating Graphics in Flash Professional

Flash Professional includes several drawing tools, which work in different drawing modes. The basics of drawing tools enable you to create and edit graphics. To create basic geometric shapes, Flash Professional CS6 provides you various tools, such as **Line, Rectangle, Oval** and **PolyStar Tools**. The **Pencil** Tool can be used for creating freehand shapes. The Pen Tool is used for drawing Bezier curves and the **Brush** tool is for creating artistic effects.

Selection Tool, Subselection and **Lasso** Tools are used to select objects for editing and reshaping the objects. There is another set of tools called **Ink Bottle, Paint Bucket** and **Eyedropper Tools**, which are used to modify fill and outlines of the objects.

Memorize

In order to create curves, indicate the anchor points, which limit curvature, and then drag the tangent on them.

Extra Byte

In Timeline, the red rectangle will move across the Timeline to show you the current frame on the Stage.

Selecting Objects

To edit or modify an object, you must first select different parts of it. In Flash Professional CS6, you can select objects with the **Selection**, **Subselection**, or **Lasso Tools**. Flash provides you the following tools to select shapes and objects.

Using Selection Tool

Selection Tools look like Arrow Tool. You can use this tool to select a single or multiple objects on the **Stage**.

To select the objects with the Selection Tool, do this:

- To select a filled object, click the Selection Tool in the **Tools panel** and click in the fill area. On a merged object, the selected fill is highlighted as shown in Figure 8.1 (a).
- To select both fill and outline, double-click the fill area with the **Selection Tool** as shown in Figure 8.1 (b).
- To select the stroke of an object, click on the Object's stroke with the **Selection Tool**.
- To select two or more objects together, click on the first object with the **Selection** Tool and then hold down the **Shift** key and click all other objects together. Or

Figure 8.1: Using the Selection Tool to fill and stroke

You can also create a marquee selection to select multiple objects on the **Stage**. The **Selection Tool** can be used to reshape objects on the Stage. You can modify the segments or move the endpoints to reshape the curve.

To reshape the object with the Selection Tool, do this:

1. Click the **Selection Tool** in the **Tools panel**.
2. Move the pointer around the segment, which you want to modify. The **Selection** Tool cursor will display with a curve under it (See Figure 8.2).
3. Click and drag the cursor to move the desired segment.

Figure 8.2: Reshape an object using the Selection Tool

Extra Byte

If you wish to select several objects together hold down the SHIFT key or use a the lasso or a selection box

Subselection Tool

You can use the **Subselection Tool** to modify the shapes created with **Pen, Pencil, Brush, Rectangle** or **Oval** Tool. The **Subselection Tool** enables you to move or edit individual anchor points on lines or outlines.

To use the Subselection Tool, do this:

1. Draw a shape using any drawing tool. For example, we have created a square as shown in Figure 8.3.
2. Click the **Subselection Tool** from the **Tools Panel** and then click the Outline of the shape. The outline will be selected and square handles appear along the outline of the shape (See Figure 8.3).
3. Click the square handle, and keep the mouse-button pressed. Drag to reshape the shape. Once you have finished the reshape, release the mouse button (See Figure 8.3).
4. Reshape of the square object looks like a flower shape as shown in Figure 8.3).

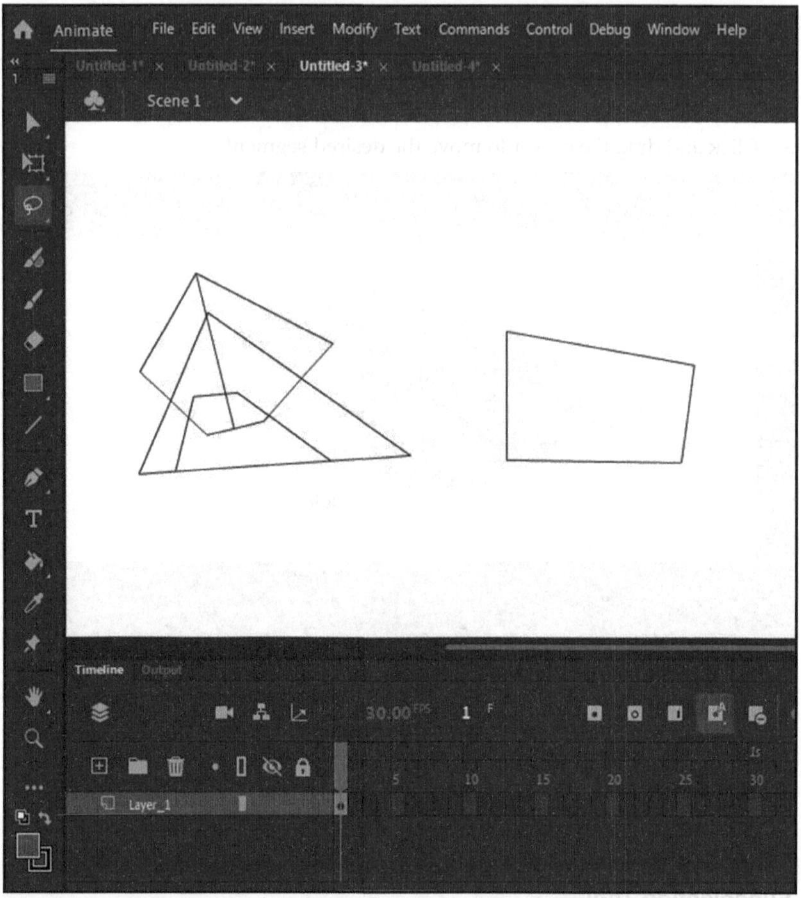

Figure 8.3: Using the Subselection Tool to reshape the circle

Lasso Tool

Another way to make a selection is to use the **Lasso** Tool. The **Lasso** Tool provides more flexibility than the **Selection** Tool when selecting object(s) or parts of an object on the **Stage**. The **Lasso Tool** lets you select an irregular part of a graphic, which you can then move, scale, rotate, reshape, or delete.

The **Lasso Options** area contains the following modifiers:

Magic Wand—Magic Wand Tool is useful for selecting areas of similar color in a bitmap graphic you have broken apart.

Polygon Mode—Polygon Mode option is useful for drawing straight lines and connect them to form a shape that will select any object(s) within the shape.

Selection using a Lasso Tool

To make a selection using Lasso Tool, do this:

1. Open an image.
2. To break apart graphic, select the image and then click on the **Modify** menu and select **Break Apart** option (See Figure 8.4). Alternatively, press **Ctrl+B** keys together to break apart the graphics.
3. Image after breaking apart looks like as shown in Figure 8.5.

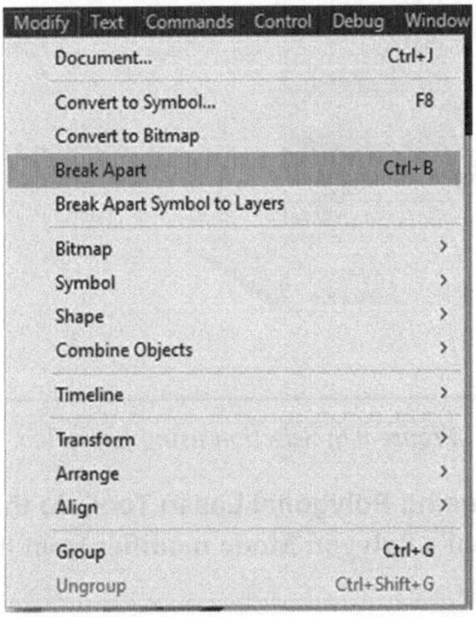

Figure 8.4: Break Apart option selected in Modify menu

Figure 8.5: Effect of Break Apart feature on selected Image

4. Click the **Lasso** Tool from **Tools panel**. Place the mouse pointer over the image and drag it around the neck of the bird and end the loop approximately where you started (See Figure 8.6).

Lasso Tool with Polygon Modifier

Polygonal Lasso Tool draws straight segments.

Figure 8.6: *Selection using Lasso Tool*

To make a selection using Polygonal Lasso Tool, do this:

1. Select the **Lasso tool's Polygon Mode modifier** from the **Options area** of the **Tools panel.**
2. Click to set the starting point.
3. Position the pointer where you want the first line to end, and click. Continue setting end points for additional line segments (See Figure 8.7).
4. To close the selection area, double-click.

Figure 8.7: *Polygonal Selection of an image*

Draw Rectangles and Ovals

The **Oval** and **Rectangle** Tools let you create basic geometric shapes. In addition to the **Merge** and **Object drawing modes**, the **Oval** and **Rectangle tools** also provide the **Primitive Object drawing mode** as described earlier in this following section.

When you create rectangles or ovals using the **Rectangle Primitive** or **Oval Primitive tools**, Flash draws the shapes as separate objects. After you create a primitive shape, you can alter the corners of rectangles, the start and end angle and the inner radius of ovals using controls in the **Properties Inspector**.

Rectangles and Squares

Rectangles and squares are the basic shapes available with most drawing software packages. Flash Professional lets you draw rectangles and squares with ease.

To draw rectangle and square, do this:

1. Click the **Rectangle Tool** in the **Tools panel**. Make sure the **Object Drawing mode** icon is not selected in the **Options area**.
2. Click and drag the mouse on the **Stage** until the rectangle is of the size you want. (See Figure 8.8). If you want to draw a square, press and hold down the **Shift** key, while dragging until the Square has the size and form you want (See Figure 8.8).

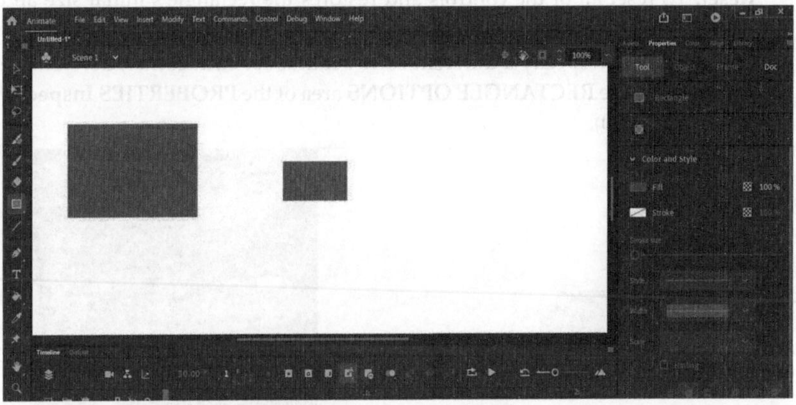

Figure 8.8: Using Rectangle Tool to draw square and rectangle

To draw rectangle using Rectangle Primitive Tool, do this:

1. Click the small black arrow on the **Rectangle Tool** in the **Tools panel**. The **Rectangle Tool** flyout is activated as shown in Figure 8.9.
2. Click the **Rectangle Primitive Tool.**

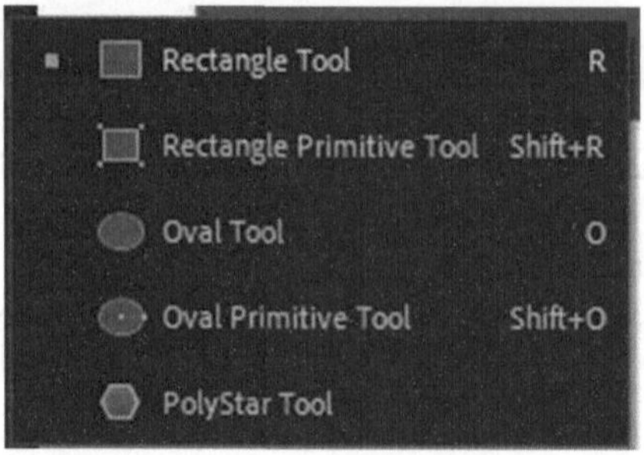

***Figure 8.9:** Rectangle Tool flyout (or hidden tools)*

3. Drag the mouse on the **Stage** until the rectangle has the size and form you want.
4. In the **PROPERTIES Inspector**, select the one of the following options: **Rectangle Corner Radius Controls:** To specify the corner radii for the rectangle, enter a numeric value for the inner radius in each text box.

   Entering a negative value creates an inverse radius. You can also deselect the constrain corner radius icon, and adjust each corner radius individually.

   Reset: To reset all of the controls and restores the rectangle's initial size and shape.

   Lock Corner: To specify a different corner radius for each corner, deselect the **Lock icon** in the **RECTANGLE OPTIONS** area of the **PROPERTIES Inspector** (See Figure 8.10).

***Figure 8.10:** Rectangle Primitive Tool properties*

Oval and Circles

Oval, also known as Ellipse, can be drawn in Flash Professional using the **Rectangle Tool** in the **Tools panel.**

To draw oval and circle, do this:

1. Click on the small black arrow on the **Rectangle Tool** in the **Tools panel**. The **Rectangle Tool** flyout is activated as shown in Figure 8.9.
2. Click the **Oval Tool.**
3. Click and drag the mouse on the **Stage** until the Oval is of the size you want. (See Figure 8.11). If you want to draw a Circle, press and hold down the **Shift** key while dragging until the Circle has the size and form you want. (See Figure 8.11).
4. If desired, change the stroke color, fill color, height and style in the **Properties Inspector**. (See Figure 8.11)

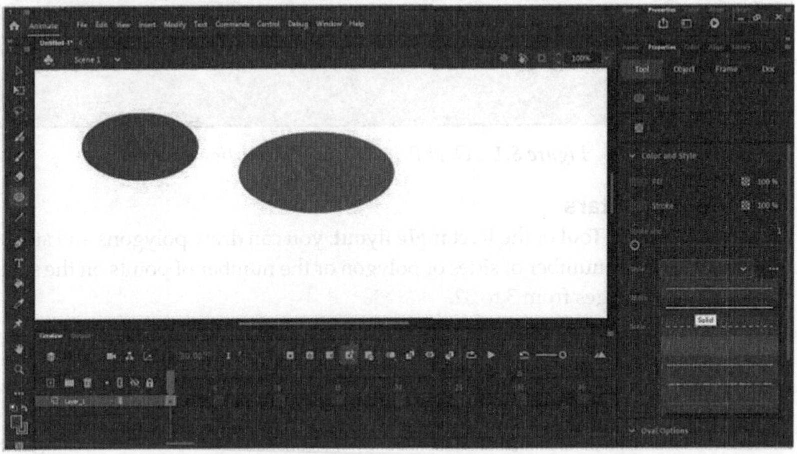

Figure 8.11: Drawing Oval and Circle

To draw oval using Oval Primitive Tool, do this:

1. Click on the small black arrow on the **Rectangle Tool** in the **Tools panel.** The **Rectangle Tool flyout** is activated as shown in Figure 8.9.
2. Click the **Oval Primitive Tool.**
3. Drag the mouse on the **Stage** until the oval has the size and form you want.
4. In the **PROPERTIES Inspector**, select the one of the following options:

   Start Angle/End Angle: These controls are useful for easily modify the shape of ovals and circles into pie slices, half circles, and other creative shapes (See Figure 8.12).

   Inner Radius: It is an inner radius (or oval) within the oval. To set inner radius, you have to either enter a numeric value for the inner radius in the box or click the slider and interactively adjust the size of the inner radius.

   Close Path: It determines whether the path of the oval is closed. If you specify an open path, Close path option is unchecked and no fill is applied to the resulting shape, only the stroke is drawn (See Figure 8.12). Close Path is selected by default.

Reset: It resets all of the Oval Primitive Tool which controls and restores the oval primitive shape has drawn on the Stage to its initial size and shape (See Figure 8.12).

Figure 8.12: Oval Primitive Tool properties

Polygons and Stars

Using the **PolyStar Tool** of the **Rectangle flyout**, you can draw polygons and stars. You can choose the number of sides of polygon or the number of points on the star. The size of star ranges from 3 to 32.

To draw polygon and polystar, do this:

1. Select the **PolyStar** tool from the **Rectangle flyout** as shown in Figure 8.9.
2. Then click on the **Window menu** and then choose **Properties** option.
3. In the **PROPERTIES Inspector**, click the **Options...** button as shown in Figure 8.13 in the **Tool Settings** Section The Tool Settings dialog box appears (See Figure 8.14). In the **Style:** drop-down list, select **Polygon** or **Star** whichever you want to draw.
4. In the **Number of Sides:** text box, enter a number between 3 and 32.
5. If you are drawing star, then in **Star point size:** text box, enter a number (from 0 to 1) to specify the depth of the star points. But, if you are drawing a polygon, leave this setting unchanged.
6. Click the **OK** button.
7. Drag on the **Stage**.

Using Symbols

One of the most important features in Flash Professional is that it gives the ability to create a prototype we can use, change and reuse with a movie. This prototype is called a *symbol*. A symbol can include artwork that you import from another application. Any symbol that you create automatically becomes part of the library for the current document.

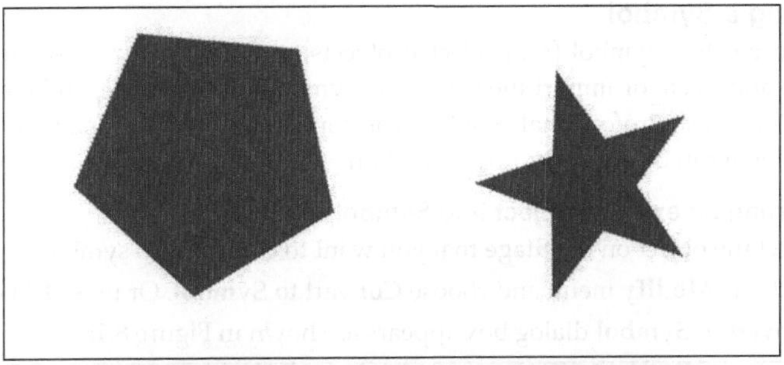

Figure 8.13: Option... button in PROPERTIES Inspector

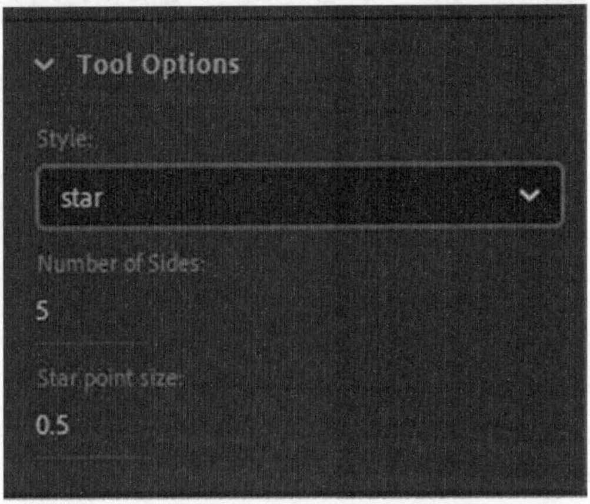

Figure 8.14: Tool Settings dialog box

An *instance* is a copy of a symbol which is either located on the Stage or inside another symbol. An instance can be different from original symbol in size, color, etc. While we edit the symbol, it will update all the instance of symbol. But, editing one instance of symbol can change only that instance, not all the instances of the symbol. Flash Professional CS6 uses four types of symbols. These are:

(a) **Graphic symbols:** These symbols are used for static images. Therefore, sound will not work in graphic symbols. Graphic symbols add less to the FLA file size than buttons or movie clips because they have no Timeline.

(b) **Button symbols:** These symbols are used to respond with the mouse clicks, rollovers, or other actions.

(c) **Movie clips:** These symbols are used to create reusable piece of information. It can contain interactive controls, sound and even other movie clip instances. Movie clip symbols contain their own independent Timeline. You can have an animation inside a movie clip symbol just as easily as you can have an animation on the main Timeline.

(d) **Font symbols:** These symbols are created from font files to make them available for use in dynamic text fields.

Creating a Symbol

You can create a symbol from selected objects on the **Stage** or create an empty symbol and make or import the content in symbol-editing mode, and create font symbols in Flash Professional. Symbols can contain all the functionality that Flash Professional can create, including animation.

Converting an existing object into Symbol, do this:

1. Select the object on the **Stage** that you want to convert into symbol.
2. Click the **Modify** menu and choose **Convert to Symbol**. Or press **F8** key.
3. **Convert to Symbol** dialog box appears as shown in Figure 8.15.

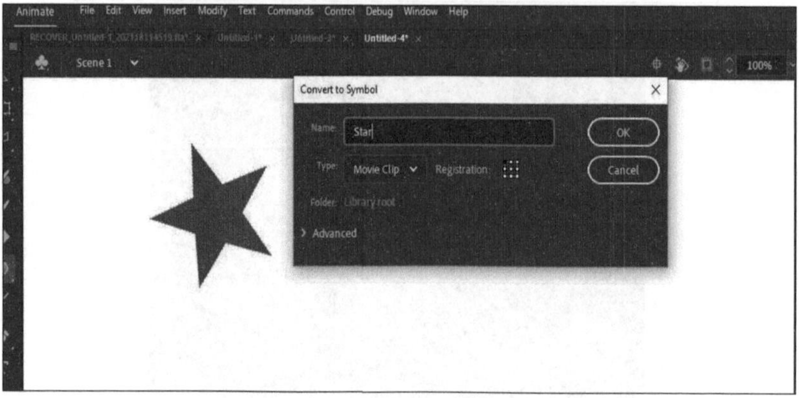

Figure 8.15: Convert to Symbol dialog box

4. Enter a name for the symbol in the **Name:** text box.
5. Choose a behavior type for the symbol from the **Type:** drop-down list.
6. Click the **Registration grid** to position the registration point for the symbol. Registration point of the symbol refers to the point of reference on the symbol. The registration point is the axis around which the symbol rotates, and the point along which the symbol aligns.
7. Click **OK** button. The object is now converted to a symbol and appears in the **Library panel**. The selected object becomes instance of the symbol in the **Library** and a registration point placed in it (See Figure 8.15).

Creating a New or an Empty Symbol

The new symbol is created in the symbol-editing mode.

To create new symbol, do this:

1. Click the **Insert** menu and choose **New Symbol...** . Or press **Ctrl+F8** keys together. The **Create New Symbol** dialog box appears as shown in Figure 8.16.

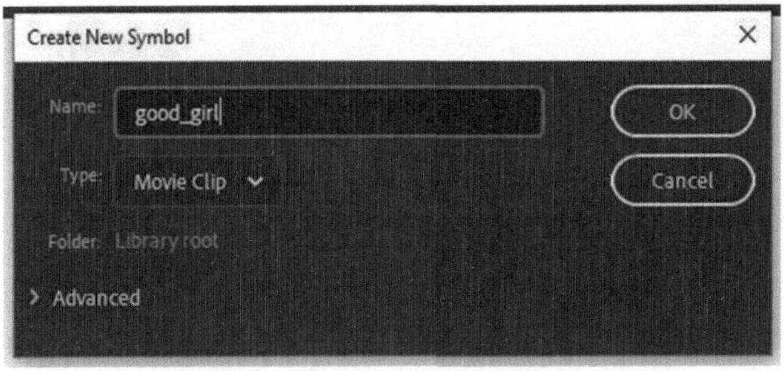

Figure 8.16: *Create New Symbol Dialog box*

2. Enter a symbol name in the `Name:` text box. For example, we have given symbol name as **good_girl**.
3. Select a behavior type for the symbol in the `Type:` drop-down list box. For example, select **Graphic** as a type of symbol.
4. Click **OK** button to close the dialog box. The dialog box will get closed, symbol adds to the library and you will be moved to the *Symbol Editing Mode*. In this mode, the name of the symbol appears above the upper-left corner of the **Stage**, and a cross hair indicates the symbol's registration point (See Figure 8.17).

Figure 8.17: *Symbol Editing Mode*

5. Create a symbol content using drawing tools, **Timeline**, import media. For example, we import a file from Illustrator.
6. To import a file from Illustrator, click the **File** menu, choose **Import** and then select **Import to Stage**. An **Import** dialog box appears as shown in Figure 8.18.

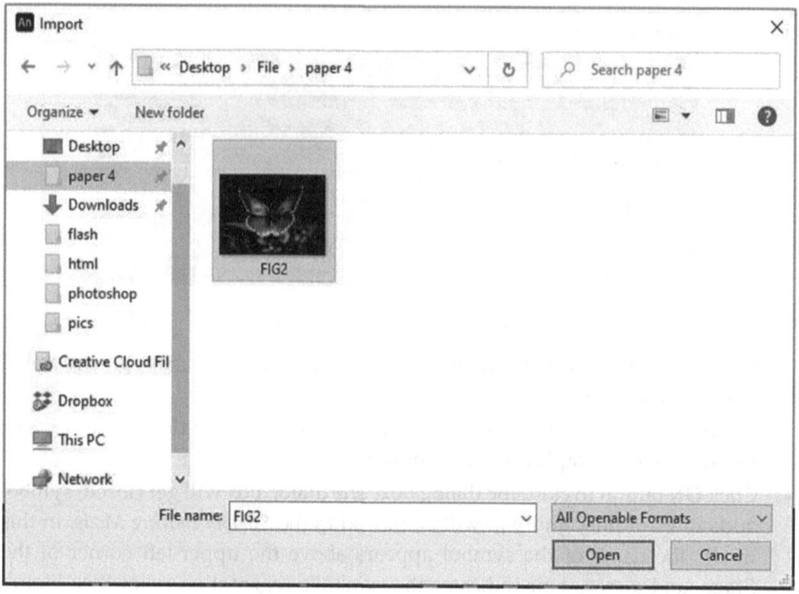

***Figure 8.18:** Import dialog box*

7. Here, navigate an Illustrator file (**.ai file**) from your local computer, and click **Open** (See Figure 8.18).
8. After that, in **Import <file name> to Library** dialog box as shown in Figure 8.19, make sure all layers have been selected. A check mark should appear in the check box next to each layer.

***Figure 8.19:** Import <file name> to Library dialog box*

Create Instances

After you have created a symbol, you can place number of instances of the symbol on the **Stage**, including inside other symbols.

You can give names to instances from the **Properties Inspector**. To specify color effects, assign actions, set the graphic display mode, or change the behavior of new instances, use the **Properties Inspector**.

To create an instance of a symbol on the Stage, do this:

1. Select a layer in the **Timeline**.
2. Click the Symbol name or the symbol image in the **Library** and drag it on the Stage (See Figure 8.21).
3. Release the mouse at location on the **Stage** where you want to place the instance. Figure 8.21 shows the instance of the Star symbol placed on the **Stage**.

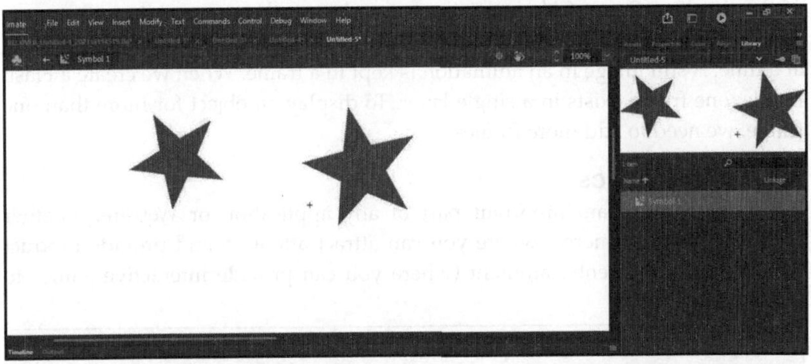

Figure 8.21: Instances of symbol placed on the Stage

Editing Instance Properties

Each instance on the **Stage** has its own properties that are saved with it and every instance's properties are separated from the symbol's properties. You can change instance's properties, such as *tint, transparency*, and *brightness*, redefine how the instance behaves and much more. You can also *skew, rotate*, or *scale* an instance without affecting the symbol.

Working with Timeline

The **Timeline** organizes and controls a movie's contents over time. With the help of Timeline, you can determine and change what will be happening in a movie, frame-by-frame. You can also determine which objects are animated, what types of animations are being used, when the various objects will appear in a movie, when changes are made to the properties of an object, which objects will appear on top of others, and how fast the movie will play. Features of the Timeline are shown in Figure 8.22.

Figure 8.22: Timeline features

Concept of Frames

Like films, Flash Professional documents are divided into lengths of time and frames. In the Timeline, you can work with these frames to organize and control the content of your document.

A *frame* is the little rectangular cell in a Timeline. Frames are numbered at the top of the timeline. Every fifth frame is gray and rest others are white with a gray outline. Timeline displays all the frames, but we can see only one frame's content at a time. A still image in an animation is kept in a frame. When we create a Flash movie, one frame exists in a single layer. To display an object for more than one frame, we need to add more frames.

Animation Basics

Animation can be an important part of any application or Website, whether we focus on e-commerce (where you can attract attention and provide product demonstration), or entertainment (where you can provide interactive games to the user).

> **Definition:** Animation is the process of creating a continuous motion and shape change illusion by means of a rapid display of a sequence of static images that minimally differ from each other.

How does Animation Work?

Animation is like a motion picture, which is made up of a series of still images. Animation can be as simple as moving a box across the Stage from one frame to the next. It can also be much more complex. The perception of motion in an animation is actually an illusion because our eye captures and holds an image for one-tenth of a second before processing another image.

By retaining each impression for one-tenth of a second, we perceive a series of rapidly displayed still images as a single, moving image. This is known as persistence of vision. It provides the basis for the frame rate in animation. Frame rates of 10–12 frames per second (fps) generally provide a smooth computer- based animation. Lower frame rates result in a jerky image, while frame rates over 30 fps may result in a blurred image. Flash uses a default frame rate of 24 fps.

Creating Animation

Creating animation is one of the most powerful features of Flash. However, developing basic animations is a simple process. Flash allows you to animate many different aspects of a single object. You can change an object's position on the Stage, change its color or transparency, change its size or its rotation, and even animate the special filters. You also have control over an object's path of motion, and even its easing, which is the way an object accelerates or deaccelerates. Animations are created by changing the contents of successive frames.

Types of Animation

Flash Professional provides several ways to create animation and special effects. Each method provides you with different possibilities for creating and engaging animated contents. These are:

1. Tweened Animation
2. Frame-by-Frame Animation
3. Inverse Kinematic

Tweened Animation

Tweened animation is an effective and efficient way to create movement and changes over time while minimizing file size. In tweened animation, only the values for the property keyframes you specify are stored in the FLA (Flash) file and published as SWF (ShockWave Flash) file. Tweened animations can be again divided into three types. These are the following.

Motion Tweens

Motion tweens are useful for creating animation that consists of continuous motion or transformation of an object. Motion tweens appear in the Timeline as a contiguous span of frames that can be selected as a single object by default. Motion tweens are powerful and simple to create. In a motion tween animation, you have to specify the position of the object in the beginning and in the ending frames and Flash fills in the in-between frames.

Classic Tweens

Classic tweens are like motion tweens in which you can create animations that change the properties of an object over time. Motion tweens are easier to use and allow the greatest degree of control over tweened animation. But Classic tweens are a bit more complex to be created, however, they provide certain capabilities that some developers desire.

Shape Tweens

Shape tweening is a technique for interpolating amorphous (shapeless) changes between shapes in different keyframes. For this, you have to draw a shape at one specific keyframe in the Timeline, and change that shape or draw another shape at another specific keyframe. Flash then interpolates the intermediate shapes for the keyframes in between and Shape tweens make it possible to smoothly morph one shape into another. For example, animation of clouds, water, or fire is perfect for shape tweening.

Frame-by-Frame Animation

Frame-by-frame animations are useful when you want to change individual parts of an image. Frame-by-frame animation changes the contents of the Stage in every frame and is best suited to complex animation in which an image changes in every frame instead of simply moving across the **Stage**. Frame-by-frame animation increases file size more rapidly than tweened animation.

Inverse Kinematics

Inverse Kinematics (IK) allows you to easily create character animations. It allows you to stretch and bend shape objects, and link groups of symbol instances to make them move together in a natural way. Once you have added bones to a shape or a group of symbols, you can change the position of the bones or symbols in different keyframes.

Classification of Animations in the Timeline

Flash distinguishes different types of animations in the Timeline by displaying different indicators. These indicators and their animation types are given in Table 8.1.

Table 8.1 *Different Indicators of different Animations in Timeline*

Indicators	Types of Animation
	**Motion Tween Animation** A *black dot* in the first frame indicates that the tween span has a target object assigned to it. *Black diamond* indicates the last frame and any other property keyframes.
	**Motion Tween Animation** A *hollow dot* in the first frame indicates that the target object of the motion tween has been removed. The tween span still contains its property keyframes and can have a new target object applied to it.
	**Inverse Kinematics** Pose layers contain Inverse Kinematics armatures and poses. Each pose appears in the Timeline as a black diamond. Flash interpolates the positions of the armature in the frames in between poses.
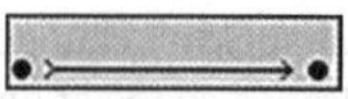	**Classic Tween** A *black dot* at the beginning keyframe with a black arrow and blue background indicates a classic tween.
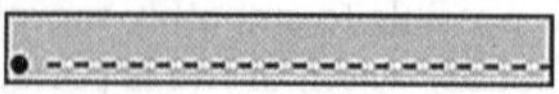	**Classic Tween** A dashed line indicates that the classic tween is broken or incomplete when the final keyframe is missing.
	**Shape Tween** A black dot at the beginning keyframe with a black arrow and a light green background indicates a shape tween.

Indicators	Types of Animation
	**Single Keyframe** A *black dot* indicates a single keyframe. *Light gray frames* after a single keyframe contain the same content with no changes. These frames have a *vertical black line* and a *hollow rectangle* at the last frame of the span.
	A *small* a indicates that the frame is assigned a frame action with the Actions panel.
	A *red flag* indicates that the frame contains a label.
	A *green double slash* indicates that the frame contains a comment.
	A *gold anchor* indicates that the frame is a named anchor.

Understanding Motion Tweens

In a *motion tween* animation, you can specify the position of the object in the beginning and ending frames and Flash fills in the in-between frames, a process known as *tweening*. You can also change several properties with one motion tween. For example, you can place a symbol to the left of the **Stage** in frame 1, and move it to the right of the **Stage** in frame 20.

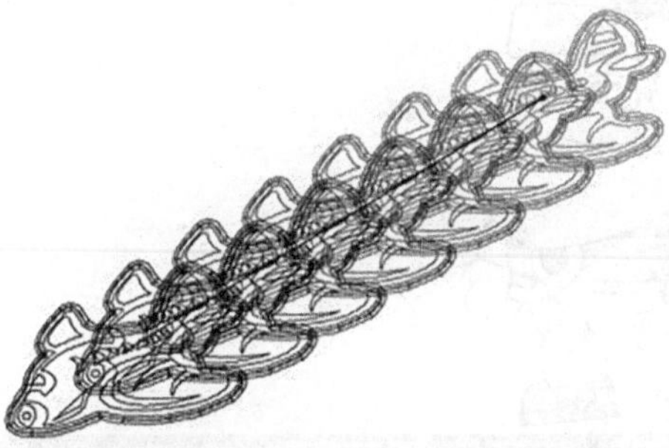

Figure 8.23: Sample motion tween animation

At the same time, you can change the size of the symbol to give the impression that the symbol is moving away from the viewer. After that when you create a tween, Flash calculates all the positions and change the size of the movie-clip symbol in between. The result is an animation of the symbol moving from left to right, from frame 1 to frame 20.

The Onion Skin feature is enabled so that outlines of the plane are displayed for each frame of the animation as shown in the Figure 8.23.

Tween Span

A *tween span* is a group of frames in the **Timeline** (See Figure 8.23). It appears in the **Timeline** in a single layer with a blue background. These tween spans can be selected as a single object. Only one object on the **Stage** can be animated in each tween span. This object is called the *target object* of the *tween span*.

Motion Path

A *motion path* shows the path of the tweened object taking during its movement on the **Stage**. Each dot on the path corresponds to a frame on the Timeline and indicates the location of the object when the frame is played (See Figure 8.23). A motion path can be altered by dragging a point on the path using the Selection Tool or by using the Subselection Tool.

Property Keyframe

Property Keyframe is a keyframe which indicates a change in a Flash movie, such as the start or ending of an animation.

To create a Motion Tween animation, do this:

1. Select a symbol, instance or a text field to tween on the **Stage**.

   If the selection contains other objects, a dialog box appears giving you a warning that your selected object is not a symbol. Motion tweens require symbols. Flash asks if you want to convert the selection to a symbol so it can proceed with the motion tween. Click **OK**. Flash automatically converts your selection to a symbol, which is stored in your **Library panel**.

2. Then click **Insert** menu and then choose **Motion Tween** (See Figure 8.24).

Figure 8.24: *Tween layer*

3. Flash converts the current layer to a Tween layer so that you can begin to animate the instance. Tween layers are distinguished by a special icon in front of the layer name, and the frames are tinted blue as shown in Figure 10.

4. The tween span appears on the **Timeline** as shown in Figure 8.25.
5. Drag the object to the right side of the Stage as shown in Figure 8.25. A motion path appears on the Stage with dots indicating the position of the object for each frame (See Figure 8.26). A diamond symbol appears in the last frame, which is the end of the tween span.
6. Point to the end of the tween span, when the pointer changes to a double arrow, drag the tween span in the **Timeline** to shorten or extend the span to the desired number of frames.
7. Click the frame 1 on the **Timeline**, then press the period (•) key to move the playhead one frame at a time and notice the position of the plane for each frame.
8. Click **Control** menu and then select **Play** or alternatively press **Enter** key to play the movie (See Figure 8.27).

Figure 8.25: Playing the animation

Extra Byte

The more frames per second (fps), the smoother the animations. 12 should be the minimum, although keep it in mind that it looks choppy. 30 frames per second are nice and smooth, just make sure your animations don't go by too quickly.

Shape Tweening

Shape tweening is a technique for interpolating amorphous changes between shapes in different keyframes. Flash Professional can tween the location, size, color, and opacity of shapes. To apply shape tweening to groups, instances, or bitmap images, you must first break these elements apart. For shape tweening, you have to draw a shape at one point in time, and then change that shape or draw another shape at another point in time.

Creating a Shape Tween Animation

To create an animation using shape tweening, you shall convert the shape of square into an Oval.

To create a shape tweening animation, do this:

1. Open a new Flash document.
2. Draw a square at Frame 1. (See Figure 8.26)
3. On the same layer, right-click on Frame 30 and choose **Insert Blank Keyframe** from the menu as shown in Figure 8.26.
4. In Frame 30, draw an oval using **Oval tool**. Now you have a keyframe in frame 1 with a square and a keyframe in frame 30 with an Oval.

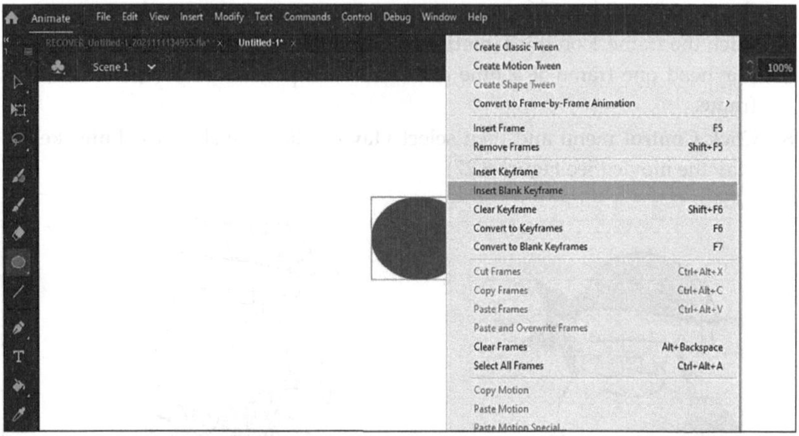

Figure 8.26: *Inserting Blank Keyframe*

5. Click anywhere on the same layer between frames 1 and 30.
6. Right click on the Shape and select Shape crate tween.
7. Click on play button.

Memorize

When you want to change the content, you insert a keyframe. The keyframe indicates a change.

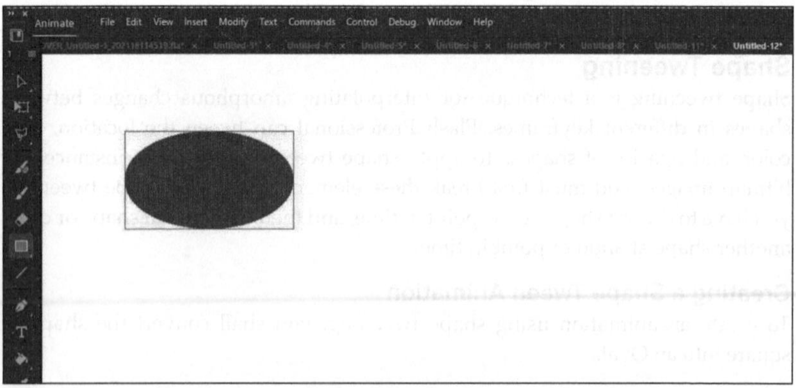

Figure 8.27: *Interpolating the shape between the two keyframes*

Keyboard Shortcut

You can also add individual frames by choosing Insert > Timeline > Frame (F5), or remove individual frames by choosing Edit > Timeline > Remove Frames (Shift + F5).

Understanding Actions

In a simple movie, Flash plays the frames sequentially without stopping the user input. However, if you want to provide the ability to the user to interact with the movie by allowing them to perform actions, such as starting and stopping the movie or jumping to a specific frame in the movie. One way to provide user interaction is to assign an action to the Down state of a button. Then, whenever the user clicks the button, the action occurs. Flash Professional provides a scripting language, called ActionScript 3.0, that allows you to add actions to buttons and frames within a movie. For example, you can place a stop action in a frame that pauses the movie and then you can assign a play action to a button that starts the movie when the user clicks the button.

Add a code snippet to an object or Timeline frame

To add an action that affects an object or the playhead:

1. Select an object on the Stage or a frame in the Timeline.

   If you select an object that is not a symbol instance, Animate converts the object to a movie clip symbol when you apply the snippet.

   If you select an object that does not already have an instance name, Animate adds one when you apply the snippet.
2. In the Code Snippets panel (**Window > Code Snippets**), double-click the snippet you want to apply.

   If you selected an object on the stage, Animate adds the snippet to the Actions panel in the frames containing the selected object.

   If you selected a Timeline frame, Animate adds the snippet to just that frame.
3. In the Actions panel, view the newly added code and replace any necessary items according to the instructions at the top of the snippet.

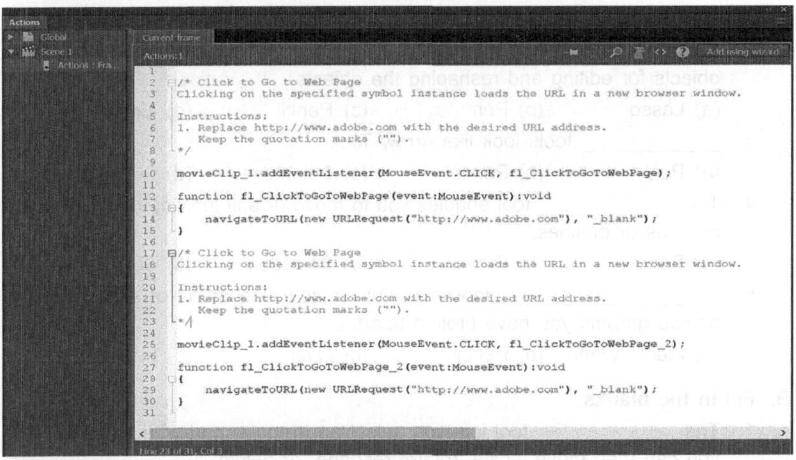

***Figure 8.29:** Code snippet in actions panel*

Add new snippets to the Code Snippets panel

You can add new code snippets to the Code Snippets panel in two ways:

- Enter a snippet in the **Create New Code Snippet** dialog box.
- Import a code snippet XML file.

To use the Create New Code Snippet dialog box:

1. In the Code Snippets panel, choose Create New Code Snippet from the panel menu.
2. In the dialog box, **Enter** the Title, Tool tip text, and JavaScript or ActionScript 3.0 code for your snippet.

   You can add any code that is currently selected in the Actions panel by clicking the Auto-Fill button.
3. Select the Automatically replace instance_name_here check box if your code includes the string "instance_name_here" and you want Animate to replace it with the correct instance name when the snippet is applied.

Animate adds the new snippet to the Code Snippets panel in a folder called **Custom**.

To import a code snippet in XML format:

1. In the Code Snippets panel, choose **Import** Code Snippets XML from the panel menu.
2. Select the XML file you want to import and click Open

To see the correct XML format for code snippets, choose **Edit** Code Snippets XML from the panel menu.

To delete a code snippet, right-click the snippet in the panel and choose Delete Code Snippet from the context menu.

EXERCISES

A. Multiple Choice Questions.

1. The ____________ tool can be used for creating freehand shapes.

   (a) Pen (b) Pencil (c) Oval (d) Line
2. Selection tool, Subselection and ____________ tools are used to select objects for editing and reshaping the objects.

   (a) Lasso (b) Pen (c) Pencil (d) Line
3. ____________ tools look like Arrow Tool.

   (a) Pen (b) Pencil (c) Selection (d) Subselection
4. The ____________ tool enables you to move or edit individual anchor points on lines or outlines.

   (a) Pen (b) Pencil (c) Selection (d) Subselection
5. ____________________ tool is useful for selecting areas of similar color in bitmap graphic you have broken apart.

   (a) Magic Wand (b) Pencil (c) Oval (d) Line

B. Fill in the blanks.

1. The ____________ tool lets you select an irregular part of a graphic, which you can then move, scale, rotate, reshape, or delete.

2. ____________ shortcut keys together to break apart the graphics.
3. ____________ tool draws straight segments.
4. Oval, also known as ____________, can be drawn in Flash Professional using the rectangle Tool in the Tools panel.
5. The size of star ranges from ____________.

C. State whether the following statements are True or False.

1. Ink bottle is used to modify fall and outlines of the object.
2. In Timeline, the blue rectangle will move across the Timeline to show you the current frame on the Stage.
3. The first prominent use of the Adobe Flash animation format was by Ren & Stimpy creator John Kricfalusi.
4. When you want to change the content, you insert a keyframe. The keyframe does not indicates a change.
5. If two shapes are the same color, then they are merged into one shape.

D. Answers the following questions.

1. Explain subselection tool.
2. What is the purpose of Lasso tool?
3. How to create a New symbol in Flash animation?
4. Discuss the classification of animations in the timeline.
5. Define animation and how does animation work?

9 Working with Adobe XD

Learning Objectives

After studying this chapter, you should be able to do:

- Get started with Adobe XD interface • Understand to create layout in design view • Discuss to start a new design • Explain to create background of prototype • Identify to set header • How to insert the background for content area • Explain to create grid • Discuss to create Artboard • Understand to setup homepage • How to create interaction

Introduction

Here you will be learning the basic concepts of Adobe XD and understand its interface. You will be designing Artboards and making connections between them, so that your Artboards can interact with each other. Let's have a look at it now and get started.

Get started with Adobe XD interface

When you first open Adobe XD the tool, you are greeted with a Welcome page and with different types of projects that you can select and start working with. Using Adobe XD is not at all complicated. It is very simple and easy to use tool. The interface is very user friendly and you would not find it difficult to use at all. It has similar ease of use as its other companions in the creative cloud. It offers a lot of platforms that you can use for prototyping. If you have to name some, then they would be as follows- Mobile phones, Tablets, Websites, or any custom size of your choice.

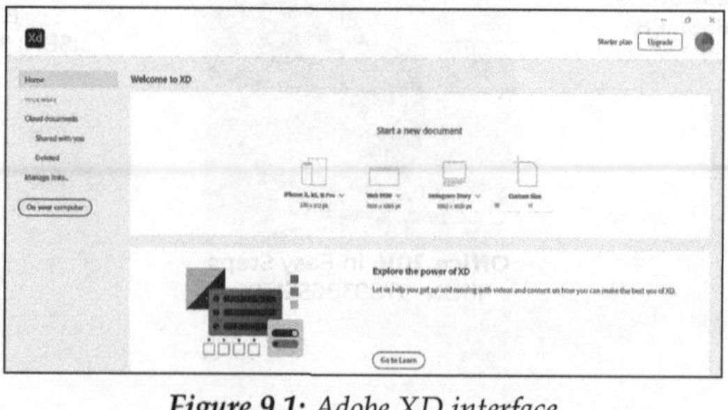

Figure 9.1: *Adobe XD interface*

FACT

On October 18, 2017, Adobe announced that Adobe XD was out of beta.

Creating layout in design view

If you talk about the Adobe XD screen, it is divided into two views, which are namely- The **Design view** and **The Prototype** View. Both of these views can be accessed from the top left.

Now let us talk about the design view. The design view can be used by designers to create beautiful designs. They can also use the different features and tools that are offered by Adobe XD. They can give life to their ideas and design here with better integration of other Adobe tools as well, like **Photoshop** and **Illustrator**. You can import resources and then incorporate them into your design and create something beautiful.

The other view offered by the Adobe XD is the **Prototype view**. It enables the user to add connections to their Artboards or pages. Not only this, but it also helps the designer to add interaction to these images and then previews the final prototype. It is also useful to showcase how the artboards will be interacting with each other.

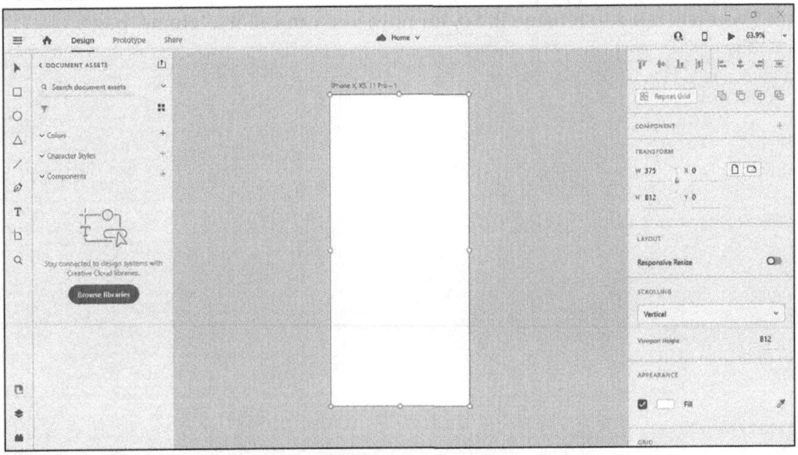

Figure 9.2: Layout

Extra Byte

Adobe XD is the Adobe prototyping tool for user experience and interaction designers. Adobe XD features are used for creating wireframes, prototypes, and screen designs for digital products such as websites and mobile apps.

Starting a new design

Here, you can select any of the projects from the options provided to us. Different options are provided as shown in the below image. You have- different versions of iPhone, web, custom size, tablet.

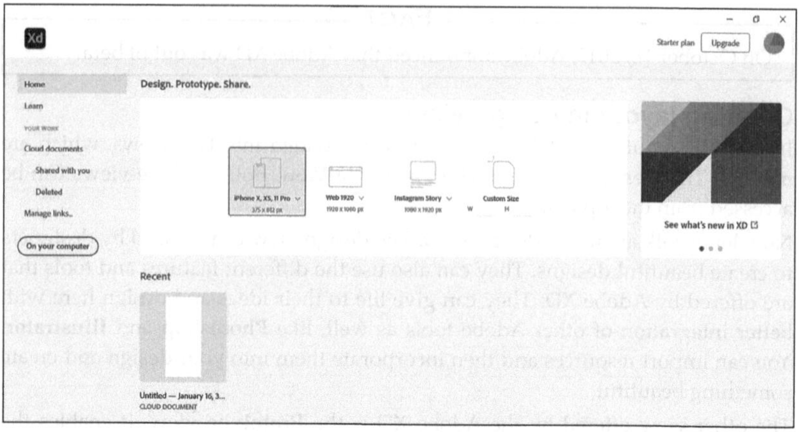

Figure 9.3: Share Protoype

Here you will select the iPhone and click on its icon to successfully create the project. You will get all the UI elements from the Apple iOS of the iPhone which will help us in prototyping. Now you will have successfully created the artboard and you will need to rename it. So, for now, you can call it a 'Home' page.

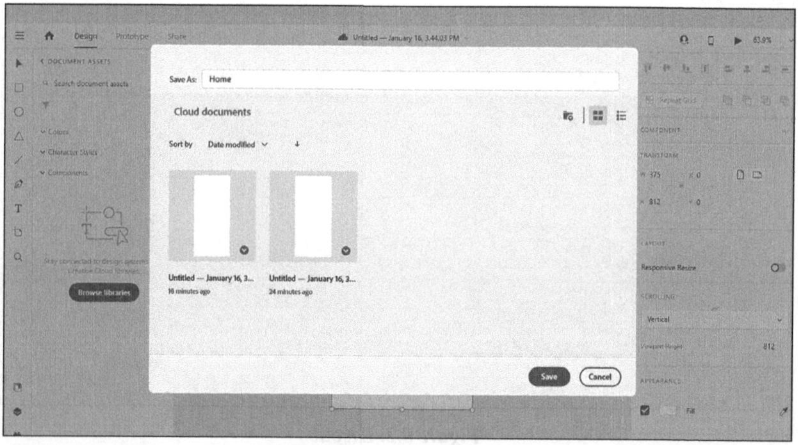

Figure 9.4: Save Prototype

Note: Designers can copy design elements directly from these applications and then paste them into the selected artboard as a vector.

Create background of prototype

For creating the prototype background, you will be using the Artboard. You will have to click on the Artboard in order to view its properties. After clicking, the properties of the Artboard will be displayed. Now from the right-side panel, you will be clicking on the **Fill color** option. Now, from the dialog box, you will be selecting any color of your choice that you want to use as your background color.

Here, in this case, you will be selecting a Black color. Please refer to the below image for your reference.

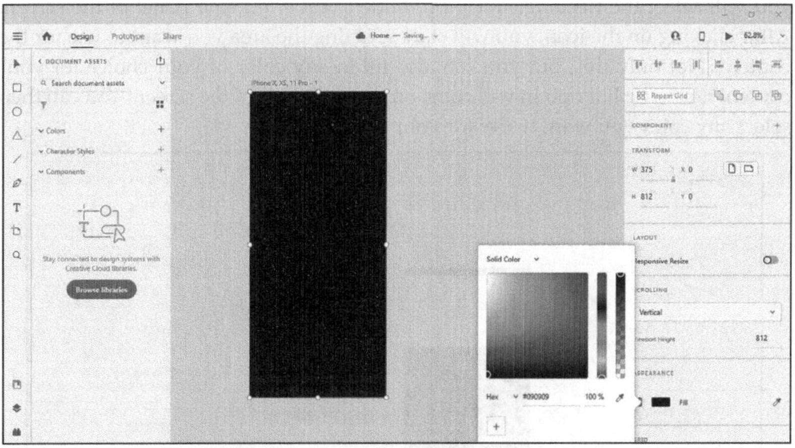

***Figure 9.5:** Prototype Background Creation*

As you can see in the above image, you have selected black color as the background color for your prototype.

Setting header

Prototype: In this step, you will be setting up the header for your prototype project. You will go to the **File** menu, then click on **Import**, and you can import any image of your choice from your computer system. And you will place it in the header.

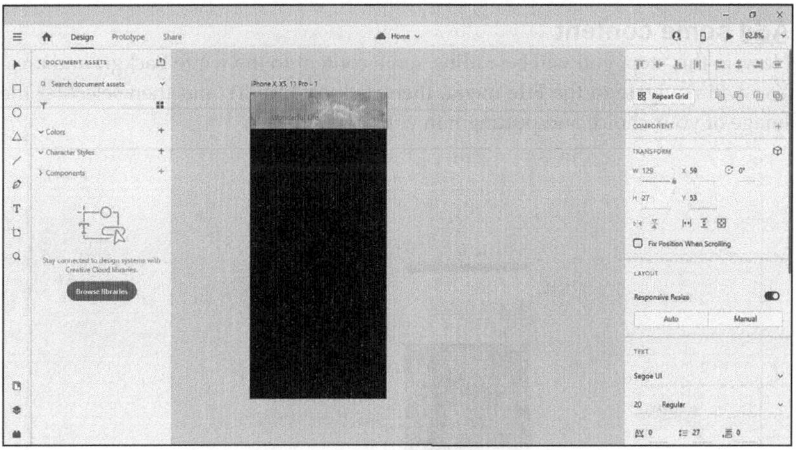

***Figure 9.6:** Setting Header*

As you can see in the image above, you have set the header for your project. In addition to the image, you have also added some text in the header. It will provide a Title for your Home Page.

Inserting the background for content area

Now you will take a look at how to insert the content area background. Here you will select the Rectangle shape provided in the left side panel of the screen. After clicking on the icon, you will start selecting the area you want to use for the content. Not only this, but you can also fill in any color of your choice for your content area. The Fill option will come on the right side of the screen. You can then select any color you want to use for your background.

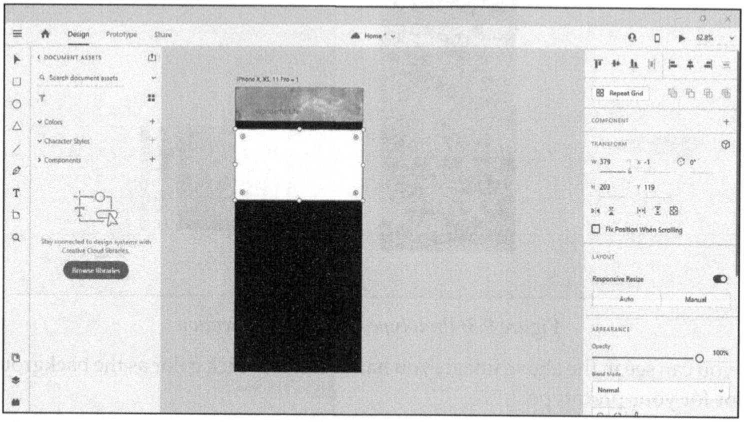

Figure 9.7: Inserting the background

As you can see in the above image, how you have selected the required area to be your content area and then provided it a white color. Now, you can start working on this area by putting text or images over it.

Add some content

Now, in this step, you will be adding some content to the white background area. You will navigate to the **File** menu, then click on **Import**, and then selecting the image of your choice and putting it in your content area.

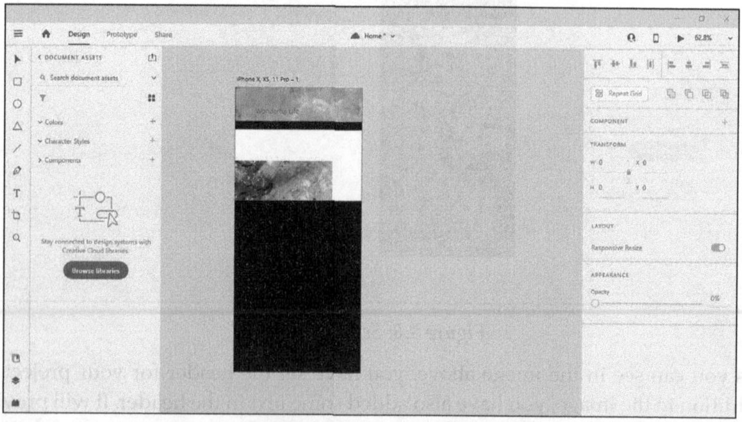

Figure 9.8: Content Addition

As you can see in the above image, you have successfully added the image to your content area. Now you will proceed by adding some text over the content area. You can provide any text of your choice. You just have to select the **Text** icon from the left side panel. And then you can add any text successfully.

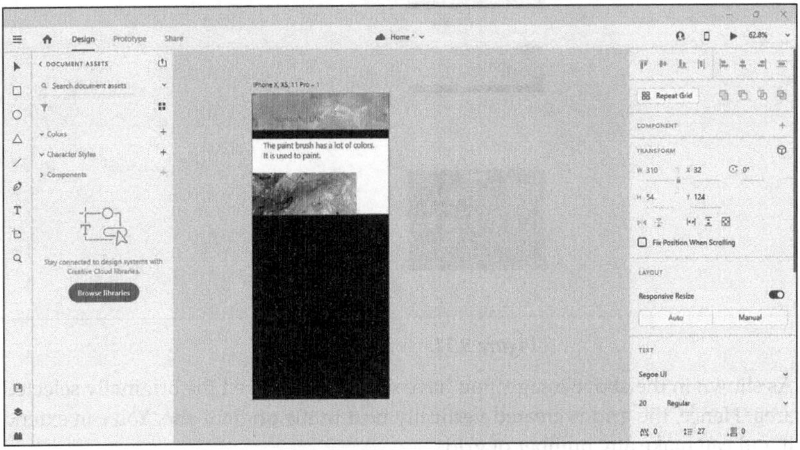

Figure 9.9: *Text Added*

Now if you refer to the above image. You have added the text of your choice successfully. You can go to any text.

Creating grid

Now in this step, you will be adding the Grid to our project. Now select the **Add Grid** option from the right side of the panel, as shown in the image below. Then you will have to **Select** your area which you want to make a grid of automatically.

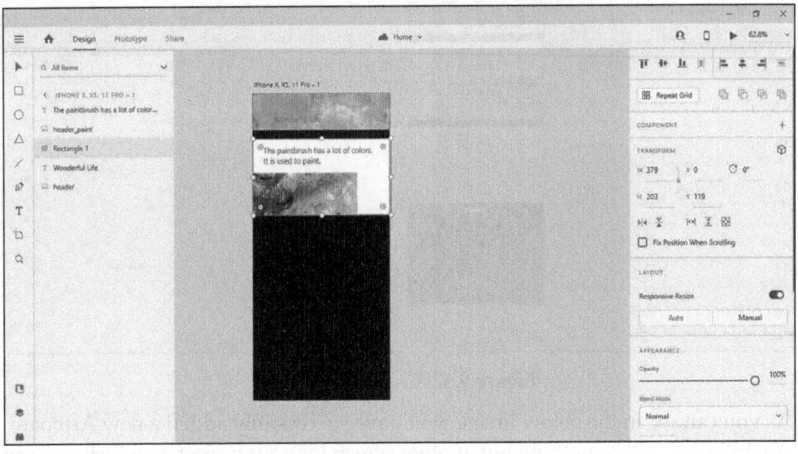

Figure 9.10: *Creating grid*

In the above image, you have selected the area you want to make a grid of. **Grids** can be added **vertically** or **horizontally**, depending on your requirement you can select accordingly.

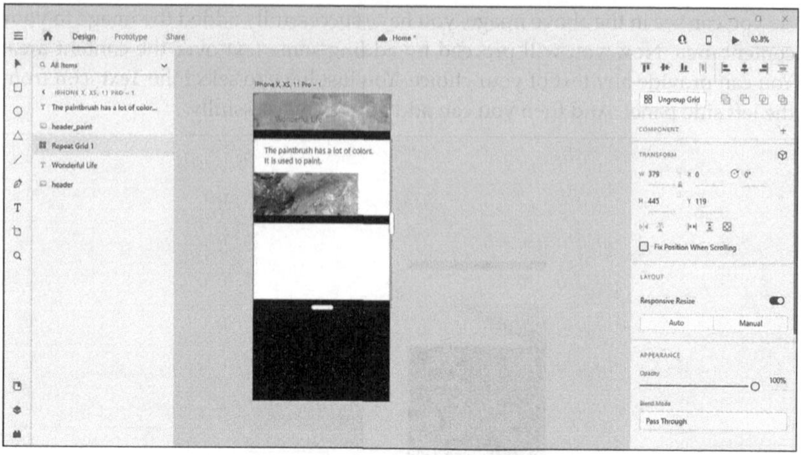

Figure 9.11: vertical grid added

As shown in the above image, you have vertically dragged the originally selected area. Hence, the grid is created vertically next to the original one. You can extend it and can make any number of grids.

Creating Artboard

In this step, you will be adding more Artboards in your design area. You will be simply clicking on the Left side panel icon, as shown in the below image. Then you will be able to add as many Artboards as you need.

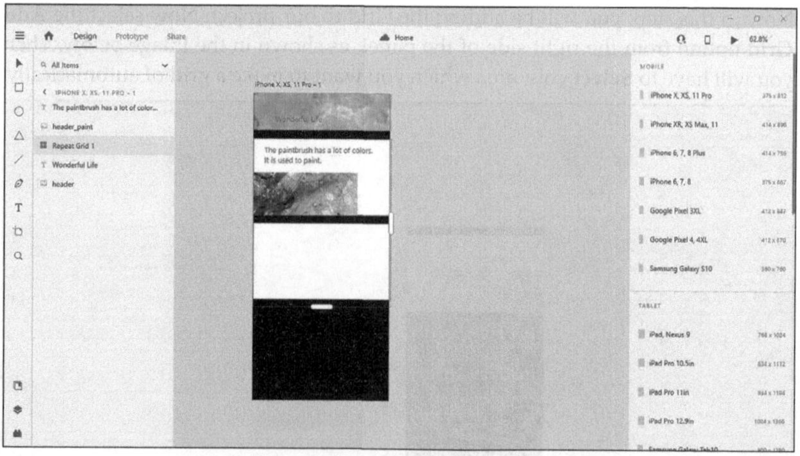

Figure 9.12: Creating Artboard

As you can see in the below image, you have successfully added a new Artboard. An Artboard will be nothing but another screen for your project, to which you can navigate from your homepage.

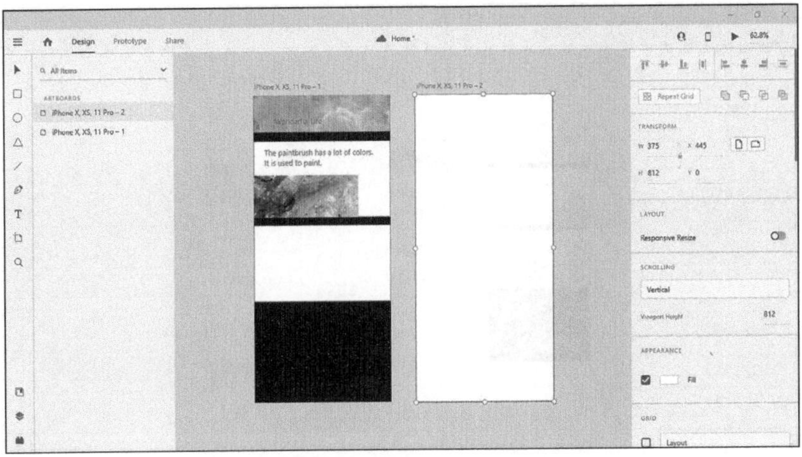

Figure 9.13: Added a new Artboard

Here you have successfully added a new Artboard. Now, in a similar way, you will be adding one more Artboard, so that you can navigate to more than one screen.

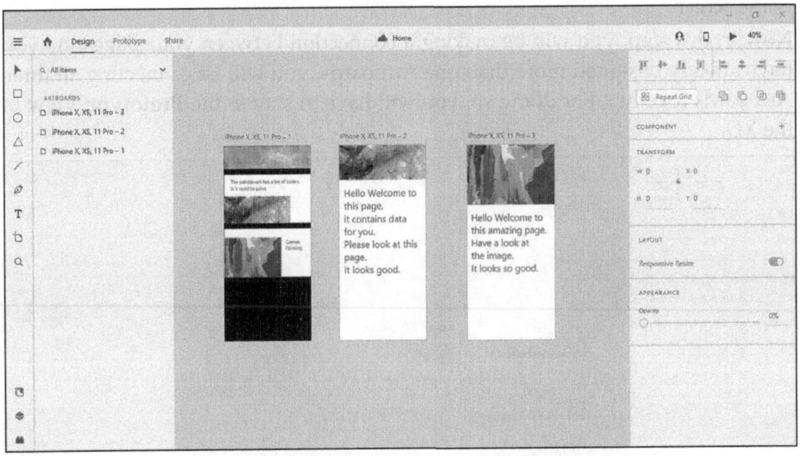

Figure 9.14: Added two new Artboards

As you can see in the above image, you have successfully added two new Artboards. Not only Artboards, but you have also added some content on both of the Artboards. Now that content has been added, you will proceed.

Setup homepage

Now, you will be setting up your home page in this app. You will now have to navigate to the Prototype screen. Here you will be making your screen a home screen. You will have to select the screen you want to make a Home screen and you can click on the home icon from the above menu.

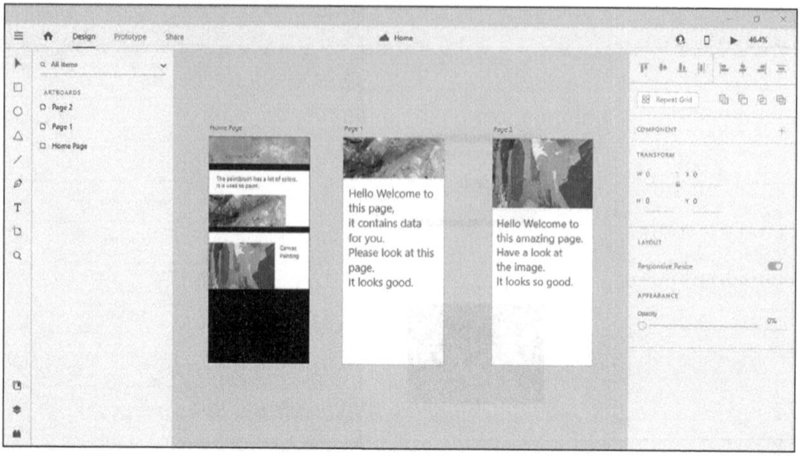

Figure 9.15: *Setup homepage*

As you can see in the above image, you have selected the first screen or Artboard, and you can see the small home icon on your screen which signifies that it is the home screen.

Now in this step, you will be making a connection between your pages. As you have already designed more than one Artboards, you will be connecting all three Artboards together. For doing so, you will have to stay in the **Prototype View** of the XD.

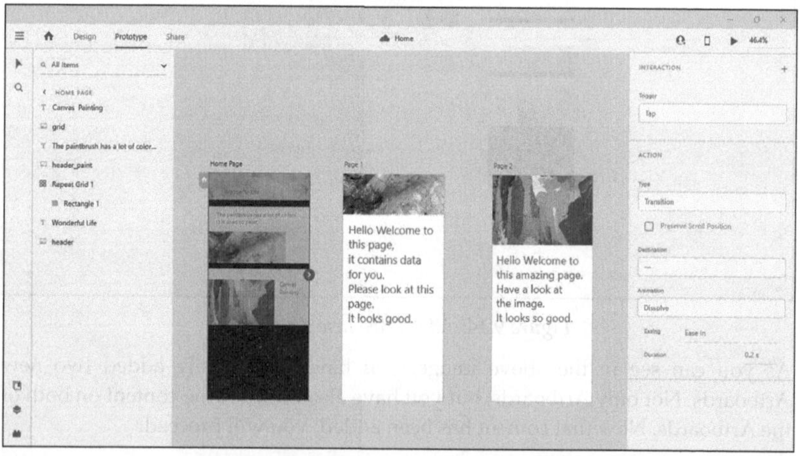

Figure 9.16: *Connecting pages*

As you can see in the above image, you can see the arrow on the right corner of the selected area, which will help us to make connections between the different Artboards.

Creating interaction

In this Step, you will be designing the interaction of different Artboards. Similar to the earlier step. The connection will be providing interaction between them.

As you can see in the below image, you have added the interaction of the first rectangular section to the second Artboard.

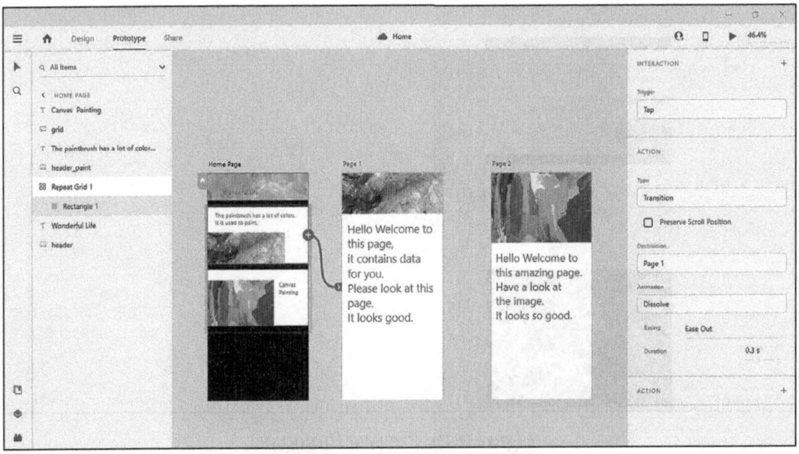

Figure 9.17: Creating interaction

As shown in the image above, a connection between the first section and the second Artboard has been made successfully.

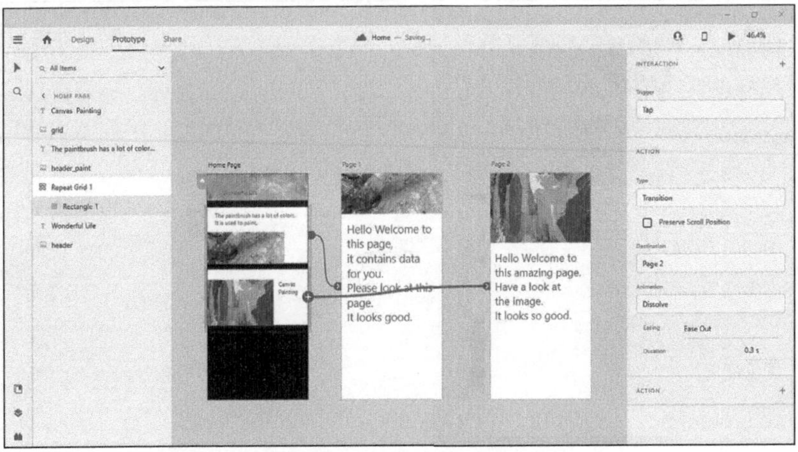

Figure 9.18: Added the interaction

As you can see, you have added the interaction between the Second rectangular box to the third Artboard.

Preview Prototype

In this step, you will be Previewing your prototype project. For this, you will have to navigate to the play button on the rightmost corner of the top menu. Then you can click it and your preview will just start simply.

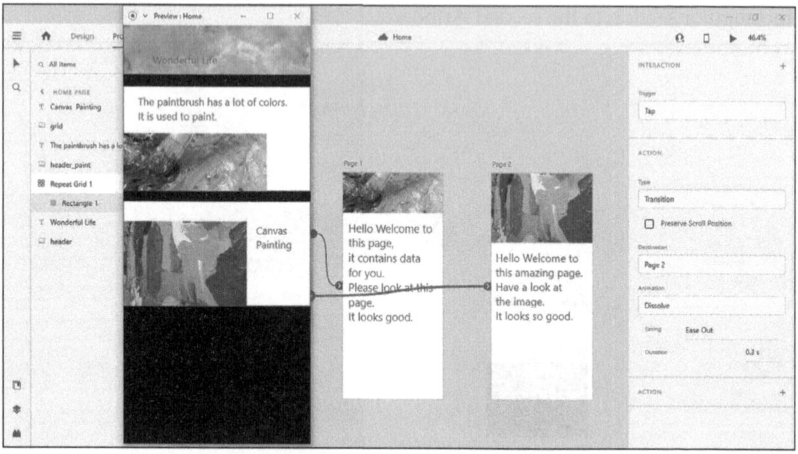

Figure 9.19: Preview Prototype

As you can see here, the preview has started, it tells us how your project will look and work on the targeted device. Now if you click on the first rectangular section, you will land on the second Artboard.

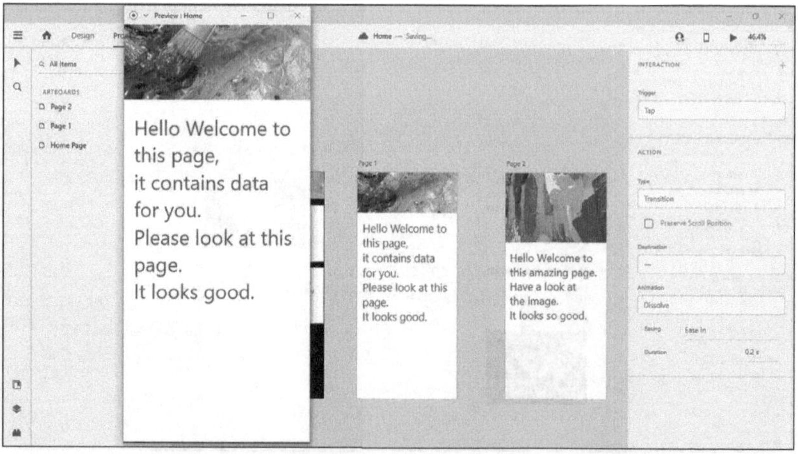

Figure 9.20: successfully landed on the second Artboard

As you can see, you have successfully landed on the second Artboard. In a similar way, you can navigate to the third Artboard by clicking on the second rectangular section.

EXERCISES

A. Multiple Choice Questions.

1. On October ___________, 2017, Adobe announced that Adobe XD was out of beta.
   (a) 16 (b) 17 (c) 18 (d) 19
2. Adobe XD is the Adobe prototyping tool for ___________ and interaction designers.
   (a) User Experience (b) User Designers (c) User field (d) User protocol
3. The ___________ view can be used by designers to create beautiful designs.
   (a) Prototype (b) Design (b) Both (a) and (b) (d) None of these
4. ___________ can be added vertically or horizontally, depending on your requirement you can select accordingly.
   (a) Home Page (b) Adobe XD (c) Grids (d) Artboard
5. Adobe XD screen is divided into two views: Design view and ___________ view.
   (a) Artboard (b) User (c) Designer (d) Prototype

B. Answers the following questions.

1. Explain Adobe XD and its features.
2. Discuss how to set homepage in Adobe XD.
3. Write down the steps for Creating Artboard.
4. How to preview prototype in Adobe XD?
5. How to add some content in the content area?